EPIDEMIC
America's Trade in Child Rape

LORI HANDRAHAN, PHD

Published by:
Trine Day LLC
PO Box 577
Walterville, OR 97489
1-800-556-2012
www.TrineDay.com
trineday@Icloud.com

Disclaimer: The position/job title and place of employment at the time of the arrest have been cited throughout this book. Upon arrest employers may or may not terminate the defendant. Some people remained in their position, on paid or unpaid leave, while charges were pending with cases taking one-two years or more to move through the system. Other times people have been allowed to quietly retired, some were forced to resign and some people were terminated immediately. Because the arrests represent a snap-shot in time, information regarding the cases included in this book may have changed. The title/employer cited is not necessarily still current – it was only current at the time of arrest.

Library of Congress Control Number: 2017952754

Handrahan, Lori
–1st ed.
p. cm.

Epub (ISBN-13) 978-1-63424-160-1
Mobi (ISBN-13) 978-1-63424-161-8
Print (ISBN-13) 978-1-63424-159-5
1. Child Abuse, Sexual -- epidemiology. 2. Child sexual abuse -- Investigation -- United States. 3. Child sexual abuse -- United States -- Statistics. 4. Child pornography. 5. Child sexual abuse -- Prevention. 6. Children -- Social conditions. I. Handrahan, Lori. II. Title

FIRST EDITION
10 9 8 7 6 5 4 3 2 1

Printed in the USA
Distribution to the Trade by:
Independent Publishers Group (IPG)
814 North Franklin Street
Chicago, Illinois 60610
312.337.0747
www.ipgbook.com

"Let unwelcome truths be told."

– Paul Farmer, M.D, *Pathologies of Power*

Dedicated to my daughter Mila

Acknowledgments

R esearching these crimes against our children, I have been fortunate to receive support from courageous friends who held me up and pushed me to keep researching, writing and publishing. So America would know. So our children could be protected. This book would not exist without the people who have sustained me and this research. You know who you are. Thank you.

One of the most persistent champions has been Gary Heidt of Signature Literary Agency. Gary pitched this book to publishers over several years. Many publishers rejected the book explaining the subject was too horrific; Americans did not want to read about this crime. No one would buy the book because it was too disturbing. Publishers said, we cannot make a profit. Sorry.

When my research on professors and staff arrested for trading in child rape went viral, Gary decided to pitch the book one more time. Trine Day immediately responded. I am grateful to Kris Millegan of Trine Day for believing in this book and offering a contract just when hope was dissipating.

Gratitude is also due to the Justice Department's public affairs officers who answered my questions and provided court documents. Likewise, I am grateful to court clerks, law enforcement officers and prosecutors across the country who took time to speak with me and send public documents.

I owe a debt of gratitude to everyone who clicked and shared the research I have so painstakingly and stubbornly been gathering. This book found a publisher because thousands of people, expressing outrage at what pedophiles are doing to our children and indignation at mainstream media's refusal to report on the epidemic of child sex abuse, shared my research.

Thank you.

Table of Contents

Foreword

The rape and torture of thousands of children in America is shared every day in videos, photos and live-streams. Men, and some women, are raping children, including infants and toddlers, and distributing evidence of the crime on the Internet in epidemic numbers. These offenses against our children are flourishing, in part, because we refuse to move beyond our collective denial that this criminality, often called child pornography, has reached catastrophic levels in America.

We are sustaining crisis-level numbers of seemingly normal, often powerful and successful men involved in America's illegal child sex-abuse industry. It does not matter if the perpetrator is on the demand-side, with an incessant appetite for brutal child rape to achieve sexual gratification, or the supply-side of raping children, often their own or those of friends and relatives, and trading this abuse online. Both supply and demand of child pornography, which almost always intertwine, have reached epidemic proportions and too few are talking about it.

The current child rape crisis is also a serious community and national security concern, given how many government employees at the local, state and federal levels, including in the military, law enforcement, judicial and education sectors, are being arrested on child exploitation charges.

The problem of child sex abuse and its cover-up is real. A generation of American children are being destroyed. If you think this happens to someone else's children and your children are safe, you are mistaken. Your children might be enduring sexual abuse right now while you remain dangerously ignorant. America's appetite for child pornography puts all our children at risk.

Your children and mine. Whether you acknowledge it or not.

This book is a wake-up call about a subject too few people want to discuss. That is, while no one was watching, America has become a child-pornography nation.

Lori Handrahan, Ph.D.
Washington DC
July 2017

Introduction

The incidence of child sexual exploitation has reached staggering proportions.
– US Department of Homeland Security's Special Agent John Reynolds
Los Angeles Times 21 June 2016[1]

THE BOOK

This book is the result of a difficult journey. It is not research I wanted to do. It is research I have been compelled to do. I have learned more than I ever wanted to know about how pedophiles destroy our children, families and communities. This knowledge has altered how I view the world and changed how the world regards me. It has cost me a great deal. I have lost friends. My career has been targeted. My ability to earn a living has been restricted. I have persisted because this is a labor of love for children and adult survivors harmed by this crime and for dedicated investigators and prosecutors working to achieve justice.

Researching child pornography is difficult both because there is a data problem and because the subject is overwhelmingly painful. While so many journalists and academics, earning full salaries and benefiting from institutional support, are apparently unable or unwilling to report or research America's child pornography epidemic, the research in this book has been eked out, literally, with blood, sweat and tears. Sweat from working as a gardener. Tears over the harm being done to our children. Blood when, overwhelmed by the magnitude, I sometimes tug unconsciously at my cuticles as I type.

Acting Director of Cyber Security at the Department of Health and Human Services (DHHS), Timothy DeFoggi, was sentenced, in 2015, to 25 years in federal prison for participating in a child pornography ring "so depraved, it even shocked veteran investigators." DeFoggi "expressed an interest in the violent rape and murder of children" and planned with other pedophiles to rape and murder children.

I have been researching America's child pornography epidemic for seven years. When I was a professor I focused on child pornography as a national security issue. Far too many federal and state employees in positions of power are engaged in the crime-making it a serious national security issue that has been ignored. *Forbes, Washington Times* and others published this research.[2] Fox News and Canadian TV invited me for interviews.[3] When I lost my university position my credible and funded platform vanished and so did my ability to continue publishing and raising awareness.

Good research is expensive, tedious, and absorbs a great deal of human labor. Losing my academic position, I lost graduate research students, library access, a salary and community support. Unable to sell the book I had originally intended to write and unable to pursue the research in the manner I was trained – as a social scientist at The London School of Economics – I stumbled along with this research in fits and starts.

As I sought new employment and was unable to secure a position, I started landscaping in my community. I spent months planting flowers, re-conditioning soil, spreading mulch and trimming roses. In between time in gardens, I kept researching, working in local coffee shops and posting raw data and essays on the social media platform Medium, in what I considered a rather futile effort to raise awareness about the scope of this crime. I struggled along applying for job after job only to be continually rejected. As I asked people if they would hire me and/or support this research, I was told "No, sorry," in varying degrees, and often a total lack of kindness. Was documenting a crime committed, often, by men in positions of power harming my career?

In October 2016, WikiLeaks published the Podesta emails and a popular movement called #PizzaGate emerged. My Twitter account was flooded with people sharing my work. An essay about government employees arrested on child pornography charges called "State Dept Dan Rosen's Arrest: Cheat Sheet for Journos" went from 12,000 shares to nearly 60,000 almost overnight. My personal philosophy is deeply rooted in non-violence and so when a man with a gun went to a pizza place near where I live in Washington, DC I was horrified. PizzaGate worried me, and

> Homeland Security's Operation Sunflower rescued 120 children including a 19-day-old baby. 44 children were living with their abusers; 70 were girls and 53 were boys. Those arrested included a first-grade teacher and a pilot. Homeland said the trend in child rape was, "younger children were more often abused and more women were directly involved in carrying out the abuse."

I stayed far away. As time passed, PizzaGate morphed into #PedoGate representing a movement raising awareness about child sex abuse. The hashtag became a symbol of America's pedophile crisis and was no longer focused on any single allegation. A popular uprising expressing outrage about impunity for child sex abuse was beginning to emerge.

The essay, "State Dept Dan Rosen's Arrest: Cheat Sheet for Journos," that captured so much interest was originally posted in February 2015, three days after the State Department's Director for Counter-terrorism was arrested for attempted sodomy with a child under 14-years-old; in reality an undercover police officer in Fairfax, Virginia. I had a list of government employees arrested on child pornography charges because of the research

I had been doing for this book that no one wanted to publish. As I watched mainstream media report on Dan Rosen's arrest, I became exasperated. Not one journalist conducted even the most basic search of government employees arrested on similar charges. I posted my essay expressing frustration with amateur reporting and called it a "Cheat Sheet for Journos."

Shane Harris, then with The Daily Beast and now with the *Wall Street Journal*, contacted me. He said he was shocked by my list. He had no idea. He planned to issue a four-part series profiling the hundreds of arrests I had gathered. Harris published "The Sickening Child Porn Crisis Infecting U.S. Government Agencies," referencing my research but his intended series never materialized. I do not know why. Harris stayed in touch for a while and then went silent. My essay received about 12,000 shares and stagnated until, nearly two years later, when the PedoGate crowd discovered it and shared it widely.

In mid-February 2017, I posted "Professors & Staff Arrested for Trading in Child Rape." This essay received 8,000 shares overnight and escalated to 20,000 and then 30,000 shares a day. Within four weeks the essay had over 400,000 shares. People began asking me to include professors who were absent from my list. Clyde Fant, a former dean at Stetson University, was one request. When I contacted Stetson University to ask if this former dean still had *emeritus* status, despite his federal conviction for trading in pre-teen hard core (PTHC) – the brutal rape and torture of very small children, Stetson, unaware of Fant's conviction, held an emergency meeting of their Board of Trustees. They immediately revoked Fant's awards and *emeritus* status. Stetson also issued a press release stating unwavering opposition to crimes against children. If only all institutions took such an immediately powerful public stance. Fant's arrest was not covered by the media and represents the importance of reporting on child pornography crimes.[4] Had Fant's arrest been reported, Stetson would have been able to act at the time of his arrest.

Chart of the number of shares and views on my essay, posted on Medium, about professors and staff arrested on child pornography charges.

I have structured this book in a manner I hope will enable readers to understand the extent of extreme sexual violence being perpetrated against our children. Arrest samples are in text boxes throughout the book and within each chapter. Longer lists of arrests are on my Medium profile. The compiled arrests are not complete data sets but are rather sample raw data. The scope of the crime is so immense it is impossible for one person, with no institutional support, to build a complete data set of all child pornography arrests in America. The data collected so far is the best I can do with limited resources. I have focused, mostly, on government employees in our military, law enforcement, judiciary, prosecutorial offices and education system. There are many arrests in religious communities, among coaches, child protection staff, children's charities, the mental health profession, the medical community and other professional categories.

This book is just the beginning. More than anything else, it establishes the critical need for comprehensive, demographic data on child pornography arrests in America. The website www.Data4Justice.org describes the vision for this kind of database. I hope to secure employment and funding to build a public database allowing transparency and analysis of the child rape epidemic sweeping America. Perhaps this book will attract the attention of an employer and donor willing to make this possible. I hope people will read this book and take action; document the epidemic, create public policies and demand our government allocate resource to halt this crime that is destroying a generation of American children.

Endnotes

1. Veronica Rocha, "238 arrested in sweep of suspected child sex predators," Los Angeles Times, June 21, 2016, accessed July 14, 2017, http://www.latimes.com/local/lanow/la-me-ln-operation-broken-heart-arrests-20160621-snap-tory.html.

2 Lori Handrahan, "To Catch Government Workers with Ties to Child Porn, call the IRS," Forbes Magazine, 19 September 19, 2012, accessed July 14, 2017, http://www.forbes.com/sites/85broads/2012/09/19/to-catch-government-workers-with-ties-to-child-porn-call-the-irs/ and Lori Handrahan, "Executive Branch Porn Problem," The Washington Times, August 10, 2012, accessed July 14, 2017, http://www.washingtontimes.com/news/2012/aug/10/executive-branch-porn-problem.

3 "Can the IRS Prevent Child Porn?" Canadian Television (CTV), September 21, 2012, accessed July 14, 2017. http://www.ctvnews.ca/video?clipId=-1.

4 Stetson University, "Statement from Stetson University Regarding Clyde E. Fant," March 9, 2017, accessed July 14, 2017, http://www.stetson.edu/administration/public-relations/media/stetson-statement.pdf?ad=160310.

1

The Crime

> area. The child is depicted as being bound, with her hands behind her back, ankles are bound with handcuffs, there is a leash hanging down the front of her body and a gag in her mouth. An adult woman is standing over this child. This image is entitled "old young bond6f9f9d_500.jpg". Mr. Levin commented on this photo to Gray, stating:
>
> *"mmm, so hot to imagine a mother doing that to her girl to please her lover"*.

– Benjamin Levin's Statement of Facts
University of Toronto Professor & Deputy Minister of Education

CHILD PORNOGRAPHY

In America child pornography is a legal term used in the criminal justice system. There is a growing movement objecting to the term and a corresponding debate about what this crime should be called. Some argue child sex abuse is not adequate because sex describes legal, consenting adult behavior rather than the illegal rape of children. Child exploitation, others say, is a weak phrase that does not capture the reality of the crime. These arguments are accurate. What is being done to our children is not child pornography, exploitation or sex. It is rape and torture often meeting the Convention Against Torture (CAT) definition.[1]

Pedophiles frequently discuss being aroused by committing and watching others commit violence against children. They say they want the child to suffer. They want to "see blood." Children are often bound, gagged and violently assault-ed. Pedophiles like Benjamin Levin, a former University of Toronto pro-fessor and Depu-

> . Mr. Levin instructed D.C. Blackadar to "play" with this child in order to "prepare her for being fucked". He also instructed D.C. Blackadar to spank this child for her own pleasure and digitally penetrate her. Mr. Levin asked D.C. Blackadar if she would hurt her child to "please him".

Benjamin Levin's Statement of Facts describing his online activity

ty Minister of Education in Canada, say things like they want "to "f—— all three (of her children) in front of you with your help … would they submit or would I need to tie them?"[2] Pedophiles ask for images of babies being raped saying, "the bloodier the better."[3]

Pedophiles also discuss, and are involved in, killing children with what seems to be alarming frequency. In 2000, for example, the Guardian reported on a British child-snuff network which included a video series titled Necros Pedo where children were raped and tortured until they died. Many of the children had been taken from Russian orphanages.[4] In June 2017, Australian Federal Police (AFP) Commander Lesa Gale warned about child snuff films seen by the AFP in their investigations.[5] More than a few of those arrested in America, including people holding government positions, have discussed killing children. People like the former Acting Director of Cyber Security at the Department of Health and Human Services (DHHS), Timothy DeFoggi, who "expressed an interest in the violent rape and murder of children" and planned these crimes with other pedophiles.[6]

Additionally, murdering and/or attempting to murder the child witness is not uncommon. As Rita Karakas, of Save the Children Canada, explains "sexual abusers kill children to eliminate witnesses."[7] Such as Michael Gardner, Democratic Party Chair in Falls Church, Virginia. Gardner attempted, from jail, to have the children he abused killed so he might avoid prosecution. He had used his own children as bait, as pedophiles often do, to sexually assault their

> Using the screen name 'pedoyou,' Raymond Cain traded in child pornography including of infants and toddlers. Cain told investigators he was "turned on" by images of infant rape. He requested images of babies being raped, saying "'the bloodier the better.'"

friends during a "slumber party for his daughter's 10th birthday."[8] If pedophiles are killing children for pleasure, as documented by investigators and media reports of arrests, then murdering a child to avoid prosecution is not surprising pedophile behavior.

The "trade in child rape and torture" is the phrase I am most comfortable with because that is what is occurring. Although I agree with Interpol's position "terms such as 'kiddy porn' and 'child porn' are used by criminals and should not be legitimate language used by law enforcement, judiciary, the public or media," I do use "child pornography" throughout this book because it is still a current legal description in the United States.[9] Of course, this term needs to change. The crime should be legally called what it is and prosecuted as such. Prosecutors should use the Convention Against Torture. Organizations devoted to ending torture, such as Amnesty International, should focus on aiding American children depicted in these crime scenes.

PEDOPHILIA

There is also a debate about the word "pedophilia." Some believe the term should be "pedosadism" because what is being done to children is not "child love," as pedophilia implies, but sadistic, violent abuse; sadism. While I agree with this logic, I use the term pedophile because it is commonly understood in America. I do not use any of the terms that seek to differentiate pedophiles, like hebephilia, because I find the views of some mental health professionals who use these various terms to be incorrect and, perhaps, based on false premises.

This crime is not about sexual attraction. The "sexual attraction to pubescent youngsters" is not normal – as some mental health professionals argue.[10] It is important to note, when considering the mental health research, that more than a few in the mental health sector have been arrested for trading in child rape. So many, indeed, it is a subject for an entirely separate book. Mental health experts making the argument that pedophilia is normal may be creating a legal cover to justify their own crimes. In naming the crime, it is important to consider three key flaws with the mental health argument about "attraction."

First, from my own extensive reading of hundreds of child pornography arrests, what pedophiles most often discuss is a desire to harm children – not an attraction to children. They trade files labeled "torture12.jpg."[11] They write "slut hurt me" across the bodies of small children before raping them. They want to see the children bound and gagged, hurt, bleed and sometimes murdered. If there is any "attraction" within this crime in America, judging by the arrest records, it is white men in leadership positions "attracted" to their own power to harm society's most vulnerable; our children.

> The type of images in Garner's collection is also relevant under the Guidelines. Garner admits that the images he possessed included images of prepubescent minors and material portraying sadistic or masochistic conduct or other depictions of violence. (Plea ¶ 2) Included in the images possessed by Garner are the following five examples:
>
> ! IMAGE #1
>
> "mar32089.jpg" is a color image of one (1) white, naked, brown haired female, approximately 7-10 years old, lying on her back on top of a bed. The bed has a tan colored sheet. She is holding a black plastic sword with both hands above her chest. Written on her chest and stomach, in red, are the words "slut hurt me." The female's legs are spread apart exposing her vagina. On her right knee is what appears to be a sticker or fake tattoo of a green frog. In the upper left hand corner of the image, there is a text in red letters reading: "nifty-star.com, home-made pictures."

The Dean of Education at University of San Francisco - William Gardner's Criminal Complaint describing what he was trading in.

Second, it is documented that most offenders "do not automatically have a sexual preference for children."[12] Pedophiles rape and abuse children because it is easy to do. The more vulnerable the child the better. They do this because they care about obtaining gratification for themselves, regardless of the damage it does to anyone else. In fact, the pain they inflict on others is often what gives them gratification. Children are easier to control and abuse than adults, with a far greater chance of impunity for the crime. That is why pedophiles target children. They are an easy and safe mark. It is a strategic choice, not a sexual preference.

Third, the extensive involvement of organized crime in the trade of child rape is well established. Organized crime's sexual exploitation of children "is motivated by the vulnerability of the child rather than a specific sexual interest in children."[13] People who obtain pleasure watching, possessing, trading and producing the rape and torture of children are criminals. Pedophiles are situational offenders who rape children and trade in child rape because they can, "simply because it is available."[14] Because we, as a society, have allowed child pornography to be easily and profitably accessible.

Because we have failed to protect our children.

BACKGROUND

It is beyond the scope of this book to provide a detailed description of the history of child pornography and legal statutes prohibiting the offense. It is also outside my remit to include a complete analysis of all the literature. Instead, I provide a brief overview of key literature for those interested in reading more extensively about this crime. The body of academic research on child pornography is not extensive, largely out-of-date and broadly divided into three categories: (1) legal analysis of prosecution and sentencing guidelines, (2) investigative techniques and (3) mental health/therapy for perpetrators, with a notably limited focus on victims. The best journalistic work has been done by Julian Sher in his book *Caught in the Web: Inside the Police Hunt to Rescue Children from Online Predators*.[15] Research by government agencies appears to be the most detailed and current. The International Centre for Missing and Exploited Children (ICMEC) provides information on child pornography laws in 196 countries.[16]

In America until 1977, when The Protection of Children Against Sexual Exploitation Act was passed, there was no federal law against child pornography.[17] Child pornography was legal in Europe in the 1970s with Denmark and the Netherlands producing magazines exported to America. Publications were also domestically produced and, apparently, freely available. Says Philip Jenkins, author of *Beyond Tolerance: Child Pornography on the Internet*, "it was easy to walk into a store in New York, Los Angeles, or London

> Robert Geist, police chief of Brecknock Township, Pennsylvania, was arrested in 2013. He was trading files including "6Yo babyj – Bedtime rape." Geist pled guilty on three counts and received five years probation and 100 hours of community service. Geist was the "number one possessor and distributor of child porn" in Pennsylvania.

and purchase what was frankly advertised as child porn."[18] Pedophiles also openly organized groups such as North American Man-Boy Love (NAMBLA) and the Pedophile Information Exchange (PIE). In 1996, the Child Pornography Prevention Act was passed in America, criminalizing sexual images of individuals under eighteen.[19]

While there is now a federal child pornography statue, at the state level definition and sentencing vary widely. Usually but not always when federal prosecutors take over a case, the state will drop charges. The state can and sometimes does pursue charges concurrently with the federal government. What a pedophile is sentenced to is extremely inconsistent at both the state and federal level, despite the federal statue. Sentencing depends on the judge in the district and the person being prosecuted.[20] A police chief, like Robert Geist, Pennsylvania's number one possessor and distributor of child pornography trading in files like "6Yo babyj – Bedtime rape," may not spend a day in jail, while people who do not enjoy government positions or personal wealth, like Patricia and Matthew Ayers, can be sentenced to 1,590 years and 750 years, respectively, in prison.[21]

It is important to note that the investigation and prosecution of child pornography in America occurs within the context of a broken, sexist and racist judicial system. If you are unaware of how corrupt our courts are, please read Matt Taibbi's *The Divide: American Injustice in the Age of the Wealth Gap and Just Mercy: A Story of Justice and Redemption* by Bryon Stevenson.[22] The judicial system in America is widely documented, by a vast body of literature, to protect the rich, white and male. Women, people of color, and the poor are destroyed by America's judicial system. Why? In my opinion, far too many white, racist, sexist men dominate our criminal justice system and more than a few have been caught engaged in trading in child rape and torture themselves. This is further discussed in Chapter Six on the legal profession.

GOVERNMENT REPORTS

International government and law enforcement agencies are producing important reports. In June 2017, the national police in the Netherlands issued their Annual Trend Report, describing, for the first time, child pornography as a "threat to Dutch society."[23] Europol, the European police agency, is releasing perhaps the most detailed reports. Europol's Commercial Sexual Exploitation of Children Online 2015, and Strategic Assessment of Commercial Sexual Exploitation of Children Online 2013, are excellent sources of knowledge on the crime. Australia's 2016, Online Child Exploitation Material – Trends and Emerging Issues Research Report of the Australian National University Cybercrime Observatory with the Office of the Children's eSafety Commissioner, is also a must-read. The National Rapporteur on Trafficking in Human Beings in the Netherlands also issued a comprehensive report in 2011, Child Pornography: First Report of the Dutch National Rapporteur.[24] In April 2017, the European Parliament released Combating Sexual Abuse of Children Directive.[25]

In America, the most recent U.S. Sentencing Commission report is from 2012, *Report to the Congress: Federal Child Pornography Offenses*. The U.S. Department of Justice (DOJ) published *The National Strategy for Child Exploitation Prevention and Interdiction* in 2016, updating the first *National Strategy for Child Exploitation Prevention and Interdiction,* from 2010. DOJ's Child Exploitation and Obscenities Section (CEOS) has some material available in their resource section, the most recent from 2010, and the latest Congressional Testimony, with one exception, from 2006. The Bureau of Justice Statistics (BJS) most recent report is "Federal Prosecution of Child Sex Exploitation Offenders, 2006."[26] BJS is currently completing a report on commercial exploitation of children, including child pornography, expected to be released in 2017.[27]

Action Item
The U.S. Sentencing Commission welcomes public comment on issues people would like the Commission to focus.
Contact Liz Dawson, Publishing and Public Affairs Specialist, Tel: 202-502-4633 🐦 @theusscgov & PubAffairs@ ussc.gov
Request the USSC update their 2012 child pornography report and include detailed demographics of child pornography arrests, including profession and place of employment.

This crime is expanding so fast that material more than a few years old is already out of date. It is not clear why the U.S. government lags behind in reporting on this crime compared with Europe and Australia. Current and detailed U.S. government data and reporting on this crime is urgently needed. If you agree, contact the U.S. Sentencing Commission and ask for an updated report on child pornography.

ACADEMIC RESEARCH

Regarding the academic literature, legal and investigative research has been done by Europeans like Ethel Quayle at the University of Edinburgh who published, with Max Taylor in 2003, *Child Pornography: An Internet Crime.* Quayle also co-published, in 2012, with Kurt Ribisl, *Understanding and Preventing Online Sexual Exploitation of Children*. Alisdair Gillespie at Lancaster University in the UK published, in 2012, *Child Pornography: Law and Policy*. Yaman Akdeniz published *Internet Child Pornography and the Law*, in 2008, covering legal approaches in America, Canada, Europe and the United Nations.[28]

Anti-Slavery Australia, based at the University of Technology in Sydney, and the law firm of Norton Rose Fulbright, released, May 2017,

"Behind the Screen: Online Child Exploitation in Australia," providing an overview of the "legal landscape of online child exploitation crimes" in Australia.[29] In America, Chad Steel, author of *Digital Child Pornography: A Practical Guide for Investigators,* published an excellent overview of child pornography law in America. In 2016, Carissa Byrne Hessick, a law professor at the University of North Carolina, published *Refining Child Pornography Law: Crime, Language, and Social Consequences.* In Canada, Francis Fortin and Patrice Corriveau, published *Who Is Bob_34?: Investigating Child Cyberpornography* in 2016.[30]

The other area of academic research on child pornography, as mentioned, is by the mental health profession, such as *Illegal Images: Critical Issues and Strategies for Addressing Child Pornography Use* by Elizabeth Griffin, a marriage and family therapist, and David Delmonico, an education professor at Duquesne University. Or, *Treating Sex Offenders: An Evidence-Based Manual* by Jill D. Stinson and Judith V. Becker. In Canada, Michael Seto, a psychologist, has published *Internet Sex Offenders,* in 2013, and *Pedophilia and Sexual Offending Against Children: Theory, Assessment, and Intervention* in 2007.[31]

Some of the mental health research employs a disturbing tone of empathy for pedophiles. Given that pedophiles exhibit sadistic pleasure in harming children and rarely demonstrate even the pretense of remorse for the crimes they commit, a mental health focus on empathy for pedophiles, and not the child victims, is misplaced. There is also a suggestion in some of the literature that pedophiles should be "cured" by therapy rather than sentenced to jail. Of course, it would benefit the mental health profession, enormously, if judges started issuing court-ordered therapy across the country instead of jail time. Many therapists would earn a lucrative living. Some in the mental health sector also argue pedophilia is a sexual orientation, not a crime.[32] This junk science is being distributed by mainstream media like *Gawker* "Born This Way: Sympathy and Science for Those Who Want to Have Sex with Children," *The Atlantic* "What Can Be Done About Pedophilia?" and *Salon* "Meet Pedophiles Who Mean Well."[33]

> Kimberly Epperson, a Signals Intelligence Analyst with the 401st Military Intelligence Company, was sentenced in 2013, to 28 years for raping her three-year-old son. She sent videos and live-streams to Wade Allen Perkins, a Geospatial Intelligence Imagery Analyst, with the 306th Military Intelligence Battalion. He requested Epperson include her infant son in their "sex life." Epperson was pregnant at the time. Perkins was sentenced to 30 years in jail.

Child pornography, the trade in child rape, is not a "mental health" condition to be "treated with therapy."[34] It is not a sexual orientation among consenting adults. It is a horrific crime perpetrated, most often, by organized crime and men in positions of power against the most vulnerable in our societies – our children. The only acceptable legal and societal response to this crime is prison for the perpetrators followed by life-time supervised release and life-time sex offender registration. Mandatory chemical castration should also be considered. Yes, pedophiles should receive therapy – in jail. If mental health professionals had to visit pedophiles in prison to provide court-ordered therapy, I suspect the call for therapy as a policy solution to this crime would decrease substantially.

CLOSING THE DATA GAP

There is a near total gap in the literature, both in governmental reports and academic research, in documenting and detailing the scale of the epidemic. Most of the research on child pornography begins with a disclaimer explaining that there is little research being conducted and, as a result, there is no definitive data on how many children are being destroyed, how many and who engages in the crime, what the arrest rates are, how much illegal money is generated, how profits are being laundered, how and where supply-lines to children are established, how many and which government employees have been arrested, etc.

Despite the need for in-depth and complete data, the government is not stepping up and there is not one U.S.-based public policy organization or academic institution devoted to supporting a child pornography research center to gather the data. Because there is no comprehensive data on child pornography arrests in America, journalists do not have academic studies or government data to report on. Consequently, a lack of media attention to the epidemic means that most people in America have no idea a child pornography epidemic is even occurring. As a result, the criminals know far more about this crime, and how to avoid prosecution, than almost anyone else. Without the data, there is no problem. Right?

This book attempts to establish the need to fill this data gap. The dimensions of the epidemic must be clearly established.

As soon as possible.

THE NUMBERS

> *FBI's Assistant Director of Criminal Investigation Joseph Campbell,* says *child sex trafficking and pedophilia* have reached *epidemic levels.*
>
> – BBC Interview July 2015[35]

No one knows the numbers because no one is gathering the data. We *don't know* how many children are being raped, how many people are trading in these rapes, or how much money is being made through this crimewave. At the moment, we can only guess. The numbers in this section do not represent any complete set of comprehensive, analyzed data. Instead, they are small bits of partial knowledge; windows into the scope of the epidemic. A complete statistical analysis of estimated and partial data gathered by various organizations should be performed to obtain credible average quantitative data. I regret that I have not yet done so. This task is on my future research agenda, once I receive funding and support to continue this work.

Behind every number there is a child. A real child. Someone's son or daughter. Maybe yours. The production of child pornography depends on the sexual abuse of children – American children. When a journalist reports on an arrest with 10,000 child pornography images, these are real children being raped by someone they know, trust and love. Children are being abused by teachers, coaches, religious leaders, baby-sitters, grandfathers and fathers. Indeed, child exploitation rings led by fathers have become, what some are calling, a "widespread tragedy."[36] It is almost certain, given the numbers, someone in your social, professional or family circles is trading in child rape. It is highly probable you know a child being sexually abused. Unbeknown to you, your own child might even be in a video shared widely on the Internet. You may not know of your child's abuse for decades – if ever.

WEBSITES AND SERVERS

In terms of websites trading in child rape, there is some reliable data. The Internet Watch Foundation (IWF) reported, as early as 1999, America was hosting 40 percent of the world's child-sex abuse images/videos. In 2006, IWF reported 82 percent of all web domains hosting child pornography were in America. The European police, Europol, reported, in 2013, that nearly half of all servers hosting child pornography were located in the United States.[37] Europol's 2015 report details a dramatic increase in U.S.-based sites from 516 sites in 2013 to 2,617 sites in 2015; far greater than any other country.

American journalists never reported on these statistics. Not once. Why not?

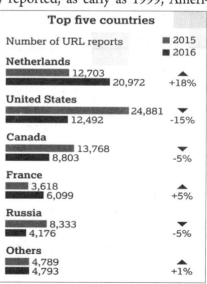

Internet Watch Foundation (IWF) 2016 Report, pg. 12.

In 2014, the Australian Communications and Media Authority reported a 500 percent increase in child pornography sites with 64 percent on U.S.-based servers. Australian authorities estimated 80,000 children had been trafficked to produce these images/videos with the majority being girls under thirteen-years-old.[38] Anti-Slavery Australia reported, in May 2017, that child pornography is now a "crime epidemic" with images/videos depicting "highly depraved acts of sexual violence and torture" against "young children."[39] As of 2016, Europe, primarily the Netherlands, hosts more websites than anywhere else with 60 percent of the global total.[40]

In 2016, the Internet Watch Foundation (IWF) logged onto a child pornography website every five minutes and removed 57,335 webpages from the Internet. Fifty-three percent of children on these sites were ten-years-old or younger.[41] In 2015, IWF removed 1,000 webpages every week with 69 percent of the children on these sites under ten-years-old and 1,788 of the children two-years-old or younger.[42] In 2015, the FBI shut down one U.S. based website called Playpen that had 214,898 members trading in child rape and torture.[43] Just one website out of thousands. Imagine. In 2017, Canada released a report detailing a six-week period when the Canadian Centre for Child Protection's Project Arachnid processed over 230 million child pornography web pages with over 40,000 unique images of child sex abuse.[44] A small sample of the staggering volume of child rape being traded on the Internet.

The National Center for Missing & Exploited Children (NCMEC) reported from 2007 to 2013, a 5,000 percent increase in child sex abuse images/videos and an estimated 22 million images/videos available on the market. In 2014, NCMEC processed 24 million child sex abuse images/videos – a 48,000 percent increase since 2002. Of these, 75 percent were of children under twelve-years-old and ten percent were infants and toddlers. Microsoft, working with NCMEC, says 1.8 billion images of child sex abuse are shared online every day. Terre Des Hommes estimates there are 750,000 pedophiles online every second worldwide.

Imagine how many children are being abused to produce this kind of volume.

PROFITS

The global industry may be yielding $20 to $50 billion or more per year.[45] No one knows for sure. An estimated 1.2 million children are trafficked globally every year.[46] One investigator calls the child pornography industry "very tempting" with lots of "sales to be made."[47] For example, in 2013, Germany estimated some 250,000 Germans spent $27 billion U.S. dollars on child pornography. Twenty-seven billion in just one year, by a quarter of a million people.[48]

A total of 5236 URLs suspected of the commercial distribution of CAM in 2013 divided into hosting countries[36] (for countries with more than 20 reports) as follows:

INHOPE Commercial URLs by hosting country	2013
1. United States	2617
2. Netherlands	942
3. Russian Federation	437
4. Japan	322
5. Ukraine	182
6. Canada	177
7. Czech Republic	125
8. Germany	81
9. Luxembourg	77
10. Singapore	60
11. Korea, South	51
12. Kazakhstan	42
13. United Kingdom	34
14. France	27

This distribution is broadly similar to INHOPE statistics in the two other periods:

The hosting countries (for countries with more than 20 reports)	October - December 2012	The hosting countries (for countries with more than 20 reports)	January - June 2014
1. United States	516	1. United States	2048
2. Russian Federation	121	2. Japan	455
3. Kazakhstan	119	3. Netherlands	156
4. Japan	83	4. Russian Federation	88
5. Netherlands	67	5. Ukraine	59
6. Ukraine	58	6. Canada	23
7. Germany	50	7. Germany	22
8. Czech Republic	40		
9. Hungary	24		

Europol's Strategic Assessment of the Commercial Sexual Exploitation of Children On-line, 2015. pg 15.

According to Europol, "child sexual exploitation material (CSEM) is increasingly produced for financial gain."[49] The easy profit-model of child rape is rapidly overtaking drugs and guns as organized crime's preferred money-maker. Children are a renewable resource. They can be sold multiple times a day over many years and are easy to transport. Their rape can be sold online and in-person. Their organs can be sold on the black market.

As early as 2012, child sex trafficking was reported to be America's fastest growing crime, expanding by some 150 percent each year.[50] The Department of Justice reported, in 2012, pedophiles can earn $1,000 per night raping children in front of a live web camera.[51] In March 2015, the Ontario Provincial Police in Canada seized a data-hosting server with 2,200, out of a total 7,500, Internet provider (IP) addresses based in America. Germany had 843 users. There were 534 in Japan, 457 in Russia, 394 in Canada, 380 in the United Kingdom and 374 in France. In this one bust, Canadian investigators seized over 1.2 petabytes of data – more than four times the amount of data in the U.S. Library of Congress. This one server netted $18 million in revenue over a three-month period.

AMERICAN CHILD PORNOGRAPHY ARREST AND PROSECUTION DATA

Currently, there is no coordinated reporting and data collection among federal or state law enforcement agencies on child pornography arrests. Therefore, to my knowledge, no one has calculated the total number of federal and state child pornography arrests per year. This lack of coordination and data collection underscores the need for a national child pornography arrest database housing complete arrest and prosecution records.

The Department of Justice (DOJ) reported between 2011-2016, federal prosecutors filed 20,260 child pornography cases against 19,111 defendants.[52] According to DOJ's Bureau of Justice Statistics (BJS), from 2010-2014, there were 17,054 child pornography arrests and 12,334 corresponding prosecutions at the federal level. Limitations on this data include at least three issues. First, the U.S. Marshals use National Crime Information Center Codes (NCIC) offense codes and BJS has "not investigated the reliability of these detailed offense codes (such as child pornography)."[53] Second, this data only represents federal agencies contributing to the Federal Justice Statistics Program.[54] In order to calculate total federal arrests, information from all federal law enforcement agencies,

Number of suspects in matters concluded by U.S. attorneys where child pornography was lead charge, 2010-2014

Fiscal year	Child pornography suspects in matters concluded Number	Child pornography suspects in matters prosecuted Number	Percent
2010	3,414	2,256	66%
2011	3,632	2,563	71%
2012	3,255	2,344	72%
2013	3,517	2,670	76%
2014	3,236	2,501	77%

Note: Child pornography inckudes Title 18 U.S.C. §§ 2251-2252 as lead charge.

Source: Bureau of Justice Statistics, based on data from the Executive Office for U.S. Attorneys, National LIONS database, fiscal year.

Bureau of Justice Statistics (BJS) Chart
Sent to author via email from BJS

such as Homeland and others, investigating child pornography is needed. Third, state level arrest and prosecution data is not included.

Other information from some federal agencies conducting child pornography arrests includes a random set of available data. This fragmented data, however, provides a scope of the epidemic. The FBI reported 2,900 child sexual exploitation arrests in 2014. Immigration and Customs Enforcement (ICE) reported 35,000 child exploitation arrests from 2003-2015. The U.S. Postal Inspectors claimed 500 arrests from 2010-2015.[55] In 2014, *USA Today* reported "last year, more suspects were arrested for child exploitation crimes – 7,386 – than at any time in the past five years, according to Justice Department records gathered from sixty-one Internet Crimes Against Children (ICACs) task forces across the nation."[56] By 2015, the ICACs had made 8,500 child pornography arrests.[57] The U.S. Marshals, from 2010-2015, arrested 2,671 people who had violated their court-ordered federal sex-offender registration obligations.[58]

LACK OF PERPETRATOR DATA

One element of perpetrator data that is known is from the U.S. Sentencing Commission. Those convicted on child pornography charges in America have been, overwhelmingly, white men. The U.S. Sentencing Commission documents data from federal prosecutions in 1992, 2004, and 2010. For every year, more than eight-five percent of child pornography convicts were white men averaging forty-three-years-old.[59] This perpetrator information will be discussed in greater detail in Chapter Four. The U.S. Sentencing Commission needs to update this data to determine if this trend is continuing.

What percentage of thousands of arrests reported by DOJ and others include infant and toddler rape? How many of the perpetrators were in positions of power over vulnerable children, such as pediatric oncologists, special education teachers, child protection staff or law enforcement themselves? How many were parents molesting their own children? What is the social-economic and racial composition of the perpetrators? How many were government employees? We don't know because these kinds of detailed demographics are not being tracked. We need to know the details of who is committing this crime and how, if we hope to stop the epidemic.

When it comes to child pornography arrests and prosecution demographics, no one has solid methodology. Reports, even by national law enforcement agencies, all begin with a disclaimer that researching the scope of the crime is nearly impossible because the data is not consistently documented, collected and collated at local or federal levels and not shared well across state or international borders. Researchers cobbled together methodology, attempting to create reasonably valid results. Even

---

Dear Ms. Handrahan:

This letter is a final response to your June 28, 215, Freedom of Information Act /Privacy Act request that was received in the Office of Justice Programs (OJP), Office of the General Counsel, on June 29, 2015, for processing and responding directly to you. A copy of your request is attached for your convenience.

Please be advised that a search has been conducted in the OJP, and after seeking further clarification, it appears that we do not collect prosecution rates. OJP mandate reporting for all ICAC Taskforce arrests. Therefore, we have no responsive documents. This completes the processing of your request by OJP.

Personal correspondence sent to author by DOJ in response to a FOIA request No. 15-00305

law enforcement working in cyber-crimes units, with access to data others lack, say the same thing; researching child pornography presents unique methodological problems. This "unique methodological problem" is entirely human-made. When government agencies fail, or refuse, to gather and publish the data a "unique methodological problem" does develop.[60]

The lack of perpetrator data is acutely concerning. How many teachers, lawyers, police officers, child protection staff, etc., have been arrested, at what institutions, receiving what kind of sentences and trading in what kind and volume of child rape? No one knows because the U.S. government has failed to gather this data. DOJ's Office of Juvenile Justice (OJJDP) responded to my freedom of information act (FOIA) request about prosecution data, saying OJJDP does "not collect prosecution rates" related to the ICAC arrests.[61] DOJ does not track the employment status of offenders prosecuted for federal offenses because, Bureau of Justice Statistics informed me, employment status is not a variable provided in the data received from federal law enforcement.[62]

While it is troubling that the Department of Justice is not collecting, analyzing and publishing detailed arrest and prosecution data on America's fastest growing crime, to be fair to DOJ, there also seems to be little interest or demand from academics, journalists, public policy experts, Congress or the general public to document this epidemic. It is a subject almost everyone has avoided. Nonetheless, at the very least, the U.S. government should publish annual data on how many and which government employees have been prosecuted on child pornography charges.

A WAR WE ARE ALREADY LOSING

The people who know the most about this crime, other than pedophiles, are dedicated law enforcement officers and prosecutors on the front-lines of this war being waged on our children. Behind every pedophile in jail is a team of investigators and lawyers who put their own mental health on the line to investigate and prosecute these crimes and bring justice to child victims. Prosecutors and law enforcement working this crime are under-funded and overwhelmed. There are far too many pedophiles producing mind-bending amounts of videos, images and live-streams of child rape and torture. America's criminal justice system cannot keep up because the public and our policy leaders have not demanded necessary resources be allocated. We have not insisted on substantial funding because very few people even understand that there is a war being waged against our children.

The lack of a child pornography arrest database also impedes the efforts of law enforcement and prosecutors. Prosecutors and law enforcement tell me they would benefit from a comprehensive public database.

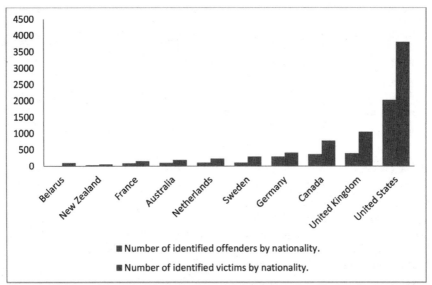

Figure 1.1 Total number of identified offenders and victims by nationality from the beginning of the ICSE database until 1 June 2016 (Source: INTERPOL ICSE). As displayed in Australia's "Behind the Screen," report, pg. 10. Interpol manages the International Child Sexual Exploitation (ICSE) image database.

Police and prosecutors ask if I know what happened with a certain case, because cases get lost in the system. For example, Julian Sher detailed how Canadian police spent two years on a case only to discover the perpetrator had been caught by the FBI and was already in jail.[63] No one can afford to investigate a case that has already been solved. Resources are too little, too late for redundant investigations. Investigators and prosecutors need easy access to individual cases and comprehensive statistics about the crime.

There is raw federal child pornography arrest and prosecution information available for a fee on Public Access to Court Electronic Reports (PACER).[64] This data has not yet been gathered and analyzed. Collecting the data and building a database using PACER data is possible. It would require reading, researching and entering information on over 20,000 federal arrests and prosecutions. This would be a time-consuming endeavor , but could be accomplished with a team of researchers employed to gather, enter and analyze the data. This book is, in many ways, a preface to that future research goal if funding becomes available.

America's fastest growing crime is one we know almost nothing about. The absence of collected and published data by the U.S. government is inexcusable. The U.S. government must publish comprehensive annual data on this crime. Private funds must be found to document the epidemic. How is it possible for child pornography to be categorized as the fastest-growing crime and there is little detailed data about this war against our children? A war we are we are already losing.

(Endnotes)

1. United Nations, "Convention against Torture and Other Cruel, Inhuman or Degrading Treatment or Punishment," General Assembly Resolution 39/46, December 10, 1984, accessed July 16, 2017, http://www.ohchr.org/EN/ProfessionalInterest/Pages/CAT.aspx

2. "Ben Levin Statement of Facts" and Arthur Weinreb, "Ben Levin: Child pornography charges were the least of it," *Canadian Free Press,* June 1, 2015, accessed July 16, 2017, http://canadafreepress.com/article/ben-levin-child-pornography-charges-were-the-least-of-it

3. "Investigators: Berkeley County Man Asked for Pics of Infant Rape" ABC News 4, December 20, 2012, accessed July 16, 2017, http://abcnews4.com/archive/court-docs-kiddie-porn

4. Jason Burke, Amelia Gentleman, and Philip Willan, "British link to 'snuff' videos." *Guardian,* September 30, 2000, accessed July 16, 2017, http://www.theguardian.com/uk/2000/oct/01/ameliagentleman.philipwillan

5 Keith Moor, "'Snuff films alarm: AFP warns of growing paedophile problem," *Herald Sun,* June 4, 2017, accessed July 16, 2017, http://www.heraldsun.com.au/news/law-order/snuff-films-alarm-afp-warns-of-growing-paedophile-problem/news-story/4c-f9a18f18348d0c2b897a4802bb1793

6. Moyer, "Former HHS official sentenced," 2015.

7. Julian Sher, *Caught in the Web: Inside the Police Hunt to Rescue Children from Online Predators* (New York: Carroll & Graf Publisher, 2007), 152.

8. Julie Zauzmer, "Defendant allegedly asked about hit man to kill child witnesses," *Washington Post,* February 19, 2015, accessed July 16, 2017 http://www.washingtonpost.com/local/crime/defendant-allegedly-asked-about-hit-man-to-kill-child-witnesses/2015/02/19/8a4fe858-b878-11e4-a200-c008a01a6692_story.html?utm_term=.211e0a02b2e6

9. Interpol, "Interpol network identifies 10,000 child sexual abuse victims," *Interpol Press Release,* January 9, 2017, accessed July 17, 2017, https://www.interpol.int/News-and-media/News/2017/N2017-001

10. Francis Allen, "Hebephilia is a Crime, Not a Mental Disorder," *Psychiatric Times,* December 15, 2011, accessed July 15, 2017, http://www.psychiatrictimes.com/articles/hebephilia-crime-not-mental-disorder

11. Sher, *Caught in the Web,* 237.

12. Alessia Altamura, "Understanding demand for CSEC and the related gender dimensions: A review of the research," *ECPAT Journal Series,* No. 7 (2013): 4, accessed July 17, 2017, http://www.ecpat.org/wp-content/uploads/legacy/ecpat_journal_jul_2013_eng.pdf

13. United Nations, "Report of the Special Rapporteur on the Sale of Children," 9.

14. Altamura, "Understanding demand for CSEC," 4.

15. Sher, *Caught in the Web.*

16. International Centre for Missing and Exploited Children (ICMEC), "Child Pornography: Model Legislation & Global Review," accessed July 17, 2017, https://www.icmec.org/research-library

17. United States Congress, "Protection of Children Against Sexual Exploitation Act," S. 1585 (95th) (Washington DC: United States Government), February 6, 1978, accessed, July 17, 2017, https://www.govtrack.us/congress/bills/95/s1585

18. Philip Jenkins, *Beyond Tolerance: Child Pornography on the Internet,* (New York: New York University, 2003), 32.

19. John Schwartz, "Congress Passes Bill Extending Definition of Child Pornography," *Washington Post*, October 4, 1996, accessed July 17, 2017, https://www.washingtonpost.com/archive/politics/1996/10/04/new-law-expanding-legal-definition-of-child-pornography-draws-fire/3259a7d5-3349-4b4b-a49a-f2d1ba534019/?utm_term=.6059aaf70d2f

20. Julian Sher describes how random sentencing can be for child pornography offenses, see: Sher, *Caught in the Web*, 205-219.

21. Bob Keeler, "Bedminster resident Robert Geist sentenced for possessing child pornography," *Montgomery News*, September 29, 2014, accessed July 17, 2017, http://www.montgomerynews.com/perkasienewsherald/news/bedminster-resident-robert-geist-sentenced-for-possessing-child-pornography/article_5666c593-2794-5857-9cb8-68d6a445dd7d.html and "Former Berks Co. police chief faces child porn charges," ABC News 6 WPVI-TV, December 12, 2013, accessed July 17, 2017, http://6abc.com/archive/9357995/ and Federal Bureau of Investigations (FBI), "Child Pornography Case Results in Lengthy Prison Sentences: Couple Abused Child in Their Care," *FBI Press Release*, November 13, 2014, accessed July 17, 2017, https://www.fbi.gov/news/stories/child-pornography-case-results-in-lengthy-prison-sentences

22. Timothy Noah, "The Justice Gap: 'The Divide,' by Matt Taibbi," *New York Times*, April 10, 2014, accessed July 17, 2017, https://www.nytimes.com/2014/04/13/books/review/the-divide-by-matt-taibbi.html and Bryon Stevenson, *Just Mercy: A Story of Justice and Redemption*, (New York: Random House, 2014) accessed July 17, 2017, http://bryanstevenson.com/the-book

23. Janene Pieters, "Explosive increase in child pornography forms national threat: Dutch police," *NLTimes.nl*, May 31, 2017, accessed July 17, 2017, http://nltimes.nl/2017/05/31/explosive-increase-child-pornography-forms-national-threat-dutch-police and Jorg Leijten, "Politie: kinderporno bedreigt de Nederlandse samenleving Nationaal dreigingsbeeld De politie krijgt veel meer meldingen binnen van mogelijke kinderporno. Ze kan lang niet alle tips goed nagana," NRC.nl, May 31, 2017, accessed July 17, 2017, https://www.nrc.nl/nieuws/2017/05/31/politie-kinderporno-bedreigt-de-nederlandse-samenleving-10812854-a1561130

24. Dutch National Rapporteur on Trafficking in Human Beings and Sexual Violence against Children "National Rapporteur presents First Report on Child Pornography to United Nations," National Rapporteur Press Release, May 6, 2012, accessed July 17, 2017, https://www.dutchrapporteur.nl/current/news/NationalRapporteurpresentsFirstReportonChildPornographytoUnitedNations.aspx

25. European Parliamentary Research Service, "Combating Sexual Abuse of Children," Directive 2011/93/EU, April 2017, accessed July 17, 2017, http://www.europarl.europa.eu/RegData/etudes/STUD/2017/598614/EPRS_STU(2017)598614_EN.pdf

26. Mark Motivans and Tracey Kyckelhahn, "Federal Prosecution of Child Sex Exploitation Offenders, 2006," NCJ 219412, Department of Justice Bureau of Justice Statistics (BJS), December 2007, accessed July 17, 2017, https://www.bjs.gov/content/pub/pdf/fpcseo06.pdf

27. Bureau of Justice Statistics (BJS), e-mail message to author, May 15, 2017.

28. Ethel Quayle and Max Taylor, *Child Pornography: An Internet Crime*, (New York: Routledge, 2003); Ethel Quayle and Kurt Ribisl, *Understanding and Preventing Online Sexual Exploitation of Children* (New York, Routledge, 2012); Alisdair Gillespie at Lancaster University in the UK published, in 2012, *Child Pornography: Law and Policy*, (New York: Routledge, 2012); and Yaman Akdeniz, *Internet Child Pornography and the Law*, (New York, Routledge, 2008).

29. Anti-Slavery Australia, *Behind the Screen*.

30. Chad Steel, *Digital Child Pornography: A Practical Guide for Investigators* (Lily Shiba Press, 2014); Carissa Byrne Hessick, ed., *Refining Child Pornography Law: Crime, Language, and Social Consequences*, (Michigan: University of Michigan Press, 2016); Francis Fortin and Patrice Cor-

riveau, *Who Is Bob_34?: Investigating Child Cyberpornography*, (British Columbia: University of British Columbia Press, 2015).

31. David Delmonico and Elizabeth Griffin, *Illegal Images: Critical Issues and Strategies for Addressing Child Pornography Use*, (NEARI Press, 2013); Jill D. Stinson and Judith V. Becker, *Treating Sex Offenders: An Evidence-Based Manual* (New York: Guilford Press, 2013); Michael Seto, *Internet Sex Offenders*, (Washington DC: American Psychological Association, 2013); and Michael Seto, *Pedophilia and Sexual Offending Against Children: Theory, Assessment, and Intervention*, (Washington DC: American Psychological Association, 2008).

32. Michael Seto, "Is pedophilia a sexual orientation?" Archives of Sexual Behavior 41 (1), (2012) :231-6, accessed July 17, 2017.

33. Cord Jefferson, "Born This Way: Sympathy and Science for Those Who Want to Have Sex with Children," *Gawker*, September 7, 2012, accessed July 17, 2017, http://gawker.com/5941037/born-this-way-sympathy-and-science-for-those-who--want-to-have-sex-with-children; Alice Dreger, "What Can Be Done About Pedophilia?" *The Atlantic*, August 26, 2013, accessed July 17, 2017, https://www.theatlantic.com/health/archive/2013/08/what-can-be-done-about-pedophilia/279024 and *Tracy Clark-Flory*, "Meet Pedophiles who mean well," Salon, July 1, 2012, accessed July 17, 2017, http://www.salon.com/2012/07/01/meet_pedophiles_who_mean_well

34. There is no credible evidence that child rapists can be "cured" by therapy. There is a volume of reports about corruption within the mental health profession around this subject. Most recently, [as reported by David Rose, "The scandal of the sex crime 'cure' hubs: How minister buried report into £100million prison programme to treat paedophiles and rapists that INCREASED reoffending rates," *The Mail on Sunday*, June 24, 2017, accessed July 17, 2017, http://www.dailymail.co.uk/news/article-4635876/Scandal-100million-sex-crime-cure-hubs.html] a British report that UK's former Justice Secretary, Liz Truss, kept hidden a report that documented "rehabilitation courses taken by thousands of jailed rapists and paedophiles make them more dangerous once they are released. According to the study, prisoners who take the courses are at least 25 per cent more likely to be convicted of further sex crimes than those who do not, suggesting that the sessions may have created hundreds of extra victims. The controversial Sex Offender Treatment Programme (SOTP), a six-month psychological group-therapy course, is believed to have cost taxpayers well over £100 million since it was set up in 1991."

35. "Human trafficking: FBI warns of 'epidemic,'" British Broadcasting Corporations (BBC), 28 July 2015, accessed July 17, 2017, http://www.bbc.com/news/world-33682953.

36. Robert Crib, "Chilling evidence of organized child sex abuse revealed in survey," *The Star*, January 17, 2017, accessed July 17, 2017, https://www.thestar.com/news/world/2017/01/17/chilling-evidence-of-organized-child-sex-abuse-revealed-in-survey.html

37. Paul Gallagher, "Live streamed videos of abuse and pay-per-view child rape among 'disturbing' cybercrime trends, Europol report reveals," *The Independent*, October 16, 2013, accessed July 17, 2017, http://www.independent.co.uk/news/uk/crime/live-streamed-videos-of-abuse-and-payperview-child-rape-among-disturbing-cybercrime-trends-europol-report-reveals-8884198.html

38. Paddy Wood, "Online child porn inquiries rise five-fold,' *The Australian*, July 21, 2014, accessed July 17, 2017, www.theaustralian.com.au/news/latest-news/online-child-porn-inquiries-rise-five-fold/news-story/ff3662c8a85d73570bad3b8b3c48a7e4?nk=463af5693cca928371878f8f6313124b-1498337095

39. University of Technology Sydney (UTS), "Live-streamed child sex abuse part of a global crime pandemic," Press Release, May 30, 2017, accessed July 17, 2017, https://www.uts.edu.au/research-and-teaching/our-research/law-research-centre/news/live-streamed-child-sex-abuse-part and Anti-Slavery Australia, *Behind the Screen*, 5.

40. Internet Watch Foundation, *Annual Report 2016*, 12.

41. Internet Watch Foundation, *Annual Report 2016*, 9. *See also*: Olivia Gordon, "The Young Woman Behind the Software that Catches Child Predators," VICE, July 22, 2016, accessed July 22, 2017, https://broadly.vice.com/en_us/article/8qww73/Internet-watch-foundation-harriet-lester-catch-child-predators-interview

42. Internet Watch Foundation, *Annual Report 2016*.

43. Nate Raymond, "FBI seized child porn website with 215,000 users: court filing," *Reuters*, July 7, 2015, accessed July 17, 2017, http://www.reuters.com/article/us-usa-crime-childporn-idUSKCN0PH24C20150707

44. Canadian Centre for Child Protection, "Canadian Centre for Child Protection's survey speaks to damaging impacts of the sharing of child sexual abuse material," Press Release, January 17, 2017, accessed July 17, 2017, https://protectchildren.ca/app/en/csa_imagery#csa_imagery-arachnid

45. Accurate calculations of criminal activity always present data problems and due to the lack of research on child pornography, this problem is amplified. *Wall Street Journal* reporter Carl Bialik published a summary of the various reports that guest-estimate child pornography profits in 2006. Carl Bialik, "Measuring the Child Porn Trade," *Wall Street Journal*, April 18, 2006, accessed July 17, 2017, http://online.wsj.com/news/articles/SB114485422875624000.

46. United Nations, "UN Global Initiative to Fight Human Trafficking," Fact Sheet, February 9, 2014, accessed July 17, 2017, www.unglobalcompact.org/docs/issues_doc/labour/Forced_labour/HUMAN_TRAFFICKING_-_THE_FACTS_-_final.pdf

47. Rebecca Lopeze and Jonathan Betz, "University Park Woman Faces Child Porn Charges," Dallas News, June 2, 2012, accessed July 17, 2017, http://www.dallasnews.com/news/community-news/park-cities/headlines/20120602-university-park-woman-faces-child-porn-charges.ece

48. Ines Pohl, "Child pornography in doubt for the child," *Deutschlandfunk*, February 22, 2014, accessed July 17, 2017, http://www.deutschlandfunk.de/kinderpornografie-im-zweifel-fuer-das-kind.720.de.html?dram:article_id=278181

49. Europol, "Serious and Organised Crime Threat Assessment (SOCTA)," 2017, accessed July 17, 2017, https://www.europol.europa.eu/socta/2017, 31.

50. Unites States Congress, "Statement of Chairman Lamar Smith on the House Floor, H.R. 6063, the Child Protection Act," (Washington DC: United States Government) July 31, 2012, accessed July 17, 2017, http://judiciary.house.gov/index.cfm/press-releases?ID=1B-54DC42-BFFF-B0B3-7267-0CA0FAE06B4E

51. Department of Justice, "*The National Strategy for Child Exploitation Prevention and Interdiction 2010*," August 2010, accessed July 17, 2017, 32-33.

52. Department of Justice, "The National Strategy 2016."

53. Bureau of Justice Statistics (BJS), e-mail message to author, May 15, 2017.

54. U.S. Marshals, Drug Enforcement Administration, Executive Office for U.S. Attorneys, Administrative Office of the U.S. Courts, U.S. Sentencing Commission and the Federal Bureau of Prisons. The BJS told the author that Homeland Security, for example, among others may or may not be included.

55. Department of Justice, "The National Strategy 2016."

56. Kevin Johnson, "Clandestine websites fuel 'alarming' increase in child porn," *USA Today*, May 15, 2014, accessed July 16, 2017, https://www.usatoday.com/story/news/nation/2014/02/19/child-pornography-dark-web/5184485

57. Department of Justice, "The National Strategy 2016," 6.

58. Department of Justice, "The National Strategy 2016," 6.

59. U.S. Sentencing Commission, "Report to the Congress," 142.

60. Europol reports "Analysts engaged in the assessment of global criminal phenomena such as online child sexual exploitation (CSE) invariably face methodological challenges regarding data collection. In the first instance, data on online sexual offences against children is not always collected at national level: this is particularly the case where countries lack national police intelligence and recorded crime databases. Secondly, without exception data is recorded and collected at national level according to the relevant articles of national penal codes. By this token, even where national legislations are approximate, variations in the precise previsions will mean that data collected according to these specifications will never be truly comparable to those of other countries." Europol, "Strategic Assessment of the Commercial Sexual Exploitation of Children Online," October 15, 2013, accessed July 16, 2017 https://www.europol.europa.eu/content/new-cybercrime-report-examines-disturbing-trends-commercial-online-child-sex-abuse, 7.

6 1. Department of Justice (DOJ), e-mail message to author in response to FOIA request No. 15-00305, February 3, 2017.

62 Bureau of Justice Statistics (BJS), e-mail message to author, May 15, 2017.

63. Sher, Caught in the Web, 138-162.

64. Public Access to Court Electronic Records accessed July 17, 2017, https://www.pacer.gov

2

The Trade is Global

The illegal trade in children being raped and violently abused is at "a level of epidemic proportions" according to an internal government memo obtained by The Canadian Press.[1]

– Globe and Mail, 4 July 2016

EPIDEMIC PROPORTIONS

In July 2016, *The Canadian Press* reported on a government memo describing the illegal trade in child rape as having reached "a level of epidemic proportions." In addition to being an American problem, trading in child rape is also a global crisis.[2] Images, videos and live-streams of children in America are transferred internationally. Children abused elsewhere are shared across the United States. Pedophile networks do not remain within national boundaries. They are highly organized with vast transfers on file-sharing software world-wide. According to Chad Steel, a forensic investigator at George Mason University, "it is not atypical to have a single case that involves terabytes of data and over one million images and movies."[3] One terabyte fits into about 1,428 CD-ROMs holding some 3.6 million images, or 300 video hours.

All filled with rape and torture of children. In a single arrest. Shared all over the world.

Imagine.

GLOBAL TRENDS

The European Union (EU) police, Europol, issued one of the most staggering reports; *Strategic Assessment of the Commercial Sexual Exploitation of Children Online*. This report, first released in 2013 and updated in 2015, documents the "disturbing trends" of what Europeans call child-abuse material (CAM) or child sexual exploitation material (CSEM) known in America as child pornography.[4] Three developments, explained by Europol, are important to consider. Understanding these global trends is vital for those wishing to protect children in America.

First, the proliferation of online advice forums "has made even lower level offenders better informed on how to protect themselves."[5] Pedophiles protect each other. They provide advice on how to groom, access and drug children. They educate on how to avoid arrest and prosecution. Pedophiles have become so brazen they no longer only help each other in private dark web forums. In Arizona a radio station, Cave 97.7, was finally forced in May 2017 to stop playing a public service announcement (PSA) instructing pedophiles how to avoid "being caught." The radio station had been airing the PSA for two years.[6]

The second trend Europol describes is, "a higher proportion of new, home-made material has been observed."[7] More pedophiles are producing and distributing their own so-called "home-made" child pornography, i.e., the rape and abuse of children they have access to, often their own children or grandchildren. While pedophiles sometimes travel to places like Thailand, the Philippines or Cambodia to access to children, most often pedophiles look for children in their own homes, communities, workplaces, or schools.[8] In January 2017, the Canadian Centre for Child Protection released a study documenting that more than half of child survivors were abused, starting between birth and four-years-old, by a parent. Over half also reported being shared with other pedophiles.[9] Most child pornography is produced in North America and Europe.[10] Children in North America and Europe appear to be targeted by their parents, most often their fathers, and are frequently "shared."

The third trend is that as self-produced child rape videos/images proliferate, there is a parallel surge in computer security used by pedophiles which frustrates law enforcement and prosecution efforts.[11] As American journalist Lex Talamo explains, "The Internet has forced law enforcement to evolve methods of tracking and catching online predators. But they're often outgunned."[12] One example is the arrest of Jonathan Walsh, a 47-year-old pediatrician in the United Kingdom who used "military-grade" software to protect his trade in child rape.[13] Another example is a pedophile in Louisiana who had "wired his computer to wipe the hard drive if a pass code wasn't entered within the first few seconds of opening the device."[14]

JOINING PEDOPHILE NETWORKS

Pedophiles joining online networks must first prove they are pedophiles. To do this, they are required to offer images/videos of child rape to other group members. This serves as both an entry fee and verification code. Anyone viewing child rape, therefore, is also by nature of these gate-keeping strategies distributing child pornography. To have child pornography to share, a child must be sexually abused. The production of child pornography requires contact with children. Unless the pedophile is a parent, or has a relative or friend willing to share his/her children, pedophiles do not always have effortless access to children. In addition, children grow older quickly. These problem factors in accessing children result in pedophiles cultivating personalities that appear to be extremely child-friendly. Pedophiles must be likable to spouses, parents, neighbors, teachers and children.

A pedophile is not someone you look at and fear for your children's safety. A pedophile is someone you willingly leave your child with because this is a person you trust. An investigation called Project Spade, a 2013 Canadian and US Postal Inspection joint operation, provides helpful examples of average pedophile profiles. Toronto's Sex Crimes Unit said "Of concern to the investigators was the number of people who have close contact with children. The arrests included 40 school teachers, nine doctors and nurses, 32 people who volunteered with children, six law enforcement personnel, nine pastors or priests, and three foster parents."[15] All in just one investigation.

Pedophiles are close to home, familiar and in positions of power over children. Men, and it is overwhelmingly men, who trade in child rape "are for the most part educated, intelligent individuals who are well integrated into society and successful in other areas of their lives."[16] A pedophile is the priest who takes an interest in your children, the swimming coach willing to spend extra time with your son, the math teacher who stays after school to tutor your daughter, the piano teacher you leave your child with as you run errands, the relative who is always there when you need an extra hand, the decorated military veteran who volunteers with the Little League team, the lawyer who donates money to build a new playground, the grandfather always ready to babysit, the man who wants to marry the single mother with small children and on and on.[17]

> "People like to believe they could spot someone who is a source of danger to their child. In fact, most child molesters are known to the families, look pretty average and are often quite charming versus being the 'creepy looking guy who lives down the street.'"

Your friendly local pedophile, raping children here in America, is sharing these images across the globe.[18] It is entirely possible, for example, your child may be abused and these images shared without your knowledge. For example, let's say a coach has been abusing your six-year-old daughter and sharing images online. These photos are given to a pedophile in Australia who gets caught. He has, as most pedophiles do, an enormous collection of images/videos of child rape. Your daughter is only one of thousands. Most of images/videos seized in child pornography arrests are never investigated. Instead, a "dip analysis" is performed where a handful of videos/images needed for prosecution are selected and the rest are sent to a central database. The Australian National Victim Image Library, for example, has six million images.[19]

Law enforcement does not have the financial resources or the staff to go through every image and video in every arrest and locate all the children.[20] This means images, in the hypothetical case of your child in an Australian pedophile's collection, are unlikely to be seen by law enforcement. The local pedophile in your neighborhood continues abusing children even if images of children he abuses have been captured by law enforcement half-way around the world. As the Child Exploitation and Online Protection Centre explains, the "sheer number of images and limited resources makes identifying new abuse victims difficult."[21] And new victims are being added every day. Perhaps even your child. You may never even know.

> "We've seen cases lately where we can't even catalogue them all," said Lt. Chad Gremillion, who works for the Special Victims Unit of the Louisiana State Police. "We're talking about terabytes, literally hundreds and hundreds of thousands of images. Videos that are an hour in length of a child being sexually assaulted, raped, forced into oral sex and bondage scenarios."

Law enforcement is, increasingly, cooperating on international child pornography investigations, but these investigations are time-consuming, expensive and difficult. Sometimes, some of the children do get rescued. Those children are the rare and lucky ones. Most often, hundreds of thousands of images/videos are simply confiscated and dumped into various un-linked databases around the world where they remain unexamined. As Europol explains "internationally comparable crime data remains an aspiration."[22] Pedophiles know this. They know they are far ahead of the law. By and large, pedophiles have no fear they will be caught because so few are found out. They also know that if they are arrested prosecution is often light and jail can be avoided altogether.[23] As discussed in Chapter Six, in America prosecution depends on wealth and race. Judges are routinely bought.[24] Pedophile judges, as detailed in Chapter Six, do sit on the bench.[25] Pedophiles network. They know each other. They protect each other. On many levels. Locally and globally.

INNOVATIVE INTERNATIONAL POLICE WORK

When law enforcement is at their best, they also network globally and appeal to public forums for assistance, catching pedophiles and rescuing children. Europol, on the cutting-edge of innovative police work, launched, in June 2017, an initiative program called Trace an Object.[26] Background images of places and objects are posted on Europol's website. Investigators ask the public to help identify these objects and locations which may be key clues in rescuing children and arresting pedophiles.[27] When police ask for the public's help, they inspire confidence and harness a unique resource: citizens willing to devote time and energy to ending child sex-abuse and impunity for the crime. American law enforcement should comprehensively implement Europol's, Trace an Object, model. As *The Keepers,* Netflix's new popular documentary demonstrates, arm-chair detectives are a powerful investigative force; one which all police departments should make better use of in child pornography investigations.[28]

Another example of first-rate international police cooperation which included a public appeal is the case of twenty-five-year-old Corrine Danielle Motley. In 2012, Danish Police discovered images of a woman sexually abusing two children; 4 and 6-years-old. Danish police believed the images were being produced in America and contacted Homeland Security. Homeland Security asked, on social media, for public help locating the woman abusing the children. "Literally hours after we asked the public for their assistance in identifying Jane Doe, a tip came in that led to her identification and arrest," Homeland Security reported.[29] This is how all child pornography investigations should unfold. Every child in every image/video should be immediately located and the abuser arrested and prosecuted. Unfortunately, international police-public cooperation like the Danish/Homeland example is not yet the norm.

> William Gazafi, an Air Force officer, was indicted on six counts of sexually exploiting a minor to produce child pornography. He had been in incest chat rooms and bragged he drugged and raped young children including infants. Upon his arrest, he had videos/images he produced including the rape of a five-month-old baby as well as other drugged children, bound and handcuffed and raped.

GLOBAL CITIZEN ACTION

That's the bad news. The good news is that from America to Australia there is, increasingly, greater awareness of the crime and its cover-up. Private citizens, activists, politicians and law enforcement who care about children's rights and the rule of law are using social media to raise awareness, share information and demand accountability. There is a growing sense of outrage at what many are calling a global epidemic of child rape distributed online. People in America and around the world are refusing to be silent and are raising their voices for children and against pedophiles.

In Australia, prompted by Detective Peter Fox - who refused to continue be part of the cover-up, the Royal Commission into Institutional Responses to Child Sexual Abuse by child services, children's non-profits, politicians and the church was established.[30] Since 2013, this Commission has held 6,000 private sessions with people who shared information about child sex abuse. Some of these accounts are available in audio files on the Royal Commission's website. As of May 2017, 1,500 more individuals are scheduled to meet with investigators. Australia's Royal Commission is a best-practice model. The US government should follow Australia's example and create a national investigative committee examining and exposing institutional responses and cover-ups of child sex abuse in the United States.

In the United Kingdom (UK), a Member of Parliament (MP) Tom Watson dropped a bombshell, in 2012, during Parliamentary question time asking about an elite political pedophile ring, later described in Australia's 60 Minutes-style news show *Spies, Lords and Predators*.[31] Child sex abuse in the UK includes children in a care-home called Kincora, located in Belfast, Northern Ireland, raped by elite government employees as well as survivors like Esther Baker raped while police officers watched and protected the abusers rather than her – the child.[32] Tom Watson's demands, along with many other activists and survivors, resulted in the creation of the Independent Child Sex Abuse Inquiry.[33] Unfortunately, the Inquiry has been roadblocked and undermined at nearly every turn. Survivors have expressed frustration with how the government has handled the Inquiry as well as the failure to prosecute these crimes.[34] Unlike Australia, the British effort to expose child sex abuse and government elite involved in this crime is a worst-practice example.

In America, we have yet to create a national investigative inquiry, which is desperately needed; however, many individuals are organizing, raising awareness and demanding accountability. People like Jerome Elam, CEO of the Trafficking in America Taskforce, Marci Hamilton, a legal scholar working to end the statute of limitations (SOL) for child sex abuse and James Marsh of Marsh Law Firm, a lawyer leading the fight for compensation for children depicted in child pornography. Long ago, Judith Reisman exposed Alfred Kinsey's crimes against children and currently documents how Kinsey's rape of infants and toddlers is being cited in law journals and court judgment, to this day, validating child rape. Mary Mazzio's documentary, *I Am Jane Doe*, tells the story of brave mothers and child survivors who have been trying to shut down Backpage. Nikki DuBose, survivor and author, is active in leading the fight for children, as is Shaun Dougherty, a farm-to-table restaurateur and adult survivor.[35] John DeCamp and Nick Bryant exposed a child sex ring in Nebraska often called the Franklin Scandal.[36] Conchita Sarnoff, the journalist whose reporting made Jeffrey Epstein a well-known pedophile, refused a five million dollar bribe to stop publication of her book *Trafficking*.[37]

Comedian Barry Crimmins testified before Congress, July 24, 1995, about pedophiles organizing online in an era when most police stations did not even have computers.[38] The documentary film, *Call Me Lucky*, details his life and fight to stop pedophiles.[39] If only we all had listened to Barry Crimmins, and acted, we might have prevented the epidemic now destroying so many children in America.[40] In terms of good cops, like Detective Peter Fox in Australia, at the top of the list in America is Sheriff Grady Judd of Polk County, Florida; a living legend for his dedication to putting child rapists behind bars. Sheriff Judd leads one of the 61 Internet Crimes Against Children (ICAC) Taskforces, located across America.[41] Under his leadership Polk County's ICAC has made hundreds more arrests than any other ICAC. For example, while Hawaii made 86 arrests from 2009-2014, Polk County completed 2,448 arrests.[42] If only Sheriff Judd and his team oversaw all of America's ICACs.

There are many more people in America, too many to list here, dedicating their lives to ending child sex abuse and impunity for the crime. However, no matter how many citizens join this battle, without government representatives willing to make this a top priority, individuals will struggle to achieve policy changes needed to halt the epidemic. Government agencies must allocate budgets, priority directives and staff to tackle the explosion of child pornography. The problem is that when pedophiles occupy government positions they will roadblock efforts to end impunity and protect children. People fighting this crime can attest how frequently a politician, judge, prosecutor, cop or child-protection employee halted efforts of those seeking to protect children and hold abusers responsible. *Quis custodiet ipsos custodes* – who will guard the guards themselves? This is explored in Chapter Five, Six and Seven.

In addition to citizen activism, the break-up of pedophile rings by law enforcement and prosecutors is occurring, with growing frequency, around the world. In Canada, Australia, Portugal, Ireland, Spain, Wales, Jersey Islands, UK, Belgium, Norway and the Netherlands there have been major police actions and prosecutions.[43] While it is beyond my scope to detail these operations, it is important to note that elite pedophiles rings, the world over, appear to be structured in similar manners. Judges, prosecutors, police, clergy, journalists and politicians are often involved and the most vulnerable children targeted. Frequently, the children are in government care, such as Kincora in Northern Ireland, Casa Pia in Portugal, orphanages in Russia, or foster children in America.[44] Staff in child protection agencies, globally, appear to be key players in securing supply-lines of children for pedophile rings.[45]

CHILD PORNOGRAPHY IS ALMOST ALWAYS AN INTERNATIONAL CRIME

While this book is about child pornography in America, the crime cannot be divorced from a global epidemic. With one click a child's rape is shared around the world. By its very nature, child pornography is almost always an international crime. Citizen activists, researchers, law enforcement and prosecutors dedicated to ending this crime must learn to think and act like pedophiles in terms of strategy. Pedophiles protect each other. They provide advice on how to obtain and abuse children. They educate each other on how to avoid arrest and prosecution. Those fighting this crime, must do the same. We must protect each other and provide advice on how to protect our children. We must educate each other on how to end this epidemic. We must organize internationally. If we hope to halt this epidemic, we must beat pedophiles at their own game. To do that, we must think, act and network locally and globally against this crime that is destroying so many children.

Pedophile networks do not remain within national boundaries. Neither should we.

Endnotes

1. Jim Bronskill, "Canadian police unable to keep up with child porn 'epidemic': memo," The Globe and Mail, July,4, 2016, accessed July 17, 2017, https://www.theglobeandmail.com/news/british-columbia/canadian-police-unable-to-keep-up-with-child-porn-epidemic-memo/article30751112/?utm_source=twitter.com&utm_medium=Referrer:+Social+Network+/+Media&utm_campaign=Shared+Web+Article+Links and Jim Bronskill, "Ralph Goodale warned more resources needed to fight online child exploitation: Briefing notes say online child pornography a growing challenge for justice agencies," Canadian Broadcasting Corporation (CBC), July 4, 2016, accessed July 17, 2017, www.cbc.ca/beta/news/politics/child-exploitation-briefing-note-1.3664102

2. United Nations, "Child pornography flourishes in a world with no borders," Office of the High Commissioner for Human Rights (OHCHR), Geneva, February 11, 2014, accessed July 17, 2017, http://www.ohchr.org/EN/NewsEvents/Pages/ChildPornography.aspx

3. Chad Steel, Digital Child Pornography: A Practical Guide for Investigators (Lily Shiba Press, 2014), 1.

4. Europol, "Strategic Assessment 2013," 10.

5. Europol, "Strategic Assessment 2013," 10.

6. Bill Chappell, "Arizona Radio Station Stops Airing Advice On Hiding Child Pornography," National Public Radio (NPR), May 11, 2017, accessed July 17, 2017, http://www.npr.org/sections/thetwo-way/2017/05/11/527958711/arizona-radio-station-stops-airing-advice-on-hiding-child-pornography

7. Europol, "Strategic Assessment 2013," 9.

8. For background on CSE in Asia see also UNICEF, "National Responses to Online Child Sexual Abuse and Exploitation in ASEAN Member States," 2016, accessed July 17, 2017, https://www.unicef.org/eapro/Child_Protection_in_the_Digital_Age.pdf

9. Canadian Centre for Child Protection, "Canadian Centre for Child Protection's survey."

10. As NetClean's 2016 report documents, most child victims are in Europe and North America. NetClean, "NetClean Report 2016," accessed July 16, 2017, https://www.netclean.com/wp-content/uploads/2016/12/NetClean_Report_2016_English_print.pdf, 14-15. See also: Interpol Chart International Child Sexual Exploitation (ICSE) image database as displayed in as displayed in Anti-Slavery Australia, Behind the Screen, 10 and Internet Watch Foundation, Annual Report 2016, 6-13.

11. See also: "NetClean Report 2016," accessed July 16, 2017, https://www.netclean.com/wp-content/uploads/2016/12/NetClean_Report_2016_English_print.pdf

12. Talamo, "Child porn offenders in technological arms race."

13. Jimmy Nsubuga, "Children's doctor used 'military-grade' software to hide child porn on his computer," Metro UK, March 20, 2017, accessed July 17, 2017, http://metro.co.uk/2017/03/20/childrens-doctor-used-military-grade-software-to-hide-child-porn-on-his-computer-6522851/#ixzz4cN9r3TTi

14. Talamo, "Child porn offenders in technological arms race."

15. "Police arrest 348 in global child porn investigation, rescue 386 children," Reuters, November 14, 2013, accessed July 17, 2017, http://bangordailynews.com/2013/11/14/news/world-news/police-arrest-348-in-global-child-porn-investigation

16. Child Exploitation and Online Protection Centre (CEOP), *A Picture of Abuse: A Thematic Assessment of the Risk of Contact Child Sex Abuse Posed by Those Who Possess Indent Images of Children*, (United Kingdom: CEOP), June 2012, accessed July 17, 2017, http://ceop.police.uk/publications, 6.

17. "exclusively committed by men and a lot of them take positions in community service that puts them in close proximity to children," Derek Gilliam, "Child porn: Reaching epidemic status in Florida," Jacksonville, November 14, 2014, accessed July 17, 2017, http://jacksonville.com/news/crime/2014-11-14/story/child-porn-reaching-epidemic-status-florida-us

18. *See also* "NetClean Report 2016."

19. Moor, "'Snuff films alarm."

20. Netclean, "NetClean Report 2016," describes survey results form 370 law enforcement officers in 26 countries. *See also*: Ciara Byrne, *"How Video Forensics Are Changing The Way Cops Find Criminals,"* Fast Company, June 28, 2013, accessed July 17, 2017, https://www.fastcompany.com/3013653/how-video-forensics-are-changing-the-way-cops-find-criminals

21. Alexandra, Topping, "Online child abuse images 'becoming more extreme, sadistic and violent,'" *The Guardian*, June 13, 2012, accessed July 17, 2017, http://www.theguardian.com/society/2012/jun/14/child-abuse-images-more-violent

22. Europol, "Strategic Assessment 2013," 7 and Europol, "New cybercrime report examines disturbing trends in commercial online child sex abuse," October 15, 2013, accessed July 16, 2017, https://www.europol.europa.eu/newsroom/news/new-cybercrime-report-examines-disturbing-trends-in-commercial-online-child-sex-abuse

23. For example, a recent UK report found that "despite evidence that offenders possessing the worst types of sexual images, in many cases perpetrators are avoiding jail terms. In one police force only 18% of people convicted of possessing indecent images of children had been sent to prison over a three-year period." Topping, "Online child abuse images."

24. Christopher Sherman, "Abel Limas, Ex-Judge Involved In Racketeering, Gets 6 Years," *Huffington Post*, August 21, 2013, accessed July 16, 2017, http://www.huffingtonpost.com/2013/08/22/judge-abel-limas_n_3794523.html *See also* the Kids for Cash scandal exposed in Pennsylvania; Stephanie Chen, "Pennsylvania rocked by 'jailing kids for cash' scandal," Cable News Network (CNN), February 24, 2009, accessed, July 16, 2017, http://www.cnn.com/2009/CRIME/02/23/pennsylvania.corrupt.judges

25. "Ex-judge in Wash. charged with having child porn," *Seattle Times*, December 27, 2013, accessed July 17, 2017, http://seattletimes.com/html/localnews/2022546120_apxformer-judgecharged.html?syndication=rss

26. Europol website, accessed July 17, 2017, https://www.europol.europa.eu/stopchildabuse and "New website will show clues from child sex abuse cases to help track down paedophiles," *The Journal*, June 1, 2017, accessed July 17, 2017, http://www.thejournal.ie/child-sex-abuse-europol-3420059-Jun2017/?utm_source=twitter_self

27. Simon Smith, "Europol shares 20 tiny details from vile images of child sex abuse in a bid to track down perpetrators and victims," *Manchester Evening News*, June 1, 2017, accessed July 17, 2017, http://www.manchestereveningnews.co.uk/news/greater-manchester-news/europol-child-abuse-image-appeal-13120960

28. Lisa Robinson, "Victim in Netflix's 'The Keepers' speaks out: Woman details alleged abuse," NBC News WBLATV11, June 7, 2017, accessed July 17, 2017, http://www.wbaltv.com/article/victim-in-netflixs-the-keepers-speaks-out/9985199 and Ryan White, "Making 'The Keepers' Taught Me The Power Of Believing Survivors," *Huffington Post*, June 5, 2017, accessed July 17, 2017, http://www.huffingtonpost.com/entry/the-keepers-reminds-believe-assault-survivors_us_5935a7f1e4b013c4816a0f07

29. Matthias Gafni, "Captured: Child porn producer arrested in Florida, toddler victim rescued," *Contra Costa Times*, December 21, 2012, accessed July 17, 2017, http://www.contracostatimes.com/news/ci_22239485/captured-child-porn-producer-arrested-florida-toddler-victim?-source=most_viewed

30. Detective Peter Fox exposed the cover-ups of child sex abuse. Peter Fox, "Don't Block Your Ears to Abuse Mr. Premier," *The Herald*, November 8, 2012, accessed July 17, 2017, <http://www.theherald.com.au/story/757111/opinion-dont-block-your-ears-to-abuse-mr-premier. *See also*: Dan Box, "Abuse whistleblower Peter Fox admits secretly contacting journalist in wife's name," *The Australian*, January 17, 2014, accessed July 17, 2017, http://www.theaustralian.com.au/business/media/abuse-whistleblower-admits-secretly-contacting-journalist-in-wifes-name/news-story/4b4368bdf0f77f3b42d-8b086065ad625; Sarah Dingle, "Whistleblower Peter Fox says police should apologise now to abuse victims," Australian Broadcasting Corporation (ABC), January 17, 2017, accessed July 17, 2017, http://www.abc.net.au/news/2017-01-17/whistleblower-peter-fox-says-police-to-apologise/8189232 and Lori Handrahan, "Mark Thompson: From Pedophile Cover-Up to the *New York Times*," *FrontPage Magazine*, November 20, 2012, July 17, 2017, http://www.frontpagemag.com/2012/lori-handrahan/mark-thompson-from-pedophile-cover-up-to-the-new-york-times. The investigations and results of Australia's official inquiry in child sex abuse are too extensive to detail here. See also The Australian, National Affairs, Abuse Royal Commission, accessed July 17, 2017, http://www.theaustralian.com.au/national-affairs/in-depth/royal-commission and the Royal Commission into Institutional Responses to Child Sexual Abuse http://childabuseroyalcommission.gov.auT accessed July 17, 2017.

31. Dan Thorne, "MP Tom Watson warns of 'powerful paedophile network linked to Parliament and Number 10,'" *TNT Magazine*, October 24, 2012, accessed July 17, 2017, http://www.tntmagazine.com/news/uk/video-mp-tom-watson-warns-of-powerful-paedophile-network-linked-to-parliament-and-number-10; James Hanning, "Tom Watson: Why Labour's deputy leader won't stop speaking up for the victims of child abuse," *The Independent*, October 17, 2015, accessed July 17, 2017, http://www.independent.co.uk/news/uk/politics/tom-watson-why-labours-deputy-leader-wont-stop-speaking-up-for-the-victims-of-child-abuse-a6698321.html and Kirsteen Paterson, "Australian TV show 60 Minutes alleges child abuse in Westminster," *The National*, July 20, 2015, accessed July 17, 2017, http://www.thenational.scot/news/14898652.Australian_TV_show_60_Minutes_alleges_child_abuse_in_Westminster. See also Independent Inquiry into Child Sex Abuse (IICSA), accessed July 17, 2017, https://www.iicsa.org.uk and Exaro News archives and podcast from former Exaro News Editor Mark Watts - Freddy Mayhew, "Former Exaro chief launches podcast reporting on child sex abuse issues," Press Gazette, October 7, 2016, accessed July 17, 2017, http://www.pressgazette.co.uk/former-exaro-chief-launches-podcast-reporting-on-child-sex-abuse-issues also detailed in the FOIA Center http://www.foiacentre.com/news-Exaro-child-sexual-abuse.html

32. Henry McDonald, "Child abuse inquiry turns to Kincora home and claims of MI5 blackmail: Inquiry will hear from men abused as boys at Northern Ireland children's home and allegations that perpetrators were protected by working as spies," *The Guardian*, May 30, 2016, accessed July 25, 2017, https://www.theguardian.com/uk-news/2016/may/30/n-ireland-child-abuse-inqui-

ry-turns-to-kincora-home-and-claims-of-mi5-blackmail and David Barrett, "Child sex abuse: 'Police guarded paedophile ring', claims victim: Esther Baker, 32, waives right to anonymity to highlight alleged sexual abuse by prominent figures and police in the Eighties and Nineties," *The Telegraph*, May 26, 2015, accessed July 25, 2017, http://www.telegraph.co.uk/news/uknews/crime/child-protection/11630989/Child-sex-abuse-Police-guarded-paedophile-ring-claims-victim.html

33. Independent Inquiry into Child Sex Abuse (IICSA), accessed July 17, 2017 https://www.iicsa.org.uk

34. British journalist David Hencke has written extensively about the UK's child sex abuse inquiry. See David Hencke blog, accessed July 17, 2017, https://davidhencke.com/2015/07/26/child-abuse-survivors-strike-back-a-reflection-on-reflections-uk

35. Nikki DuBose can be reached on her Twitter account, accessed July 18, 2017, https://twitter.com/TheNikkiDuBose *See also:* Jeanmarie Evelly, "LIC Restaurateur and Child Sex Abuse Survivor Pushes for Changes to NY Law," *DNA Info,* May 12, 2017, accessed July 17, 2017, https://www.dnainfo.com/new-york/20170512/long-island-city/child-victims-act-ny-statute-of-limitations-shaun-dougherty?utm_content=buffer80b2e&utm_medium=social&utm_source=twitter.com&utm_campaign=DNAinfoNY

36. John DeCamp, *The Franklin Cover-up: Child Abuse, Satanism, and Murder in Nebraska,* (AWT, Inc., 1992) and Nick Bryant, *The Franklin Scandal: A Story of Powerbrokers, Child Abuse & Betrayal,* (Oregon: Trine Day, 2009).

37. Conchita Sarnoff, *TraffKing* (Washington DC: Conchita Sarnoff 2016), accessed July 18, 2017, https://www.conchitasarnoff.com

38. Bob Goldthwait, *Call Me Lucky*, Type 55 Films, MPI Media Group, accessed July 18, 2017, http://callmeluckymovie.com *See also*: United States Congress, "Testimony of Barry F. Crimmins, Hearing on Child Pornography on the Internet," Senate Judiciary Committee, 104th United States Congress, July 24, 1995, accessed July 17, 2017, http://www.aolwatch.org/CONGRESS. Barry Crimmins can be contacted on his website, accessed July 17, 2017, http://www.barrycrimmins.com

39. Travis Andrews, "Your weekend watch: 'Call Me Lucky,' a difficult profile of comedian and crusader against child abuse, Barry Crimmins," *Washington Post*, February 10, 2017, accessed July 17, 2017, https://www.washingtonpost.com/news/morning-mix/wp/2017/02/10/your-weekend-watch-call-me-lucky-a-difficult-profile-of-comedian-and-anti-child-abuse-crusader-barry-crimmins/?utm_term=.a02902680dcc

40. Statute of Limitations (SOL) Reform, accessed July 18, 2017, http://sol-reform.com

41. Internet Crimes Against Children Taskforce, accessed July 18, 2017, https://www.icactaskforce.org

42. Data4Justice, accessed July 18, 2017, http://data4justice.org/icac-graph-gallery/2015/12/4/icac-arrests-2009-2013

43. *See also* Virtual Global Taskforce website, accessed July 18, 2017, http://virtualglobaltaskforce.com; Interpol Crimes Against Children website, accessed July 17, 207, https://www.interpol.int/Crime-areas/Crimes-against-children/Crimes-against-children; Australian Federal Police (AFP) Child Protection Operations website, accessed July 17, 2017, https://www.afp.gov.au/what-we-do/services/child-protection/online-child-sex-exploitation; Jerome Taylor, "Guilty after six-year trial, Portugal's high-society paedophile ring," *The Independent*, September 3, 2010, accessed July 17, 2017, http://www.independent.co.uk/news/world/europe/guilty-after-six-year-trial-portugals-high-society-paedophile-ring-2070112.html; "North Wales child abuse scandal: The road to Macur," British Broadcasting Corporation (BBC), March 17, 2016, accessed July

17, 2017, http://www.bbc.com/news/uk-wales-north-east-wales-35502574; "Exposed: Ireland's vile child-sex rings," *Independent*.ie, July 11, 1998, accessed July 17, 2017, http://www.independent.ie/irish-news/exposed-irelands-vile-childsex-rings-26180125.html; Camille Standen, "The Journalist Who Was Arrested for Investigating a Pedophile Orphanage," *VICE*, February 27, 2013, accessed July 17, 2017, https://www.vice.com/en_us/article/the-journalist-who-was-banned-from-investigating-jerseys-child-abuse; "Huge Canada child sex ring bust," News24, April 22, 2017, accessed July 17, 2017, http://www.news24.com/World/News/huge-canada-child-sex-ring-bust-20170422; Interpol, "Global operation targets child sexual abuse material exchanged via messaging apps," Interpol Press Release, April 18, 2017, accessed July 17, 2017, https://www.interpol.int/News-and-media/News/2017/N2017-047; Thomas Burrows, "Former child sex slave sold into Belgian aristocratic paedophile ring where boys and girls were tortured and KILLED reveals the horrors of her five years of abuse," *Daily Mail*, January 19, 2017, accessed July 17, 2017, http://www.dailymail.co.uk/news/article-4136536/Former-child-sex-slave-sold-Belgian-recalls-abuse.html; Marlise Simons, "Dutch Say A Sex Ring Used Infants On Internet," *New York Times*, July 19, 1998, accessed July 17, 2017, http://www.nytimes.com/1998/07/19/world/dutch-say-a-sex-ring-used-infants-on-internet.html and "Police break up massive Norwegian paedophilia ring," *NTB/The Local NO*, November 21, 2016, accessed July 17, 2017, https://www.thelocal.no/20161121/police-break-up-massive-norwegian-paedophilia-ring

44. Peter Popham, "Ten charged in Portuguese paedophile ring scandal," The Independent, December 31, 2003, accessed July 17, 2017, http://www.independent.co.uk/news/world/europe/ten-charged-in-portuguese-paedophile-ring-scandal-84511.html and Liam Clarke, "Richard Kerr: I was trafficked from Kincora boys home to be abused by a ring of VIPs in London," *Belfast Telegraph*, April 7, 2015, accessed July 17, 2017, http://www.belfasttelegraph.co.uk/news/northern-ireland/richard-kerr-i-was-trafficked-from-kincora-boys-home-to-be-abused-by-a-ring-of-vips-in-london-31122559.html

45. Nicholas Watt and Patrick Wintour, "Children's homes were 'supply line' for paedophiles, says ex-minister," *The Guardian*, 8 July 2014, accessed July 17, 2017, https://www.theguardian.com/society/2014/jul/08/children-homes-supply-line-paedophiles-lord-warner?CMP=share_btn_tw

3

Infants and Toddlers

> NDFL_SEVEN-DEFENDANTS_1-14-09.pdf. In some of these videos, the children can be heard screaming and crying in response to the physical assault. *See also, United States v. Cole*, 2009 WL 1443937 *1 (6th Cir. May 22, 2009) (unpublished) (defendant admitted to possessing images of adult males engaged in sexual activity with infants); *United States v. Pugh*, 515 F.3d 1179, 1193 (11th Cir. 2008) (defendant's collection included a video of an adult male raping an infant girl and a picture of an adult male having sex with a toddler who wore a dog collar around her neck).

– U.S. Department of Justice, "Response to "A Reluctant Rebellion." 1 July 2009.

INFANT AND TODDLER PORNOGRAPHY

Infant and toddler pornography is the rape and torture of children under four-years-old. As early as 2009, the Department of Justice (DOJ) warned America that infants and toddlers were being raped in increasing numbers. By 2016, DOJ acknowledged it is "routine for child pornography investigations to include files depicting the sexual exploitation of infants and toddlers."[1] This includes newborns – "children as young as days old."[2] One pedophile father, for example, posted to a child pornography trading site a sonogram of an unborn child and a text message "I have a new baby about to be added to the game."[3]

Images, videos and live-streams of infant/ toddler rape are considered platinum in pedophile circles. Any pedophile can get his/her hands on a teenager. Accessing an infant or toddler to rape is more difficult. Infants cannot walk out of the house. They are not available after school or at swim practice. Toddler and infants are not independent of their caregivers. To traffic an infant or toddler the caregiver must be involved. Caregivers involved in infant and toddler rape often appear to be fathers. As mentioned in Chapter One, child exploitation rings led by fathers have become a "widespread tragedy."[4] Infants and toddlers are being targeted.

> Gordon Oehmig, former Coach of the Year, a Texas wrestling and football coach, was arrested. He had more than 1,500 images and 900 videos of child sex abuse, including the sex abuse of toddler and infants. Oehmig had been called, in a Houston Chronicle article, "a perfect model for his athletes."

In 2014, *USA Today* reported on the rise of "homemade" child pornography, also cited in Europol's reports.[5] Kevin Johnson, the *USA Today* reporter, described "unwitting children appear holding homemade placards bearing the pseudonyms of the macabre films' makers ... children, some pleading for help, being sexually abused in torturous ways by parents, relatives or others. Among the worst: infants used as toys for the videographers' and viewers' sexual gratification."[6] While there is an increased awareness of teenage sex trafficking, there is almost no public discussion of the surging market in infant and toddler rape. Most Americans likely have no idea how extensive infant and toddler trafficking has become.

Infants and toddlers are targeted by pedophiles for an important strategic reason; children under four-years-old cannot be witnesses in court. No witness – no crime. Pedophiles like to rape pre-verbal children because these children cannot explain what happened to them, let alone defend their rights in a court of law. Therefore, they make ideal targets. As Canadian journalist Julian Sher describes, as early as 2006, there was a notable increase in pedophiles "deliberately going after pre-verbal infants because they are the perfect targets-victims who literally can't speak up." On one pedophile chat, a father who was raping his four-year-old daughter switched to raping his 18-month-old daughter, saying "I've got to start early, even though she's young ... before my daughter starts talking."[7]

> Moshe Gerstein, a 35-year-old lawyer, died in Mexico - cause of death reported as "not clear." He had fled, while on bail. Gerstein had over 5,000 images of babies and toddlers being "brutally raped and sexually abused." He was arrested as part of an investigation of a Manhattan pedophile ring that included "stockpiled images of the brutal rapes and sexual assaults of tens of thousands of real children." Gerstein attended Yale University and Harvard Law School, and worked at some of the most prestigious law firms, including Skadden, Arps, Slate, Meagher & Flom and Gibson Dunn.

Australian Federal Police cited, in June 2017, a trend of "images of children, some just toddlers, being tortured" as pedophiles compete to produce the "next level of violence" in pedophile networks.[8] Images of children being raped have taken on their own value and become a "currency." Europol reports the value is in the "novelty of the image." Images and videos have become "bargaining chips." From an investigative perspective, "new material means ongoing abuse and unidentified victims."[9] Pedophiles produce and trade in the latest abuse of children. New abuse. New children. As young as possible. They will pay top dollar for "privileged access to previously unseen material."[10] The "hallmarks" of child pornography are the "extremely young nature of the victims and growing masses of material" that pedophiles produce, collect and distribute.[11] Newborns, infants and toddlers.

How many infants and toddlers are raped in America to produce child pornography? How are pedophiles gaining regular and easy access to infants and toddlers to rape? How many of these children have been placed in the custody of their father in family court proceedings? How many were raped in day cares or by baby-sitters, unbeknownst to their parents? Of the thousands of U.S. federal prosecution records available on PACER, how many include infant/toddler rape? We do not know the answer to these questions because, as discussed, the data has not been gathered. It is evident, however, from arrest records, that infants and toddlers are being trafficked at alarming levels.

While there is no research focused exclusively on the scope, frequency and supply-sources of infant/toddler rape, references can be found in some reports. For example, as early as 2009, the UN reported more than 80 percent of child pornography featured children under twelve-years-old with 20 percent "babies and children aged under 3-years-old"12 Since 2009, the crime has exploded with younger children and more brutal abuse. The European Child Exploitation and Online Protection Centre (CEOP) reported that from 2010 to 2012, arrests showed a 70 percent increase of "female victims aged under ten."[13] How much was of infants and toddlers? We do not know.

CEOP also reported, in 2012, that child pornography is "becoming more extreme, sadistic and violent," and the abuse of very young children is becoming more extreme, including a marked increase of "penetrative" abuse; objects thrust into the cavities of young children; anal, vagina, and mouth.[14] While pedophiles previously slowly groomed children, "the restrained influencing of a child over several months has been largely replaced by rapid escalation to threats, intimidation and coercion."[15] DOJ's former director of the Child Exploitation and Obscenity Section (CEOS), Andrew Oosterbaan said, "What I've seen is an evolution in the intensity and volume of their conduct…. There is a greater demand for extreme material…. For some,

> Matthew Gigot, a 29-year-old Washington DC lawyer, was arrested, June 2015, on child pornography charges. Gigot texted an undercover cop a description of children he wanted to rape, "[h]ow young would you go…I'd do 5[,] [b]ut 0-12 is hot." Zero indicating the rape of a newborn. The cop was posing as a father sharing his 12-year-old son for rape. Gigot's user name was "pervyboy20." He is a registered sex offender.

their social status is based on production which serves as a powerful stimulus for the actual abuse of children."[16]

Type "infant pornography" as key words into a Twitter search and it is clear how frequently this crime is being shared even on public social media. Be extremely careful not click on any of the links or you will be committing a crime. If you see child rape advertised, please report the account to your local Internet Crimes Against Children (ICAC) Taskforce.[17] Infant and toddler rape is also being shared on Facebook and other social media platforms such as SnapChat and Instagram. In March 2013, the rape of an infant girl was shared on Facebook over 32,000 times, with 5,000 likes in the eight hours before Facebook removed the video. This example alone demonstrates how popular infant rape has become and how freely pedophiles are trading on public social media.[18]

JOHN GRISHAM SPEAKS OUT

It was a bizarre few days in the American news cycle during the autumn of 2014. John Grisham, crime-fiction writer, suddenly came out in defense of America's illegal child rape industry.[19] In an interview with *The Telegraph* Grisham claimed (and later retracted) that America's prisons are "filled with guys my age. 60-year-old white men ... who've never harmed anybody, would never touch a child.... But they got online one night, started surfing around, probably had too much to drink or whatever and pushed the wrong buttons and went too far and got into child porn or whatever." American prisons filled with old innocent, white men, wrongly jailed in our broken criminal justice system? "Your honor I was drunk"; which Grisham seemed to argue should be a legal defense when committing a crime? What was Grisham thinking? Disturbingly, Grisham is not alone in his views on who is the victim in America's child rape trade.

Days before the Grisham interview, Hollywood actor Stephen Collins also dominated headlines. Allegedly, Collins told his then pregnant wife he hoped their child would not be a boy because he feared he would not be able to "resist having oral sex with the child."[20] Oral sex with an infant? Yes. Disturbing and, as mentioned, apparently all too common. Just before the Collins story broke the *New York Times* published an op-ed "Pedophilia: A Disorder Not a Crime," by Margo Kaplan, a law professor at Rutgers, who argued child rapists are not criminals but rather vulnerable, disabled people who should receive "civil rights" protection under The Americans with Disabilities Act of 1990.[21]

An infant and toddler ring was busted through identification of a stuffed bunny seen in the images. The oldest child was four-years-old. The youngest child was nineteen days old. Images included a "naked 2-year-old boy in a roasting pan inside his oven," a two-year-old child bound and raped in a hotel room, and an eighteen-month-old boy molested by his day-care provider. Perpetrators included a father of three who was a Sheraton hotel manager in Massachusetts, an emergency medical technician in Kansas, and a day-care worker in the Netherlands. Forty-three men were arrested involving over 140 children.

Disability payments for someone who has performed oral sex on an infant? Impunity for someone who has live-streamed child rape? Three jaw-dropping stories. All in a row. All reported as one-off headlines. No dots connected. Connect the dots and the developing narrative is unnerving. Kaplan's op-ed appears to be part of a well-organized strategy to create laws and norms that frame pedophiles, and not our children, as the victims. Grisham's comments seem perfectly timed to support Kaplan's argument; the poor pedophiles, they are the innocent victims in all this – not the children.

Fake news? A conspiracy theory?

In 2012, pedophiles in Greece were given legal disability status.[22] Yes, it is true. The National Confederation of Disabled People says "pedophiles are now awarded a higher government disability pay than some people who have received organ transplants."[23] Headlines at the time read "Furor in Greece over Pedophilia as a Disability." Unlike the outrage in Greece, there has been no furor, and almost no reporting, in America as a pro pedophile media strategy has quietly rolled out across the country. Kaplan's op-ed is not a one-off. Pedophile puff pieces have been popping up in state and local newspapers across the country with disturbing regularity.[24] While the pro-pedophile articles are often prominently featured, the arrest reports of prestigious men arrested for trading in child rape, often of infants and toddlers, seem to be buried deep in the metro pages, if they hit the papers at all.

In addition to examples in textboxes throughout this book, listed below are arrest samples that included infants/toddlers. More arrests are located on my Medium profile. These arrests are only a few of hundreds occurring across America.

- Army prosecutor and judge advocate, Daniel Wollverton, father of two, was convicted and sentenced, in 2011 for infant sodomy. He had over 30,000 images and 1,000 videos of brutal child sex abuse including of a three-month-old infant.[25]

- Decorated Navy Veteran, Michael Jachim, was sentenced in January 2012 to four years in prison. He had 44,000 images/videos of children being raped. Prosecutors said, "This isn't Playboy magazine. These are infants and toddlers being brutally raped" including three- and four-year-old children "in bondage positions with their hands and feet tied" with hoods or masks covering their heads and children "screaming for their mommy as they were being sexually abused."[26]

- Army West Point Military Academy Cadet Ricky Patrick Hester was sentenced, January 2016, to eight years in jail for distributing sex abuse videos of young boys.[27] He had sent requests on his Yahoo account stating, "I am into 4–10-year-olds hardcore with sound."[28]

- Police Captain David Bourque of Granby Connecticut, was sentenced, February 2012, to ten years in jail for distributing and possessing more than 328,528 images and 4,000 videos from his work computer of "sadistic and violent acts" against infants and toddlers.[29]

- Police Sergeant Jonathan N. Gamson of Tampa, Florida, was sentenced May 2013 to nearly five years in jail for trading in child rape. He had images of at least one "baby" and "a little girl bound and blindfolded while being sexually assaulted." Investigators described "sadistic" and "horrific" abuse including a girl "hung by her wrists from the ceiling."[30]

Who is Trafficking Infants and Toddlers and How?

> BOX OF GMAIL ADDRESS "ANDINONAME68@GMAIL.COM". THE IMAGE WAS VIEWED AND
> APPEARED TO BE OF A YOUNG FEMALE, APPROXIMATELY 3-5 YEARS OF AGE WITH AN ADULT
> MALE'S PENIS IN HER MOUTH. ACCORDING TO THE CYBERTIP, THIS IMAGE WAS LOCATED IN
> THE BOX OF THAT AFOREMENTIONED EMAIL ADDRESS ON FEBRUARY 26TH 2015.

Jon Riveire's Officer Report Incident

The American public needs to know who is trafficking in infants and toddlers and how. Since the trafficking of infants and toddlers requires the caregiver's involvement, parents, relatives who provide care and day-care are sources of infant and toddler trafficking. As the research has established, the overwhelming majority of those involved in child rape are men and many appear to be fathers. If the mother is not involved (and some mothers are) this means infants and toddlers would be trafficked by fathers who have secured access to their children. Family courts across the country are routinely giving fathers, who are confirmed abusers and even registered sex offenders, custody of young children.[31] Is this a factor in infant and toddler rape seen by investigators in online networks?

For example, we have the case of Jon Riveire, former Assistant Director for Student Conduct in the Office of Student Ethics at Indiana University. Riveire was arrested, May 2015, and charged with six felony child pornography counts. He was trading in child rape, including toddlers, on university computers. He pled guilty to one count, November 2016, in exchange for having the other charges dropped and was sentenced, February 2017, to 2.5 years house-arrest with no jail time. He must register as a sex offender. Although Riveire is prohibited from contact with children under 16, the judge made an exception for Riverie's own children, one of whom is two-years-old, allowing Riveire to retain unsupervised access to his toddler-age children.[32] This kind of judgment, routinely seen in family courts, makes no sense. Why would a judge provide unsupervised access to a two-year old child for a criminal convicted of child sex offenses? Is the judge a pedophile like the defendant? Has this been organized?

Preschools and day-cares are magnets for pedophiles. Chapter Six discusses this in greater detail. In some cases, day-cares have been established explicitly as child supply-lines. For example, a day-care in Sanford, North Carolina served as a source for a child pornography and trafficking ring.[33] Bailey Joe Mills and his wife Elizabeth operated the day-care and "mentoring program" to "attract young girls" with the intent of producing child pornography and trafficking the children.[34] When Bailey Joe Mills was arrested

> Joint Strike Fighter Program Navy officer, Bruce Babchyck, was arrested in 2014 for downloading "hundreds of gigabytes" of young girls and bestiality on government computers. He received a one year sentence.

in January 2014, investigators found 10,000 images/videos including infants as young as one-year-old.[35] Bailey and Elizabeth Mills were sentenced, May 2015, respectively to 25 and 16 years in prison. Bailey Mills was a registered sex offender prior to his latest arrest. In March 1997, he pled guilty to raping a 4-year-old girl and was sentenced to probation and psychological treatment.

If DOJ has confirmed, as of 2016, that the sexual exploitation of infants and toddlers is now "routine," why hasn't there been an organized investigative response to protecting these children and halting this crime? Children across the country are being placed in the custody of known abusers and registered sex offenders in family courts. There must be a comprehensive and specialized investigation by federal law enforcement to identify and halt family courts that have become secure supply-lines for child sex trafficking. Day-care children are at real risk of being abused by their caregivers, often without their parents' knowledge. Much greater attention must be given to day-cares, including routine law enforcement investigations. Infant and toddler trafficking urgently demands in-depth investigation by journalists, academic researchers, policy institutions and specialized law enforcement units.

Who is trafficking infants and toddlers? How? And why has this been allowed to continue?

DAILY IMAGES OF INFANTS RAPED

Infants and toddlers, babies, are being raped across America in what appears to be large numbers. "Each day (we) receive imagery depicting infants being sexually abused," says Australian Federal Police Child Exploitation Assessment Centre Commander Lesa Gale.[36] The U.S. Department of Justice says infant and toddler rape is now "routine." American laws are not failing pedophiles, as Kaplan argues. American courts are not failing to protect white men who drunkenly download child rape, as John Grisham claimed. America, as a country, is failing to protect our youngest children. Journalists are failing to report on the wider news the Collins and Grisham stories represent. America's broken justice system is failing our children.

Accurate data must be immediately gathered to understand how prevalent the rape of infants/toddlers is, who is conducting the rape and how pedophiles are accessing the children. For example, if the data documents that fathers given custody of infants and toddlers are abusing these children, that information should have a significant impact on family court decisions. If the data informs that infants and toddlers are accessed in day-cares, this knowledge should be used to advocate for increased regulation and oversight. Until DOJ gathers and reports on the demographics of child pornography arrests, or funding is available to build a public child pornography arrest database, effective public policies urgently needed to protect our most vulnerable children will remain absent.

Should an adult who ties a small child to the ceiling and rapes her receive disability pay? Should the man who trades in and masturbates to this rape avoid jail? Grisham's comment, the Collins scandal and Kaplan's *New York Times* article, along with confirmation that infant and toddler rape is now "routine," should be America's wake-up call.

Is anyone paying attention? Will anyone protect the children? Will you?

Endnotes

1. Department of Justice, "The National Strategy 2016," 143.

2. Department of Justice, "The National Strategy 2016," 72.

3. Johnson, "Clandestine websites."

4. Robert Crib, "Chilling evidence of organized child sex abuse revealed in survey," *The Star*, January 17, 2017, accessed July 16, 2017, https://www.thestar.com/news/world/2017/01/17/chilling-evidence-of-organized-child-sex-abuse-revealed-in-survey.html.

5. Johnson, "Clandestine websites."

6. Johnson, "Clandestine websites."

7. Sher, *Caught in the Web*, 270.

8. Linda Silmalis, "Child sex abuse reports on rise and should not be taboo subject," *The Sunday Telegraph*, June 10, 2017, accessed July 16, 2017, http://www.dailytelegraph.com.au/news/nsw/child-sex-abuse-reports-on-rise-and-should-not-be-taboo-subject-expert/news-story/dfe91709b6b51e152c9f02393f01597d

9. David Gilbert, "Rising Trend of Live Streaming Child Abuse of 'Particular Concern,'" *IBTimes*, October 16, 2013, accessed July 16, 2017, http://www.ibtimes.co.uk/live-streaming-child-abuse-rising-trend-concern-514356. *See also* Europol, "Strategic Assessment 2013," 8.

10. Europol, "Strategic Assessment 2013," 8.

11. Johnson, "Clandestine websites."

12. United Nations, "Child pornography flourishes in a world with no borders," Office of the High Commissioner for Human Rights, November 29, 2009, accessed July 16, 2017, http://www.ohchr.org/EN/NewsEvents/Pages/ChildPornography.aspx

13. Child Exploitation and Online Protection Centre (CEOP), "Threat Assessment of Child Sexual Exploitation and Abuse," June 2013, accessed July 16, 2017, http://ceop.police.uk/publications

14. Topping, "Online child abuse images." 2012.

15. CEOP, "Threat Assessment," 10.

16. Johnson, "Clandestine websites."

17. Internet Crimes Against Children (ICAC) Contact List, ICAC website, accessed July 16, 2017, https://www.icactaskforce.org/Pages/ContactsTaskForce.aspx

18. Jeremey Tanner and Monica Morales, "Disturbing viral Facebook post shows man sexually

abusing child," *PIX11*, March 22, 2013, accessed July 16, 2017, http://pix11.com/2013/03/22/disturbing-viral-facebook-post-shows-man-sexually-abusing-child see also NetClean, "NetClean Report 2016," accessed July 16, 2017, pg. 14-15, https://www.netclean.com/wp-content/uploads/2016/12/NetClean_Report_2016_English_print.pdf, 18-19.

19. Foster, "John Grisham: men who watch child porn," 2014.

20. Nancy Dillon and Bill Hutchinson, "Stephen Collins' estranged wife reached out to actor's first victim after receiving anonymous letter with child sex abuse warning," *New York Daily News*, October 9, 2014, accessed July 16, 2017, http://www.nydailynews.com/entertainment/gossip/stephen-collins-told-wife-incestuous-impulses-report-article-1.1967570

21. Margo Kaplan, "Pedophilia: A Disorder, Not a Crime," *New York Times*, October 5, 2014, accessed July 16, 2017, https://www.nytimes.com/2014/10/06/opinion/pedophilia-a-disorder-not-a-crime.html?_r=0

22. "Disability Expansion Raises Ire in Greece," *New York Times*, January 9, 2012, accessed July 16, 2017, http://www.nytimes.com/2012/01/10/world/europe/greek-disability-groups-angered-by-new-categories.html

23. Nicholas Paphitis, "Furor in Greece over pedophilia as a disability," Associated Press (AP), January 9, 2012, accessed July 16, 2017, https://www.yahoo.com/news/furor-greece-over-pedophilia-disability-174002476.html

24. Alan Zarembo, "In Focus: The pedophile next door," *Portland Press Herald*, 20 January 2013, accessed July 16, 2017, http://www.pressherald.com/2013/01/20/in-focus-sex-and-society_2013-01-20

25. "West Point Army Officer Receives 37 Years in Prison," *Salem News.com*, January 7, 2011, accessed July 16, 2017, http://www.salem-news.com/articles/january072011/army-rape.php

26. Josh Stockinger, "Should Navy vet get prison for 'staggering' child porn collection?" *Daily Herald*, January 17, 2012, accessed July 16, 2017, http://www.dailyherald.com/article/20120116/news/701169906

27. Tracy Connor, "Former West Point Cadet Ricky Hester Gets 8 Years for Child Porn," NBC News, January 6, 2016, accessed July 16, 2017, http://www.nbcnews.com/news/us-news/former-west-point-cadet-ricky-hester-gets-8-years-child-n491446

28. Department of Justice, "West Point Cadet Convicted In White Plains Federal Court Of Distributing, Receiving, And Possessing Child Pornography," (Southern District of New York: United States Government), June 23, 2015, accessed July 16, 2017, https://www.justice.gov/usao-sdny/pr/west-point-cadet-convicted-white-plains-federal-court-distributing-receiving-and and "Granger Army cadet accused of emailing porn," *South Bend Tribune*, December 19, 2013, accessed July 16, 2017, http://www.southbendtribune.com/news/local/keynews/community/granger-army-cadet-accused-of-emailing-porn/article_668db94e-6915-11e3-9f90-0019bb30f31a.html

29. Dave Altimari, "Former Granby Police Captain Pleads Guilty To Child Pornography Charges," *Hartford Courant*, July 21, 2011, accessed July 16, 2017, http://articles.courant.com/2011-07-21/community/hc-bourque-guilty-plea-0722-20110721_1_images-and-videos-u-s-attorney-miller and "Ex-Granby Police Captain Gets 10-year Child Porn Sentence," *CBS News Connecticut*, February 10, 2012, accessed July 16, 2017, http://connecticut.cbslocal.com/2012/02/10/ex-granby-police-captain-gets-10-year-child-porn-sentence_

30. Patty Ryan, "Former Tampa officer gets nearly 5 years for child porn," *Tampa Bay Times*, May 8, 2013, accessed July 16, 2017, www.tampabay.com/news/courts/criminal/former-tampa-officer-gets-nearly-five-years-for-child-porn/2119960 and Patty Ryan, "Ex-Tampa police officer takes plea deal in child porn case," *Tampa Bay Times*, February 4, 2013, accessed July 16, 2017, http://

www.tampabay.com/news/courts/criminal/former-tampa-police-officer-takes-plea-deal-in-child-porn-case/1273784

31. Laurie Udesky, "Custody in Crisis: How Family Courts Nationwide Put Children in Danger," *100 Reporters*, December 1, 2016, accessed July 19, 2017, https://100r.org/2016/12/custody-2 and Joyanna Silberg, "How Many Children Are Court -Ordered into Unsupervised Contact With an Abusive Parent After Divorce?" The Leadership Council, Press Release, September 22, 2008, accessed July 19, 2017, http://www.leadershipcouncil.org/index.html

32. Ernest Rollins, "Former IU ethics office employee sentenced to 2-1/2 years for possession of child pornography," *Herald Times On-Line*, February 28, 2017, accessed July 16, 2017.

33. Deborah Hastings, "Bailey Joe Mills, 33, was the alleged ringleader of the child pornography production operation he ran from his North Carolina home, which he billed as a daycare service," *New York Daily News*, June 25, 2014, accessed July 19, 2017, http://www.nydailynews.com/news/national/n-authorities-bust-daycare-center-child-porn-ring-article-1.1844217

34. "Deputies: Day care, mentoring program a front for Sanford child porn operation," WRAL. Com, November 21, 2014, accessed July 17, 2017, http://www.wral.com/deputies-day-care-and-mentoring-program-a-front-for-child-porn-operation/13758447

35. "With third strike, Sanford sex offender faces life in prison," WRAL.com, August 12, 2014, accessed July 18, 2017, http://www.wral.com/state-law-allowed-convicted-sex-offender-to-be-removed-from-state-registry/13887111

36. Linda Silmalis, "Child sex abuse reports on rise and should not be taboo subject," *The Sunday Telegraph*, June 10, 2017, accessed July 16, 2017, http://www.dailytelegraph.com.au/news/nsw/child-sex-abuse-reports-on-rise-and-should-not-be-taboo-subject-expert/news-story/dfe91709b6b51e152c9f02393f01597d

4

Race and Child Pornography

The large majority of children in the images in the COPINE archive involving ... child pornography were white children.

  – Dutch National Rapporteur on Trafficking in Human Beings[1]

WHITE MEN – WHITE CHILDREN

There is a prominent racial element to the trade in child rape and torture. This crime appears to be committed, largely, by white men in North America and Europe. As mentioned, according to the US Sentencing Commission's most recent data, more than 85 percentage of all child pornography convictions in the U.S. were of white men.[2] This is a staggeringly significant racial demographic.

In the United Kingdom Child Exploitation and Online Protection Centre (CEOP) noted "dual offenders are almost exclusively white males ... aged between 19 and 45."[3] The CEOP report continues "the majority of ... offenders

	R/T/D						Possession					
	1992		2004		2010		1992		2004		2010	
	N	%	N	%	N	%	N	%	N	%	N	%
Race/Ethnicity												
White	57	93.4	314	92.1	710	87.6	14	87.5	270	91.2	810	89.9
Black	3	4.9	4	1.2	29	3.6	1	6.3	5	1.7	21	2.3
Hispanic	0	0.0	16	4.7	54	6.7	1	6.3	15	5.1	53	5.9
Other	1	1.6	7	2.1	18	2.2	0	0.0	6	2.0	17	1.9
Total	61	100.0	341	100.0	811	100.0	16	100.0	296	100.0	901	100.0
Citizenship												
U.S. Citizen	60	98.4	332	97.7	794	97.7	15	100.0	291	98.3	878	97.1
Non-Citizen	1	1.6	8	2.4	19	2.3	0	0.0	5	1.7	26	2.9
Total	61	100.0	340	100.0	813	100.0	15	100.0	296	100.0	904	100.0
Gender												
Male	59	96.7	336	98.5	808	99.4	16	100.0	295	99.7	899	99.5
Female	2	3.3	5	1.5	5	0.6	0	0.0	1	0.3	5	0.6
Total	61	100.0	341	100.0	813	100.0	16	100.0	296	100.0	904	100.0
Average Age	42		41		42		48		44		43	

Table 6–8
Demographic Characteristics of Offenders Convicted of R/T/D and Possession Offenses
Fiscal Years 1992, 2004, and 2010

US Sentencing Commission, 2012, pg. 142

This table excludes cases missing information for the variables required for analysis. Percentages may not sum to 100.0% due to rounding.
SOURCE: U.S. Sentencing Commission, 1992, 2004, and 2010 Datafiles, MONFY92, USSCFY04, and USSCFY10.

lived with a spouse or partner. Of that group over half were living with children. In addition to those offenders who had access to their own or a partner's children, offenders also had access through extended family, employment, voluntary work, and via friends and neighbours."[4]

White, trusted men in North America and Europe with access to your child – that appears to be the average pedophile profile.[5]

"What is striking is the absence of black children in child abuse material."[6] The majority of children, seen in at least one child pornography study conducted by COPINE, are also white. If most children are raped by their parents, usually their fathers and/or male relatives, as studies indicate, and most people caught trading in child rape are white men, this correlation makes common sense.[7] If white American men are producing and trading, more than anyone else, in child pornography, the white children they have access to, their own children, grandchildren and those of relatives and friends, would comprise the bulk of the child pornography material. Yet, despite the data on the racial elements of the crime, no policy work has been crafted to address and protect children in this segment of the population.

No one seems willing to discuss the racial element of the crime.

When I bring the distinctive racial component to people's attention, I am often met with hostile resistance and called a "race-baiter" or a liar. America's mainstream media has refused to report on racial aspects of the crime. Why? I believe our apparent collective refusal to discuss and respond to a key racial element of known child pornography data is because, in America, we have criminalized the black man and elevated the white man. Since before we even became the United States of America the alienation of black men and adulation of white men was a core component of American patriarchal structures. One that is not easily challenged or changed.

Sometimes, very infrequently, someone does ask me about the startling racial aspect of these statistics and wonders why so many white American men are involved in trading in child rape. The short answer is – I do not know. The longer response is perhaps I do know and would prefer not to think about it. The following is written in a personal essay style in an effort to reflect upon the racial element of the crime. This is an introspective response based on my experiences and thoughts and is not, necessarily, the answer to why so many white men, above all other races in America, appear to be trading in child rape.

GOING TO MEET THE MAN

During my first year at college, I fell in love. He was a football player. I was on the field hockey team. We met during fall break in upstate New York. He had just graduated from an elite private school in Connecticut. I had escaped a poor, rural public high school in Maine. Our first date was a run by the lake. The white football players told him white girls were for white men. They warned him to stay away. The black women were angry with me for "taking a good black man" and gave me hard stares when I attended a Black History Month event. I was completely baffled. I was white. He was black. Who cares? Weren't we beyond this? And why was everyone so angry? Naively, in the way only a white person can be, I thought racism was over in America. Rev. Dr. Martin Luther King had marched on Washington and ended racism in America, right?

That was 1987. Over Christmas that year, I visited his family in Connecticut. I remember, so clearly, a cold New England afternoon cozy in their living room. His father turned on haunting music on the stereo. The lyrics talked about strange fruit in Southern trees. I asked what the strange fruit was. I remember a long silence. Then my boyfriend's father gently explained who Billie Holiday was and that she was singing about the lynching of black men and boys. He told me that when the lynched men and children were still alive, white men cut off the penis and testicles and hung these from the branches of the tree. That was the strange fruit.

```
When you do this sort of work there is certain pictures you
just can't get out of your mind. For me, one is the picture of
a young girl about six or seven. She is nude, she is strapped
to a chair, and the chair has fallen over, and this child is
being sexually assaulted by a dog. The tears are streaming up
this little girl's face. And to my knowledge, she has not been
identified.
```

Flint Waters. ICAC Taskforce Wyoming October 2007 Congressional Testimony

To this day, I remember a wave of horror and disbelief flooding my being. I could not believe this. How could this happen in America? I had never learned about this in my high school history classes. And why? Why would they do that? My boyfriend's father suggested I read James Baldwin's *Going to Meet the Man.*

This began my real education about America's history.[8]

JAMES BALDWIN

During these past years, as I have been researching America's child pornography crisis, I've been thinking often about James Baldwin's *Going to Meet the Man.* My days are spent going through media reports and criminal complaints of child pornography arrests. It is almost all white, male faces staring back at me. Sometimes a white woman's face surfaces, a few black men, one or two Latino men, several Arab and Asian men and, very rarely, a black woman. But, by and large, I am looking at white male mug shots and reading about horrific violence committed against children in the videos and images these white men were caught trading.

In *Going to Meet the Man,* James Baldwin describes a white man taking his son to

Mark Ranzenberger, a journalism professor at Central Michigan University, was sentenced, January 2017, to 14 years in federal prison, for one count of child pornography possession and 14-45 years in state prison for repeatedly raping a young girl over a seven year period. At the time of his arrest, Ranzenberger had 1,000 images/videos of child sex abuse, including the rape of infants. He also had a "grooming" document instructing pedophiles how to manipulate children from birth to age 11 "to participate in sexual acts."

the lynching of a black man. This is a rite of sexual passage for the white boy to become a man. This, for the white community, was a celebrated event. The white women cooked food, put ribbons in their hair and set up a picnic. The white men felt their penises stiffen. The son of the man, who took his son to the lynching, grew up to become a police officer who achieved sexual excitement by violently beating black men and raping black women. "Sometimes, sure, like any other man, he knew that he wanted a little more spice than Grace [his wife] could give him and he would drive over yonder and pick up a black piece or arrest her, it came to the same thing" says the white deputy sheriff in *Going to Meet the Man*.

Didn't Oklahoma City police officer, Daniel Holtzclaw do the same thing?[9] Isn't this still happening today?

James Baldwin describes how the white man teaches the next white, male generation that sexual arousal is the result of brutal violence committed against vulnerable people. Child pornography is the recorded evidence of brutal violence committed against vulnerable people. Is there a link? It seems to me there may be.

It is the act of committing the violence, and watching this violence be committed, that provides the pedophile with sexual stimulation and an erection used to rape the child. As Baldwin wrote, the white man "felt himself violently stiffen" when he thought about or committed acts of violence against vulnerable black men, women and children. The white deputy sheriff in *Going to Meet the Man* can only achieve an erection, when attempting sex with his wife, by thinking about the violence he has committed against vulnerable people in the African-American community. Child pornography, like racism, is about sexual violence committed, overwhelmingly by white men, against a vulnerable population.

BEARING WITNESS

As I write this book, I often think back to 1987 and reflect on the education I received that winter afternoon in Connecticut, exposed to music, Billie Holiday, and literature, James Baldwin. I think of the power of bearing witness through words and songs and the power of love to educate about and expose injustice. I would be a very different, and much worse, person today if not for the education I received from a football player I met one fall day in upstate New York and happened to ask if he wanted to join me for a run.

Why are so many white men in America engaged in trading in the rape and torture of our children? I do not know.

I think it may have something to do with *Going to Meet the Man*.

Endnotes

1. National Rapporteur on Trafficking in Human Beings, "Child Pornography: First Report of the Dutch National Rapporteur," (The Netherland: Dutch Government, 2011), accessed July 16, 2017, https://www.dutchrapporteur.nl/current/news/NationalRapporteurpresentsFirstReportonChildPornographytoUnitedNations.aspx, 78-79

2. US Sentencing Commission, "Report to the Congress."

3. Data from British and American crimes reports document similar pedophile arrest profiles being overwhelming white and male. Child Exploitation and On-line Protection Center (CEOP), A Picture of Abuse: *A thematic assessment of the risk of contact child sexual abuse posed by those who possess indecent images of children,* June 2012, accessed July 16, 2017, https://www.ceop.police. uk/Documents/ceopdocs/CEOP%20IIOCTA%20Executive%20Summary.pdf, 7. *See also* Mary Pulido, "Internet Child Pornography: Who is at the Keyboard?" *Huffington Post,* January 9, 2014, accessed July 16, 2017, http://www.huffingtonpost.com/mary-l-pulido-phd/internet-child-pornography_b_4562194.html

4. CEOP, *A Picture of Abuse,* 7.

5. NetClean reports the majority of child victims, in their study, are from North America and Europe. NetClean, "NetClean Report 2016," 14-15.

6. National Rapporteur, "Child Pornography," 78-79.

7. Canadian Centre for Child Protection, "Canadian Centre for Child Protection's survey."

8. James Baldwin, *Going to Meet the Man,* (New York: Vintage International, 1995).

9. Sarah Larimer, "Disgraced ex-cop Daniel Holtzclaw sentenced to 263 years for on-duty rapes, sexual assaults," *Washington Post,* January 22, 2016, accessed July 16, 2017, https://www.washingtonpost.com/news/post-nation/wp/2016/01/21/disgraced-ex-officer-daniel-holtzclaw-to-be-sentenced-after-sex-crimes-conviction/?utm_term=.e848061d6e10

ANTI-PREDATOR
P R O J E C T
STANDING IN THE VOID OF JUSTICE

http://wwww.antipredatorproject.org

The Anti-Predator Project is a nonprofit organization dedicated to combating human trafficking and sexual predators in the United States through the use of specially trained private investigators. Along with providing investigative and protective services for those victims of these horrific crimes, Anti-Predator Project is also dedicated to educating the community about the reality of human trafficking in the United States. Anti-Predator Project specializes in criminal investigations into individuals and organizations that are involved in human trafficking, the location and recovery of American children that have been kidnapped or sold on the black market, witness/victim protection, and missing children. We offer our services free of charge to victims and relatives of victims.

Contact the Anti-Predator Project if you would like to volunteer or are in need of assistance http://www.antipredatorproject.org

5

The National Security Problem

40.   The link between organized crime and human trafficking is clearly established and both are often involved in supplying children for sexual exploitation. Any of the facilitators outlined above can be affiliated or controlled by such criminal networks. Additionally, criminal networks have a particular interest in the production and sale of child abuse material, which is increasingly lucrative. Moreover, organized crime groups have used child sexual abuse material to extort money and steal identities.

– 2015 Report of the United Nations Special Rapporteur on the Sale of Children, Child Prostitution and Child Pornography[1]

UNBELIEVABLE

In May 2016, the Pentagon's Defense Security Service Director, Daniel Payne told reporters the "amount of child porn" on government computers is just "unbelievable." I contacted Payne's office seeking clarification and was told, "Director Payne was speaking from his 34 years of experience in the field of counterintelligence and security, and involvement in the Inspector General community. His remarks were not Agency specific; rather, he was speaking in terms of the government as a whole."[2]

The quantity of child pornography, a crime dominated by organized crime, on government computers as a whole, is "unbelievable" and this did not even make headline news. Most Americans are unaware that the Defense Security Service Director made this remarkable statement because journalists have, largely, failed to report on the serious national security issue of government employees involved in the child-rape trade. To my knowledge, *The Christian Science Monitor* was the only major media outlet to cover Payne's statement:

> While the notion of government employees and contractors with high levels of security clearance looking at child pornography was disturbing on its own, internal records retrieved through the Freedom of Information Act revealed the problem is not limited to military and intelligence agencies. In the past three years, agencies ranging from the Postal Service to the Federal Highway Administration substantiated about 40 allegations that employees or contractors opened child pornography or provocative images of minors using government resources. The number of confirmed cases may be higher now since many federal organizations, such as the National Security Agency (NSA), did not respond to requests for records about similar investigations."[3]

While complete data is not available, it is evident that disturbing numbers of government employees, often in leadership positions, have been caught trading in child rape at the Pentagon, Department of Homeland Security (DHS), Department of Justice (DOJ), Immigration and Customs Enforcement (ICE), Department of Transportation (DOT), Transportation Security Agency (TSA), Federal Bureau of Investigations (FBI), Central Intelligence Agency (CIA), among other federal agencies and at local and state-level government offices from Maine to California.[4] The alarming number of government employees arrested on child pornography charges renders this a national security issue because these employees have opened U.S. government networks to organized crime and have also made themselves vulnerable to blackmail by hostile governments seeking to exploit America's weaknesses.

The absence of accurate data on how many federal government employees have been arrested for trading in child rape is due to the failure of the Clinton, Bush and Obama administrations to require their executive branch agencies maintain "official numbers related to employees who access child pornography on federal government computers."[5] The Trump administration has also not yet mandated that this data be gathered and made public. Likewise, at the state level, governors are not requiring their agencies to collect and report on employees arrested on child pornography charges.

Criminal behavior, particularly at the top of an organization, establishes permissible conduct for the entire workplace. This culture permeates the government – compromising national security on many levels, from classified information to the safety and well-being of law-abiding government employees and U.S. citizens. For example, an Army prosecutor and judge advocate like Daniel Wollverton, sentenced for infant sodomy and 30,000 child rape images, would have been unlikely to hold his own colleagues accountable for sexual assault against other military staff.[6] David O'Brien, a scientist responsible for monitoring global nuclear activity, was sentenced to federal prison for trading in child rape including from Russian sources on government computers.[7] He certainly compromised America's security by exposing sensitive computer networks to organized crime and hostile foreign entities. These are two examples out of hundreds, including an Undersecretary of the Navy, James Daniel Howard, and a Navy Deputy Assistant Secretary, Wade Sanders.[8]

> Former Undersecretary of the Navy, James Daniel Howard, arrested on child pornography possession and reproduction in 2013. Howard had served as special assistant to President Ronald Reagan. He pled guilty to ten child pornography counts and spent seven months in jail. He is a registered sex offender.

Disturbingly, individual arrests are not isolated events. As previously mentioned, pedophiles are highly networked. "Molesters working as a team... can cover up each other's tracks and use their connections to outwit the police."[9] By virtue of their positions, government pedophiles have a unique ability to hide their crimes, avoid prosecution or obtain light sentences if caught. When those involved in child pornography are top government employees, responsible for America's national security, it is easy to understand why this is a serious problem. Given the number of known arrests, it certainly appears pedophiles may be connected through out our military, law enforcement, and civilian governments agencies; protecting and helping each other avoid prosecution and access children for rape and torture.

This is a problem for America's children. This is a problem for us all.

THE MILITARY

Date/Time:	March 3, 2013 at 9:53 p.m. GMT
Hash Value:	57BFF2B39C496508D2DFA3C1884B4FC5
File Name:	"(Hussyfan)(pthc)******** Best Collection.avi"
Description of File:	a movie file showing a girl, approximately three to five years old performing fellatio on an adult male. The

David O'Brien's Criminal Complaint

NOT A PRIORITY

In 2011, journalist Bryan Bender, with the *Boston Globe,* reported up to 5,200 Pentagon employees with top security clearances were engaged in child pornography on Pentagon computers.[10] Many were using their government email accounts and paying with credit cards. The brazenness with which America's most elite military men committed this crime indicates a culture that tolerates, perhaps even encourages, child pornography. What's worse is there were almost no prosecutions. The Pentagon closed the investigation, claiming it wasn't "a priority."[11] Senator Charles Grassley fought a losing battle to expose the Pentagon's refusal to examine 1,700 of the 5,200 reports. Denial. Nothing to see here. Move along please. And everyone did.

In July 2012, *Bloomberg News* reported the U.S. Missile Defense Agency issued a memo reminding staff not to download pornography at work.[12] "Specifically," the memo reads, "there have been instances of employees and contractors accessing websites, or transmitting messages, containing pornographic or sexually explicit images.... These actions are not only unprofessional, they reflect time taken away from desig-

> Cassidy Harwell, a 28-year-old Air Force employee from Ellsworth Air Force Base, was sentenced to five years in jail for child pornography possession. Upon his arrest, he had more than 300 videos of child sex abuse including children as young as three-years-old.

nated duties, are in clear violation of federal and DOD and regulations, consume network resources and can compromise the security of the network."[13] When America's most elite security professionals responsible for our missile defense system need to be told not to access pornography (perhaps child pornography, the memo did not specify) on government networks, America has a serious problem.

Lt. Col. Zatyko, former Department of Defense Computer Forensics Laboratory (DCFL) Director, told journalists, in 2012, regarding child pornography investigations, "we always have cases in the queue... and more work than we can handle."[14] Merritt Baer, owner of a cyber-security firm and former clerk with the U.S. Court of Appeals for the Armed Forces, reported, in 2013, there was an "overwhelming flow of child pornography appeals" in the military's appellate court. Baer estimated two-thirds of the U.S. Court of Appeals for the Armed Forces docket were child pornography cases.[15] While complete data on how many military employees have been prosecuted for trading in child rape has not been gathered, the information that is available is shocking.

CASCADE OF CHILD SEX ABUSE

In 2016, the Los Angeles Times, called child abuse in the military a "little-noticed cascade" and reported in many cases "military officials knew or suspected that child abuse or neglect was occurring – but failed to intervene or to alert the Family Advocacy Program or state child welfare agencies."[16] Defense Department officials say child pornography arrests and convictions are not "tracked" and so it is "difficult to determine how widespread the problem might be."[17] Although the Department of Defense (DOD) issues an annual report on sexual assaults on adults in the military, this report fails to include child sexual assaults and child pornography convictions.[18] A 2015, Associated Press (AP) investigation "found the single largest category of inmates in military prisons to be child sex offenders."[19]

In 2013, the Navy pledged greater transparency regarding sexual assaults, including against children, and now provides public monthly courts-martial information available on the Navy.mil website.[20] As of April 2017, there were ten Navy military court cases involving child pornography and child rape since the start of the year. In the Army, in March 2017, six

> Marine Captain Joshua Taylor, a 28 year old Marine pilot who flew Super Stallion Helicopters, had more than 5,000 videos/images of child rape including children as young as four-years-old.

Army staff were involved in court-martial proceedings on child pornography charges and eleven on child sex abuse charges.[21] As of June 2017, 23 Marines were in court-martial proceedings for child sexual assault and/

or child-pornography related charges.[22] As of April 2017, *Stars and Stripes* had 200 articles related to child pornography arrests in the military.

The *Military Times* said, in 2013, "the Army's child abuse and neglect epidemic is tragic and rapidly getting worse."[23] From 2003 to 2012, some 30,000 Army children were abused with 1,400 cases of sexual assault and 118 child murders.[24] From 2011-2012 the Marine Corps reported 1,591 confirmed cases of child abuse. The Navy reported 3,336 cases of reported child abuse from 2009 to 2012.[25] Child abuse reports increased 25 percent in the Air Force from 2008-2012. In a one-year period, 2011-2012, in the Army, Navy, Air Force and Marine Corps there were 12,881 cases of child abuse, 753 of which were sexual assaults with 67 children killed. In 2016, Congresswoman Tulsi Gabbard from Hawaii, when Talia's Law was passed, claimed there were 29,000 cases of

> Gregory Kyle Seerden, a 31-year-old Navy SEAL, was arrested on child pornography charges in April 2017. At the time of his arrest his cell phone contained a video of him molesting a 5-year-old girl who was asleep, an infant being raped by a dog and children in bondage. Seerden's trade in child rape was discovered during an investigation into his rape of an unconscious adult woman.

child abuse and neglect in military families in the past decade.[26] The percentage of child sexual assault and/or child pornography in all the above estimates is unknown.

In 2016, after the Associated Press (AP) filed numerous freedom of information act (FOIA) requests, partial information was released by the military. AP suggested the data provided seemed low and said the "numbers fall well-short of offering a full picture."[27] Compared with military data from earlier years, cited above, the data the military provided to AP does appear to be incomplete. In addition, child pornography, specifically, was not reported. Although child sexual assault and child pornography production are often synonymous, this is not always reflected in the investigations, convictions or data.

The military reported to AP there were 1,584 cases of reported child sexual assault from 2010-2014. Most often the sexual assault was of girls by male relatives in positions of military leadership; corporals, sergeants and staff sergeants.[28] AP's findings are consistent with research, cited in previous chapters, about who trades in child rape and how they access the children; men, most often fathers, in positions of power sexually abusing their own children and/or children of family friends.[29] Like Marine Corporeal Aaron Masa, profiled in the AP article, who groomed a fellow Marine and, unbeknownst to the Marine father, used his friendship with the family to gain access to the father's 3-year-old stepdaughter and infant daughter to produce child pornography.[30]

The Policy Lab at Children's Hospital of Philadelphia has documented that an estimated one in five cases of Army children diagnosed by doctors as assault victims are never reported to the military officals.[31] Marisa Taylor, a journalist with McClatchy, confirmed that even when military staff admit to molesting children and using child pornography they are not always reported. She cites a 2010 case of an Air Force lieutenant colonel who "confessed to downloading child pornography on his Pentagon computer and to touching a child in a sexual way" during a polygraph interview for a position with the National Reconnaissance Office (NRO), the government agency responsible for overseeing spy satellites.[32] The NRO never reported the lieutenant colonel to the police or the Air Force.[33]

On Medium, I posted "Military Staff Trading in Child Rape & Torture" in 2014. As with my other research, I used simple Twitter and Google searches to locate mainstream media reports of military staff arrested on child pornography charges. This is by no means a comprehensive account. The data does provide a sense of the scale of the trade in child rape within our military; one that represents a serious security issue not only for military children but for all Americans. Comprehensive data collection on this subject is urgently needed.

A few examples of military arrests include:

- Lt. Col. Steven Jon Frederiksen, Defense Intelligence Agency (DIA) employee, was sentenced, 8 November 2016, to 20 years in prison with 20 years of supervised release for producing child pornography. He pled guilty to one count of producing child pornography and one count of attempted coercion and enticement of a minor. Frederiksen targeted and coerced, at least four girls age 14–17 years old, to produce videos/images while he was at work and from his government computer. He was also trading in the rape of prepubescent children from his government computer. Frederiksen is a West Point graduate. He joined the Army in 1995 and was a Boy Scout and church youth leader.[34]

> old. In the text conversation, Fred S sends a picture of an exposed penis from someone wearing what appears to be a military uniform to MG3. The folders with the names of females can be observed on the left side of the account. Additional SMS conversations include Fred S asking MG3 "Whatcha up to?" to which MG3 responded with "In class u?" Fred S responded "Just jerked off under my desk." In another conversation, MG3 stated to Fred S "It must be pretty easy to jack off at work cause it seems you do it a lot." Fred S responded "Hehe…just as easy as

Jon Frederiksen's Criminal Complaint

- Col. Robert Joel Rice, an Army War College war game developer, was charged, April 2013, with 130 child pornography counts. After many delays, Rice was sentenced, 28 December 2016, to 12 years in federal prison followed by 10 years of supervised released concurrent with a four-year prison sentence from a military court-martial in October 2016. The Army War College continued to employ Rice, while he was free on bail, and allowed him supervised access to Army computers pending sentencing. At the time of his arrest, Rice had more than 30,000 images/videos of child sex abuse. His wife had discovered these and notified police.[35]

• Robert Cuff, Navy Command Master Chief of Joint Task Force North at Biggs Army Airfield, pled guilty and received a life-sentence in July 2012 for child pornography charges. Cuff had been a Dreamboard member; an online group engaged in the violent sex abuse of children under twelve years old – otherwise known as pre-teen hard core (PTHC). Members were required to continually contribute new videos/images of child rape. Those who videoed themselves raping children "received elevated status." Cuff had been repeatedly raping a five-year-old child. His online names included "slapalot" and "dd0040."[36]

• Tech Sergeant Erik Dean Rabes, a 44-year-old Air Force Computer Security Specialist who had been assigned to the U.S. Strategic Command, a joint service unit that oversees the nation's nuclear arsenal and defends American interests in space, was sentenced to ten years for child pornography production. The military refused to confirm if Rabes had used military computers. He had more than 30,000 child sex-abuse videos/images. Rabes' former wife had operated a day-care facility from their residence in Colorado Springs. Unknown to his wife, Rabes had been sexually abusing children, as young as four-years-old, at the day-care and filming and distributing that abuse.[37]

• David Riley, a 37-year-old Air Force Major stationed at MacDill Air Force Base in Florida, was charged on child pornography counts after he sent "extremely graphic" child sex abuse images to an undercover Washington D.C. Metro police officer. Riley said he was "looking for other pervs in the area" and that he had sexually abused the six-year-old daughter of his former girlfriend. Riley, a married father of a six-year-old girl, said he never abuses his own daughter. The undercover officer sent Riley a picture of a child and claimed it was his

Air Force Staff Sergeant, 29-year-old Daniel Freiwald, married father of two children formerly with the 83rd Fighter Weapons Squadron, was sentenced to eight years for receiving, distributing and possessing videos/images of child rape, including infants and toddlers, on his computer at Tyndall Air Force Base in Florida. He later died, reported as suicide, in prison.

daughter. Riley asked "What is the purpose of showing me pics of your daughter? Do you want to share her? … no pressure from me. Just curious." Riley was at Fort McNair in Washington D.C., enrolled in a National Defense University course at the time.[38]

- Former Deputy Assistant Secretary of the Navy, 70-year-old retired Navy Captain Wade Sanders, pled guilty to child pornography possession. He had been awarded the Silver Star, the nation's third-highest valor award. The Navy revoked this medal after Sander's child sex abuse conviction. Sanders introduced candidate John Kerry at the 2004 Democratic National Convention. He was sentenced to 37 months in prison.[39]

NATIONAL SECURITY INFRASTRUCTURE

Men arrested for trading in child rape are often in significant positions in our national security infrastructure. The AP's investigation confirms military men in leadership positions were most frequently arrested on child sex abuse charges.[40] The arrests I have gathered so far are only a few out of hundreds. As I reviewed arrest records, I kept thinking, "surely this arrest is as shocking as it gets." Inevitably, the next case was more concerning. Such as America's chief scientist responsible for monitoring global nuclear activity at Patrick Air Force Base's Technical Applications Center's Atomic Energy Detection System, David O'Brien.

1.	"!! Tara ********liluplanet.avi"
2.	"6Yo Licks ******** (Complete).avi"
3.	"(Hussyfan)(pthc)******** Best Collection.avi"
4.	"! NEW ! (pthc) 2006 Tara 7yr ******.avi"
5.	"(Pthc) Russian Dad ******.avi"

"PTHC," as seen in the above file titles, is an abbreviation for "preteen hardcore." Filenames do not always accurately depict the contents of the file.

David O'Brien's Criminal Complaint

In May 2013, David O'Brien was arrested and charged with ten counts of child pornography possession and distribution and sentenced, October 2014, to five years in federal prison. O'Brien had a large child-pornography collection at home and on his Air Force computer. He was trading in pre-teen hard core (PTHC) – the brutal rape and torture of very young children, often infants and toddlers. He was also exchanging Russian-sourced material. O'Brien had taken pictures of his own young granddaughter and placed images of her head over images of children being raped. He also transposed photos of Air Force employees and child-sex abuse images.

The man who was monitoring global nuclear activity for the security of our country was trading in child rape, including from Russian sources, from his Air Force computer. This means America's Atomic Energy

Detection System was likely exposed to Russian organized crime. National security journalists never reported on O'Brien's arrest. Why not? O'Brien's crimes against children are also crimes against all Americans. If you share my discomfort about O'Brien's conduct, contact the Air Force and share your concerns.

> **Action Item**
> Contact the Air Force 🐦 **@usairforce** and share your concerns about David O'Brien's case. Ask why the trade in child rape is allowed on military computers?

The military has the technical capacity to block child pornography. Blocking programs are an easy technical fix. Iceland, for example, has been considering a nation-wide block on adult and child pornography.[41] The United Kingdom has also been discussing a country-wide block on child pornography and mandating that Internet service providers create an opt-in/opt-out function to access adult pornography.[42] In the U.S. some state legislatures are considering the Human Trafficking and Child Exploitation Prevention Act which would require Internet-accessible electronics to include a filter for adult and child pornography. People wishing to access adult pornography could pay a $20 tax to unlock the filter.[43] Some states have passed Internet filtering laws regulating public schools and libraries, requiring filtering software.[44] The military can prevent access to child pornography on government computers. This is a choice. Is the military choosing to allow child rape images and videos on government computer networks over America's national security?

The military, like other government agencies, is not gathering and making public comprehensive data on child pornography arrests. They should be required to do so. The Department of Defense (DOD)'s annual report on sexual assault must include child sexual assault and child pornography charges. Child sex abuse allegations are probable cause for child pornography investigations and vice versa. These investigations must be coordinated in the military. Robust and comprehensive child protection procedures must become the norm in all military investigations. Child pornography must be blocked from all military computers and regular random searches of military electronics, including personal electronic devises for those with top security clearance, must be a top priority.

Senator Kirsten Gillibrand of New York, a leading advocate for ending adult sexual assault in the military, said the AP's investigation into child sexual abuse in the military was alarming.[45] The AP reported, in 2016, Senator Gillibrand, Senator Barbara Boxer of California and Senator Mazie Hirono of Hawaii, contacted military leadership to express concerns about the alarming amount of child sex abuse within the military.[46] If you wish to help protect children of

> **Action Item**
> Contact Senator Kirsten Gillibrand 🐦 @SenGillibrand and ask that the Department of Defense (DOD) be required to block child pornography on all military networks, regularly monitor military electronics and report all child pornography arrests.

military employees and our national security, contact Senator Gillibrand and ask her to continue to push the Department of Defense for transparency, accountability and oversight and prevent all military staff from engaging in the trade in child rape.

For the sake of America's national security and all our children.

LOCAL AND STATE LAW ENFORCEMENT

> 11. In addition, I observed that many of the Shared Files have file names that by their title indicate an apparent connection to child pornography, including, among others, "(((kingpass))) 10y touch pussy webcam 3.avi"; "boy gay sexo infantil porno (37)(2).jpg"; "pthc - capb (little boy slowly fucks little girl).mpg"; "11 years old masha masturbate.avi"; "bibcam webcam ultimate 12 best boy suck & fuck(2).avi"; "13 and 12 year old brothers enjoy playing and sucking off each others dick.mpg"; "17 yo boy fuck 7 yo girl kdv.avi"; and "homemade (pthc) father with daughter 13y anal (inzest).wmv."

Brian Fanelli's Criminal Complaint – Police Chief, Mount Pleasant, New York

WHAT IF THE POLICE OFFICER IS A PEDOPHILE?

When a report is made to law enforcement about child pornography and/or child sex abuse, it is assumed the report will be taken seriously; that police will act to protect the child and apprehend the perpetrator. But what happens when the officer receiving the report is engaged in the trade of child rape him/herself? While there are many dedicated law enforcement officers (LEOs) for whom I have tremendous respect, especially those investigating child pornography, the arrests of law enforcement engaged in this crime are alarming and appear to be widespread.[47] These arrests suggest a serious problem of pedophiles in positions of power within too many local and state police agencies.

How many state and local enforcement officers have been arrested on child pornography related charges? No one knows – because law enforcement has not been collecting the data. According to the Cato Institute's National Police Misconduct Reporting Project (NPMRP), DOJ has failed to release data on a "wide range of misdeeds, crimes, and other misconduct that occur in law enforcement agencies."[48] Cato's NPMRP provides a 2010 report by David Packman documenting 618 cases of sexual misconduct by law enforcement with over half of those against children.[49] DOJ has issued data on problems with use of force by law enforcement with a 2015 report on estimated prevalence of use/threat of force and a 2006 report about citizen complaints about use of force.[50] Issues of sexual violence, including child pornography, were not included in either report.[51]

In November 2015, the Associated Press (AP) published a year-long investigation of police misconduct detailing over 1,000 officers disciplined for sex crimes, including child pornography.[52] AP said "some states did not provide information, and even among states that did, some reported no officers removed for sexual misdeeds even though cases were identified via official records and news stories."[53] California, Hawaii, Massachusetts, New Jersey, New York and Rhode Island, with some of the largest police forces, told AP they do not maintain records of officer misconduct. Several states, Louisiana, Maryland and North Carolina, refused to provide AP with any information at all. While there is a National Decertification Index (NDI) listing officers who have lost certification, this is voluntary, and many agencies simply choose not to share information. In addition, the NDI database does not provide information on offense type.

In November 2014, I placed on Medium "Police Trading in Child Rape & Torture" profiling 70 local and state police officers arrested on child pornography charges. My survey was out of date almost as soon as I hit "publish." A year later I posted "When Law Enforcement is the Perpetrator," examining only November 2015, when more than two local or state officers per week were in the news. In April 2017, I profiled 103 state and local LEOs in "Law Enforcement Arrested for Trading in Child Rape."[54] I used simple Google and Twitter searches to locate media reports of arrests.

Similar to the military, many arrested police were in leadership positions, including ten captains or chiefs, and were often trading in infant and toddler rape. Some examples include:

- Officer Michael Harding, of Port St. Lucie, Florida, was arrested September 2015, on child pornography charges. He was caught in a chatroom called #toddlerfuck. Harding was trading in child rape while on duty and possessed hundreds of videos/images including "6 yo boy sucks" and "7 yo girl fingered deep in both holes." He was Officer of the Year in 2011.[55]

- Chief Robert Geist, the "number one possessor and distributor of child porn" in Pennsylvania, caught sending images/videos including "6Yo babyj — Bedtime rape." Geist received no jail time.[56]

- Chris Bowersox, a 38-year-old Bakersfield, California police officer, was sentenced to four years in jail. He was discovered by federal investigators discussing raping and killing young boys. In one chat session another pedophile wrote, "Every time I talk someone into rape, I always get a bit sad when they're not into this." Bowersox responded, "Oh, I'm ... into it, big time." In another chat, Bowersox discussed how to locate a child to rape, torture and kill. One pedophile wrote "I know it can't happen here, it's got to be somewhere else with a bought kid or something. We'd definitely get caught if we did it here." Bowersox replied, "Cambodia ... Thailand ... Mexico ... deep deep Mexico." Images of local boys were found on Bowersox's computer.[57]

• Maine State Police Chief Andrew Demers, charged with child sex-abuse of his four-year-old granddaughter. Demers was sentenced to five years, one of which was suspended. He served 26 years with the Maine State Police and was chief from 1987 to 1993. In 2003, Demers, the most decorated officer in state police history, was named a "Legendary Trooper."[58]

• Chief Brian Fanelli, of Mount Pleasant, New York, arrested in January 2014, pled guilty to child pornography charges in July 2015. Fanelli had images/videos of children as young as seven. Other videos included 10 and 12-year-old girls engaged in sex acts and a video called "10 y touch pussy webcam." He was sentenced, January 2016, to 18 months in prison followed by five years of probation.[59]

• Gilberto Valle, a 30-year-old New York City police officer whose online name was Girlmeat Hunter was convicted, March 2013, of conspiracy to kidnap and illegal access of a federal government database. Valle engaged in online arrangements with a man who offered his three-year-old stepdaughter as a sex slave and his two nieces, age seven and nine, for rape. Valle also discussed plans to murder his wife, saying he would tie up her feet, slit her throat and watch the blood rush from her body. Valle's wife installed spyware on their home computer and discovered his online activity. She gave the computer to the FBI and fled the state with their one-year-old baby.[60]

Valle's computer was "loaded with crime-scene pictures of dead and mutilated women, twisted images of women being tortured and sexually assaulted." He illegally accessed the encrypted National Crime Information Database to research kidnapping targets and had amassed over 100 potential victims including names, photos, birth dates and bra sizes. Valle claimed, in chat sessions, that he was "drafting and revising an operation plan to abduct and cook an identified woman." He had a file called "Abducting and Cooking: A Blueprint" and had downloaded chloroform recipes to subdue his victims. A "client" asked Valle to kidnap and deliver a woman to be raped and murdered. Valle agreed to do so for $5,000 and said, "Just so that you know, she may be knocked out when I get her to you. I don't know how long the solvent I am using will last but I have to knock her out to get her out of her apartment safely." When the "client" tried to lower the price Valle said "I really need the money." The "client" wrote "Just make sure she doesn't die before I get her."[61]

Despite all this, Valle walked free. Judge Paul Gardephe over-turned a 2013 conviction, gave Valle a misdemeanor and released him on time-served, twenty-one months, and one year supervised release. Valle said he plans to become a criminal defense attorney and pursue custody rights of his 3-year-old daughter. He also hopes to return to the New York Police Department.[62]

Serve and Protect

Far too many in law enforcement appear to be engaging in this crime with what appears to be increased frequency at leadership levels. No police officer, who has sworn an oath to serve and protect, should ever be engaged in the trade in child rape. Not one. Deeply concerning is the brutal rape and violence of infants and toddlers, that so many police have been caught producing and trading. Police involved in child pornography present a serious problem for the security of America's children and for all Americans. How can any parent have faith that their families and children will be protected by local and state law enforcement, knowing how many police are participating in the crime?

Much greater oversight and accountability of America's state and lo-cal law enforcement is needed.

Immediately.

Federal Law Enforcement

No Accurate Records

Mention federal law enforcement and the Department of Homeland Security (DHS), the Federal Bureau of Investigations (FBI), the Drug Enforcement Administration (DEA) or the Transportation Security Authority (TSA) might come to mind. There are 73 federal law enforce-ment agencies, from the United States Mint Police to U.S. Postal Inspec-tors, employing, according to the most recent U.S. Bureau of Justice Statis-tics (BJS) data, some 120,000 full-time law enforcement officers (LEOs) with the legal authority to make arrests and carry firearms. Homeland Security (DHS) and Department of Justice (DOJ) are the largest federal law en-forcement agencies, employing

> **Action Item**
> Contact DOJ's Bureau of Justice Statistics at askbjs@usdoj.gov
> Ask them to report comprehensive data, an-nually, on crimes that federal law enforcement officers commit, including child pornography.

four in every five LEOs; eighty-four percent of whom are men.[63]

Like all other government agencies, there is no comprehensive data available on how many federal LEOs have been arrested on child por-nography charges. While the U.S. Bureau of Justice Statistics (BJS) documents assaults committed against federal LEOs, it fails to track and report on crimes which federal LEOs themselves commit. If you believe the U.S. government should make public crimes committed by federal law enforcement, including child pornography, please contact DOJ's BJS and ask them to report on crimes committed by federal law enforcement, including child pornography-related arrests and prosecutions.

Aliya Sternstein, a journalist with *The Christian Science Monitor,* attempted to gather child pornography related arrests of federal government employees, including federal law enforcement. She filed freedom of information requests and reported that "many federal organizations, such as the National Security Agency (NSA), did not respond to requests for records." The U.S. Postal System Inspector General (IG) did provide information reporting between 2014 and 2016, "the USPS inspector general closed 34 investigations into that category of misconduct" of U.S. postal system employees.[64] It is worth noting, the U.S. Postal System (USPS) is one of the best federal law enforcement agencies investigating child pornography crimes. USPS agents, like Brian Bone, are well-known and respected for tackling some of the most complex cases such as Project Spade.[65] USPS should receive much greater support for the work they do dismantling pedophile networks.

Perhaps the most comprehensive report available on sexual misconduct by federal LEOs is the Department of Justice's Office of the Inspector General's 2015 report, "The Handling of Sexual Harassment and Misconduct by the Department's Law Enforcement Components."[66] This report detailed cases, from 2009-2012, among federal law enforcement agencies under DOJ's supervision; the Bureau of Alcohol, Tobacco, Firearms and Explosives (ATF), the Drug Enforcement Administration (DEA), the Federal Bureau of Investigation (FBI) and the United States Marshals Service (USMS).[67] The Office of the Inspector General (OIG)'s report begins with a rather remarkable disclaimer explaining they were unable to obtain complete information because the FBI and DEA resisted providing the data.

> The OIG's ability to conduct this review was significantly impacted and delayed by the repeated difficulties we had in obtaining relevant information from both the FBI and DEA.... Initially, the FBI and DEA refused to provide the OIG with unredacted information that was responsive to our requests... despite the fact that the OIG is authorized under the Inspector General Act to receive such information. After months of protracted discussions with management at both agencies, the DEA and FBI provided the information without extensive redactions; but we found that the information was still incomplete. Ultimately, based on a review of information in the OIG Investigations Division databases, we determined that a material number of allegations from both DEA and FBI were not included

in the original responses to our request for the information. We were also concerned by an apparent decision by DEA to withhold information regarding a particular open misconduct case. The OIG was not given access to this case file information until several months after our request, and only after the misconduct case was closed. Once we became aware of the information, we interviewed DEA employees who said that they were given the impression that they were not to discuss this case with the OIG while the case remained open. The OIG was entitled to receive all such information from the outset, and the failure to provide it unnecessarily delayed our work. Therefore, we cannot be completely confident that the FBI and DEA provided us with all information relevant to this review. As a result, our report reflects the findings and conclusions we reached based on the information made available to us.[68]

Eventually, the OIG documented 621 cases of sexual misconduct and harassment among four federal law enforcement agencies. Over half, 343 cases, were in the FBI. The FBI also had the majority, 18, reported child pornography/child sex abuse cases. ATF reported two child pornography/child sex abuse cases, the DEA reported five cases and the U.S. Marshals provided two reports. The OIG noted that none of the agencies have systems in place to monitor employee's computers. Therefore, the reported cases likely represent a small percentage of overall engagement in the crime. Many, if not most, pedophiles are apprehended because of a mistake they make rather than routine monitoring and oversight. Only the FBI, of the four agencies, monitors text messages but claims it is "hampered in its ability to archive all text messages ... due to technological limitations." The FBI also "disabled the ability to send images on employee Blackberry devices."[69]

It is concerning that federal law enforcement agencies are not only failing to maintain accurate records of employee arrests but are also refusing to share information with their own Office of Inspector General (OIG). When federal law enforcement agencies refuse to comply with legal requests from the OIG, it is nearly impossible for an unfunded researcher, like myself, to obtain comprehensive statistics. In order to acquire data on child pornography arrests for all 73 federal agencies, I would need to obtain Inspector General reports for every agency over a ten-year period, file multiple freedom of information act requests and purchase and analyze over 20,000 federal prosecution records. This kind of research is certainly possible with funding.

Unable to conduct the kind of comprehensive research this subject demands, I focused on the more powerful and well-known federal law enforcement agencies, like the FBI and Homeland Security. I did some limited searches of the many smaller law enforcement agencies and sometimes accessed Inspector General (IG) reports.[70] Given that federal LEOs have refused to comply with DOJ's Inspector General and Homeland Security's former Inspector General, Charles Edwards, was forced to resign when he came under investigation for covering up and white-washing reports, even the accuracy of IG reports are suspect.[71] A limited list of federal LEOs arrested on child pornography charges is located on my Medium profile.

Samples of arrests under DOJ's supervision include:

FEDERAL BUREAU OF INVESTIGATION (FBI)

• Brian Haller, a 40-year-old cyber-security expert contractor with the FBI, was arrested, April 2015, on child pornography charges. He was sentenced April 8, 2016, to two days and one night in jail followed by ten years of supervised release. Haller was caught in the FBI's bust of a child rape website called Playpen. At the time of his arrest he had over 600 files of child rape and abuse. His on-line name was "jb" short for "jailbait" and his collection included a 40-minute video showing the sexual exploitation of an 11-year-old girl. Haller directed a FBI/private-sector cyber-security group in Seattle, Washington and had access to a secure FBI online platform and email system.[72]

• Donald Sachtleben, a 54-year-old former FBI Agent was arrested May 2012, and charged on child pornography charges. He pled guilty to distribution and possession and was sentenced November 14, 2013, to eight years in prison. He was also sentenced to unrelated charges of disclosing and possessing classified information. Sachtleben was Director of Training at the Center for Improvised Explosives at Oklahoma State University and was with the FBI from 1983 to 2008 as a bomb technician and counter-terrorism investigator. Sachtleben's email was pedodave69@yahoo.com. He wrote to other pedophiles, "Saw your profile on (a file sharing network). Hope you like these and can send me some of ours (sic). I have even better ones if you like."[73]

• Samuel Kaplan, a 64-year-old FBI information technology program manager, was arrested and pled guilty June 2010, to child pornography possession. Kaplan was sentenced, August 27, 2010, to just under four years in jail followed by 15 years of supervised release. Kaplan worked in the FBI's Chantilly, Virginia office and used "the FBI's network to facilitate sexually explicit communications."[74]

• Keith Dietterle, a 28-year-old FBI Analyst, was arrested November 2012, on child pornography charges. He pled guilty to possession and was sentenced, September 2013, to more than three years in prison. Dietterle was caught when he sent child sex abuse images/videos to an undercover Metro D.C. Detective. The detective was posing as a man sexually abusing his three-year-old nephew and 12-year-old daughter. Dietterle described the rape of the children as "So hot man ... how'd it start?" and discussed meeting the detective with the intention of sexually abusing the three-year-old boy.[75]

Drug Enforcement Agency (DEA)

• Darren Argento, a 47-year-old, DEA Agent, was arrested, August 2010, for child pornography possession and distribution. He was sentenced August 17, 2011, to seven months in jail followed by five months of supervised release. At the time of his arrest, Argento had over 73,000 images and over 723 videos of child rape. He was caught when he brought his personal laptop to the DEA office and asked an IT employee to help back up his files. Argento is listed as a registered sex offender.[76]

• James Patrick Burke, a 39-year-old DEA Agent, was arrested August 2015, on child pornography charges. He pled guilty, June 2, 2016, and was sentenced, April 6, 2017, to 7 years in jail followed by 15 years of supervised release. At the time of his arrest, Burke had over 2,760 images/videos of the rape and torture of children, including infants and toddlers and children being raped when bound and gagged. Burke must register as a sex offender.[77]

United States Marshals Service (USMS)

> 2.   In July 2010, agents with the Department of Justice Inspector General's Office responded to a call from the U.S. Marshals Service in Arlington, Virginia. After arriving, the agents seized two CD disks labeled "Teen2" and "Teen Sluts" from the desk in the office belonging to CHRISTOPHER MCKEE, an employee with the U.S. Marshal's Service. The

Christopher McKee's Criminal Complaint

• Christopher W. McKee, a 37-year-old intelligence analyst with the U.S. Marshals, was arrested on three counts of child pornography. McKee pled guilty April 2013, and was sentenced August 15, 2013, to five years of probation with no jail time. McKee kept a collection of child sex abuse labeled "teens" and "teen sluts" in his Arlington, Virginia office and downloaded thousands of images/video of child sex abuse on his work computer. McKee is a registered sex offender.

DEPARTMENT OF HOMELAND SECURITY (DHS)

DHS protects itself from infamy. Often news of convictions appear, then disappear.[78]

-Julia Davis, National Security Reporter, March 2014-

There has been a fair amount of media attention devoted to arrests of Homeland employees as well as Homeland's refusal to provide data about employee misconduct.[79] No one knows how many Homeland Security employees have been arrested on child pornography charges because Homeland is refusing to provide public information about these crimes. If you wish to take action and help obtain the data, please contact the Senate Committee on Homeland Security and Government Affairs and express your concerns.

The highest-ranking Homeland employee to be charged on child pornography-related crimes is former Deputy Press Secretary Brian Doyle. Doyle was sending child sex abuse images/videos to an undercover officer in Polk County, Florida. "Doyle couldn't have been more brazen, giving out his title, calling from his DHS office, even sending a photo showing his Department of Homeland Security identity card along with his genitals."[80] Sheriff Grady Judd, one of America's leading LEOs, said of Doyle's actions, "It doesn't come any more hard-core. He graphically explained to a 14-year old girl what he would like to do to her and what he would like her to do to him." Doyle was charged with sixteen counts of transmission of harmful material to a minor and seven counts of using a computer to seduce a child and sentenced to five years in jail.[81] He is now a registered sex offender.

In January 2017, the *New York Times* reported that Citizenship and Immigration Services (CIS) investigators, under Homeland Security, have "repeatedly warned top managers that unaddressed allegations of corruption among contractors could put the immigration system at risk" citing nearly 70 cases, including distribution of child pornography on government computers, that have not been investigated. It is unclear how many of these cases involved child pornography. Nearly half of CIS employees, about 10,000, are contract staff subject to almost no oversight. The *New York Times* said Homeland did not respond to questions about why misconduct investigations of CIS staff have been prevented.[82] Homeland Security's Inspector General's report for 2013, reports a "CIS employee pled guilty to possession of child pornography, and was sentenced to 37 months incarceration and 120 months of supervised release." No further details were provided.

Pro Publica reported, February 2016, on misconduct among federal Air Marshals, under Homeland's supervision. The government responded, after seven years, to journalist Michael Grabell's freedom of information request. From 2002 to 2012, almost 150 Air Marshals were arrested for criminal behavior, 250 Air Marshals were terminated for misconduct and 400 were allowed to resign or retire when under investigation.[83] Details are located on Pro Publica's database. Child pornography and child sex abuse are not listed in separate categories, but appear to be under the general heading of criminal conduct/criminal arrests. In addition, employee names were not provided. Thus, making it nearly impossible to

> **Action Item**
> Contact the Senate Committee on Homeland Security and Government Affairs 🐦 @SenRonJohnson
> & 🐦 @mccaskilloffice Tel: 202 224 4751
> Ask that Homeland be required to produce public, comprehensive annual reports of employees arrested on child pornography related charges, including employee name and position.

determine how many Air Marshals have been caught engaging in child pornography-related crimes.

The Center for Investigative Reporting's journalist, Andrew Becker, reported that prospective Homeland employees sometimes confess during polygraph interviews. These confessions were not always reported, investigated or prosecuted.[84] For example, 22-year old Cody Slaughter told a Customs and Border Protection examiner that he had molested his best friend's two-year-old sister and engaged in bestiality with his horse, a dog and a pig. Although the polygrapher reported these crimes, local prosecutors refused to prosecute Slaughter.[85] Another example is Joseph Montross, a 28-year-old combat-tested Marine with a security clearance, who confessed he sexually abused children to produce child pornography. Investigators found more than 9,000 images/videos of child sex abuse. Montross was arrested and sentenced to jail.

As with my other research, I used simple Google and Twitter searches to locate media reports of Homeland employees arrested on child pornography related charges. A more comprehensive list is on my Medium profile. Examples of federal law enforcement, under Homeland's supervision, arrested for child pornography related offenses include:

CUSTOMS AND BORDER PROTECTION (CBP)

> sexually explicit conduct and the depiction was of such conduct, specially: the defendant accessed and
>
> viewed images of child pornography from a Russia website using his government issued computer, and
>
> that had been mailed, shipped and transported in and affecting interstate or foreign commerce by any

Nicholas Bolden's Criminal Complaint

- Nicholas Bolden, a 40-year-old Homeland Security Customs and Border Patrol Agent, was arrested, April 2013, on child pornography charges. He pled guilty April 30, 2013, and was sentenced July 31, 2013, to six and half years in federal prison followed by 24 years of supervised release. Bolden was accessing Russian child rape and torture websites from his government computer. A CD containing child pornography was also found in his office desk.

• Gilbert Lam, a 38-year-old Homeland Security Customs and Border Protection Agent who worked at San Francisco airport, was arrested and charged March 2013, on child pornography charges. He was found guilty in December 18, 2014 and sentenced to just over a year in jail. Investigators said Lam's electronic resources were "elaborate" and included "a whole closet ... independent server, several computers, several hard drives..." Lam was trading in a known series call the Vicky Series. He appealed the court order that he pay $3,000 in restitution to the child victim and lost his appeal.

¹ The file names of the videos that Hardrick was charged with knowingly receiving (the charged videos) were "pthc - little boy fucks 4yo girl licks moms pussy - R@ygold - PTHC - Pedo -Hussyfan - Babyshvid - Zadoom - Childfugga - Lolita - Kiddy - Child Porn - Illegal - Ddoggprn.jpg.mpg" and "9yo littlegirl displays her sweet yng cunt - PART2 - Pussy licking now (2min7sec) (orig duogill) - reelkiddymov lolita preteen young incest kiddie porno sex xxx ddoggprn.mpg."

Lawson Hardrick's Appellate Decision

• Lawson Hardrick, a 64-year-old retired Assistant Director of the Calexico, California Ports of Entry with Customs and Border Protection, was arrested on child pornography charges. He was found guilty, January 24, 2013, and sentenced April 2013, to ten years in jail. Hardrick was trading in pre-teen hard core (PTHC) the brutal torture and rape of very young children, including infants and toddlers. Hardrick appealed his sentence and lost his appeal. He must register as a sex offender.

IMMIGRATION AND CUSTOMS ENFORCEMENT (ICE)

• Anthony Mangione, 50-year-old Director of Immigration and Customs Enforcement (ICE) for South Florida, was arrested on "extreme child abuse" charges in September 2011. He was sentenced in November 2012 to nearly six years in prison. Mangione is a 1982 graduate of the University of Maine Orono (UMO) where former Senior Child Protection Services (CPS) Cynthia Wellman claimed CPS was operating a child sex ring on campus. Originally from Rhode Island, Mangione arrived in Orono in August 1978.[86]

TRANSPORTATION SECURITY ADMINISTRATION (TSA)

• Thomas Gordon, a 46-year-old TSA agent in Philadelphia, was sentenced for possession and distribution of child pornography. He had over 600 images and videos of child sex abuse, including children as young as six years old, which were described as "horrific." He had as many as six fake Facebook accounts he was using to distribute child sex abuse.[87]

• Thomas Harkin, a 65-year-old former Catholic priest who had been removed from the church for the sex abuse of an eleven-year-old girl, among possible other victims, was then employed by TSA at Philadelphia airport.[88]

• Miguel Angel Quinones, a 38-year-old who worked at Manchester airport in New Hampshire, was indicted on 20 counts of child pornography possession. He had more than 1,000 child sex abuse images and videos. He kept his child pornography in his airport work locker.[89]

Coast Guard (USCG)

• **File name:** !!!New!!! Amber - 7Yr Old Pedo-Preteen-Bondage (Selective Trade) (1).wmv
Location: Western Digital hard drive path: Elements[NTFS]/[orphan]/Pics/Giga//Vids/
Description: This is a video file that depicts a prepubescent girl on her knees with her hands bound to her feet with duct tape so that her buttocks are in the air. The hand of what appears to be an adult male then rubs her genitals and anus.

• **File name:** - x 0 Bree 001-and Big Sis.wmv
Location: Western Digital hard drive path: Elements[NTFS]/[orphan]/Pics/Giga//Vids/
Description: This is a video file that depicts what appears to be an adult female performing oral sex on a female toddler.

• **File name:** stil_1389773320_1597655_105.png
Location: Dell desktop path: New Volume[NTFS]/[root]/Users/Christopher Craft/AppData/Local/Shalsoft/GigaTribe/1597655/resources/
Description: This is a still image file that still image that depicts a close-up of what appears to be an adult male penis against a prepubescent girl's genital area.

Christopher Craft's Criminal Complaint

• Christopher Craft, a 41-year-old Warrant Officer with the Coast Guard, was arrested on child pornography charges, pled guilty and was sentenced July 8, 2016, to five years in jail followed by ten years of supervised release. Craft was trading in pre-teen hard core (PTHC). Descriptions of some of the images/videos he was trading in appear in his court documents and are noted here. Upon his arrest, he had more than 480 images and 111 videos of children being sexually exploited, including images and videos depicting sadistic or masochistic conduct. Craft must register as a sex offender.

Secret Service (SS)

• Lee Robert Moore, a 37-year-old Secret Service Agent, stationed at The White House, was arrested November 9, 2015, for soliciting sex with a child while he was on duty. He had sent pictures of his penis to an undercover police officer in Delaware. Moore was indicted in June 2016 in Florida on charges of child pornography receipt and attempting to entice a minor. He pled guilty in March 2017 to both the Delaware and Florida charges. Moore was caught attempting to sexually abuse a 14-year-old girl, who was, in reality, an undercover investigator in Delaware. The undercover investigator communicated with Moore for about two months, during that time Moore's second child was born. Moore was arrested when he made arrangements to meet the 14-year-old "girl." Moore also had contact with about ten real children. In text messages he said he was "a cop," a "federal officer" and said "Like the Rolling Stones sang, 'every cop is a criminal.'" Moore has been in custody since his arrest.

FEDERAL EMERGENCY MANAGEMENT AGENCY (FEMA)

• Brian J. Murphy, a 48-year-old Federal Emergency Management Agency (FEMA) employee, was arrested June 2001 on child pornography charges. He was sentenced, October 2002, to just over two years in jail. He was trading in child rape from his government computer. He must register as a sex offender.

OVERSIGHT IS NEEDED

Homeland Security admitted to *Christian Science Monitor* journalist Aliya Sternstein that their firewalls lack the capacity to recognize, block and report child pornography. DHS also confirmed that they "do not investigate the behavior of individual employees."[90] In contrast, The Federal Trade Commission (FTC) and the Commerce Department have security systems that alert officials when child sex abuse is shared on their networks. If the FTC and the Department of Commerce do this, why isn't this mandatory for Homeland Security as well as all federal, state, and local law enforcement agencies?[91] Given the numbers of arrests of state and local law enforcement combined with Director of the Pentagon's Defense Security Service statement that the "amount of child porn" on government computers is just "unbelievable," it is reasonable to assume if that law enforcement were required to pro-actively monitor their networks the number of LEOs arrested for this crime would dramatically increase.

Federal law enforcement officers are powerful. The scope of their ability to arrest and investigate is substantial. Their ability to protect themselves and hide their own crimes, and those of others, is considerable. As with local and state law enforcement, a system of consistent oversight and electronic monitoring must be developed. Every federal law enforcement officer should be required, as part of their hiring package, to sign a code of conduct that includes permission for random searches of their work and personal electronics and IP networks. On a rotating basis one federal law enforcement agency, perhaps the U.S. Postal System, should oversee random monitoring of all other agencies. Arrest and prosecution data must be gathered and made public.

No federal law enforcement officer should ever be engaged in the trade in child rape and certainly not on government computers. Pedophiles should not be able to gain access to and enter federal law enforcement agencies. American children should not be raped and their rape images traded by men and women who have sworn an oath of office to protect and serve America. Our children's safety and our national security depends upon effective oversight of federal law enforcement agencies' electronic networks. We can and must do better.

Not one pedophile should ever be employed in federal law enforcement. Ever.

OTHER GOVERNMENT EMPLOYEES

The text conversation continued for a period of time and arrangements to meet and have sexual intercourse developed. Mr. Rosen was very hesitant to meet until he had proof that he was texting with a real live fourteen year old. Substantial efforts were made to provide Mr. Rosen with the proof he was requesting. When one such requested proof was sent to Mr. Rosen, he stated "Good. Now let's get naked lol." At a later time, Rosen stated the following, "Maybe I'll use it when I'm behind you, █████████ wrap it around your neck and hold on to it… You want to learn how to █████ ████ I'll teach you ☺"

Daniel Rosen's Search Warrant

FROM LOSKARN TO ROSEN

When Senator Lamar Alexander's Chief of Staff, Ryan Loskarn, was arrested in 2014 for trading in child pornography, no journalists provided context to the story. The media reported Loskarn's arrest, and subsequent suicide pending trial, as if it were a one-off event. As if no other high-level government employees were being arrested on child pornography charges. In 2015, when the State Department's Director of Counter-terrorism, Daniel Rosen, was arrested on charges of computer solicitation of sex/sodomy for a child under 14, two journalists attempted to provide context. Paul Farrell, with *Heavy*, and Shane Harris, with *The Daily Beast,* respectively wrote, "the Second Child Sex Scandal to Hit D.C. in 12 Months" and "3rd U.S. Official Hit With Child Sex and Porn Charges." Both were far off the mark. A simple Twitter search reveals far more than two or three government staff arrested for trading in child rape.[92]

In addition to government employees in our national security agencies, military and local, state and federal law enforcement, there are an estimated two million federal civilian government employees and five million people employed in state governments. Some fourteen million people are employed by local governments.[93] Most state and local employees are employed in education, with 48% at the state level and 55.4% at the local.[94] All totaled, there are an estimated 21 million people employed in federal, state and local government. How many have been arrested on child pornography related charges? No one knows. A national child pornography-arrest database would provide the answer.

In the next chapters I discuss government employees who are prosecutors and educators. In this section, I review a small sample of civilian government employees arrested on child pornography related charges. The Department of Health and Human Services, U.S. Department of Agriculture, Bureau of Indian Affairs, National Children's Museum, the Internal Revenue Service, the Environmental Protection Agency, the State Department along with many others, have all had employees arrested on child pornography charges, often involving work computers.[95] Yet, to date, very little action has been taken to prevent government employees from trafficking in children – which is what child pornography is – on government computers.

In 2014, Congressman Mark Meadows from North Carolina put forward the Eliminating Pornography from Agencies Act HR 901. Meadows re-introduced this again in January of 2017 as HR 680 – Eliminating Pornography from Agencies Act.[96] This bill, if passed into law, would stop federal employees from accessing, watching or sharing pornography on government-issued computers and devices. There has been an ongoing battle waged by technology and telecom firms, along with privacy experts, who do not want this legislation passed. Nei-

> **Action Item**
> Ask Congressman Trey Gowdy, Chair of the House Oversight and Government Reform Committee, to bring HR 680 to a full House vote.
> 🐦 @TGowdySC
> Tel: 202 225 6030
> Contact your own Representative and ask him/her to co-sponsor HR 680.

ther HR 901 nor the improved HR 680 have made it to a full House debate or vote. Instead, weak and vague wording requiring some, but not all, federal agencies to prevent pornography on the computer networks has been buried deep in continuing resolutions.

For example, the most recently HR 244 Consolidated Appropriations Act of 2017 has, among others, the following sections:

- (Sec. 106) Specifies that grant recipients may continue to deter child pornography, copyright infringement, or any other unlawful activity over their networks.

- (Sec. 504) Prohibits the use of funds made available in this division for a computer network that does not block pornography, except for law enforcement purposes.

- (Sec. 532) Prohibits funds provided by this division from being used for a computer network that does not block pornography, except for law enforcement purposes.

- (Sec. 742) Prohibits funds provided by this division from being used for a computer network unless pornography is blocked, with the exception of law enforcement, prosecution, or adjudication activities.

- (Sec. 8129) Prohibits funds provided by this division from being used for any computer network that does not block access to pornography websites, with exceptions for criminal investigations, prosecution, or adjudication activities; or for any activity necessary for the national defense, including intelligence activities.[98]

All of the above sections in HR 244 are essentially meaningless. Congress must pass comprehensive legislation, complete with robust oversight, reporting and monitoring mechanisms, rather than worthless policy riders. If you think HR 680, or an improved version, should be put before the full House for a vote, contact your own U.S. Representative and ask them to sign and support HR 680. Contact Congressman Trey Gowdy, Chair of the House Oversight and Government Reform Committee, and share your thoughts about HR680.[99] Shouldn't even member of Congress sign this proposed legislation?

At the state level, Maine's Governor, Paul LePage issued one of the first of its kind Executive Orders in 2015, prohibiting Maine state employees from accessing pornographic or sexually explicit material on state computers or devices even when they are off duty on personal time.[100] Every governor should pass similar executive orders. Mayors should do the same at city levels, inclusive of robust monitoring and oversight. Also, as previously mentioned, some state legislatures are considering the Human Trafficking and Child Exploitation Prevention Act which would require blocking adult and child pornography.[101]

The list of civilian government employees arrested on child pornography charges is long. Very long. As with my other research, I've used simple Google and Twitter searches. A longer list of government employees arrested for trading in child rape is on my Medium profile. This is only a small sample of arrests. The amount of civilian government employees, at all levels, that appear to be engaged in this crime is distressing.

A few examples include:

- Timothy DeFoggi, 56-year-old Acting Director of Cyber Security for the Department of Health and Human Services (DHHS), was sentenced, January 2015, to 25 years in federal prison for participating in a child pornography ring that "shocked veteran investigators." DeFoggi was a registered user of an online child rape and torture trading site and expressed an interest in the violent rape and murder of children. He discussed meeting, at least, one other member to make plans to locate children to rape and then murder them.[102]

- A Google image search for "XXX, Super Lolita Kid Teen Pthc IN E...," which returned an image of a nude female child. Based on my training and experience, the term "Pthc" refers to "Preteen hard core".

- Google image search for "ls magazine," a Russian website known for young naturist and child pornography photos. The activity occurred on April 5, 2016 at 6:46 pm on the USPS Workplace Computer and a screen capture of an image obtained from that search is attached hereto as **Exhibit 5**.

Stephen Mantha's Criminal Complaint

- Stephen Mantha, a 62-year-old electronic technician with the U.S. Postal Service, was arrested and charged September 22, 2016, with possession of child pornography and accessing with intent to view child pornography. Mantha was using his government computer to trade in brutal abuse and rape of young children, including children as young as three, the anal rape of children as young as five. He also accessed Russian child pornography trading sites. On October 18, 2016, he was arrested again when investigators located a video of Mantha sexually assaulting a young boy. The USPS continued to employ Mantha until October 2016, when he was allowed to retire. Mantha was under house arrest but, after his second arrest, he was taken into custody pending sentencing. As of July 2017, sentencing had not yet been set.[103]

- Michael Beeman, a 62-year-old regional public relations officer with the Army Corps of Engineers in Winchester, Virginia, was arrested January 20, 2014, and pled guilty in October 2015, to four counts of child pornography possession and one count of child pornography transportation. On April 14, 2016, he was sentenced to 30 years in prison. Investigators seized over 250 electronic devices with thousands of images of child pornography from Beeman's residence. Beeman had been producing child pornography by filming the rape of boys as young as eight since the 1980s, including the rape of a boy at Patrick Air Force Base where Beeman previously worked. He gained access to his victims by offering his services as a baby-sitter on the military base and developing a "father-like relationship" with the boys he targeted. He had been a government employee for over 40 years.[104]

- Gons Nachman, a 42-year-old former U.S. diplomat, who "admitted taping his sexual encounters with teenage girls while stationed in Brazil and the Congo" was sentenced, August 2008, to 20 years in prison. Nachman also pled guilty to child pornography possession. One of his videos was titled "Congo 2004 Sexual Adventures." His law degree is from the University of Pennsylvania, where he was president of the Naturist Student Association and "led demonstrations involving public nudity in 1995."[105]

• James Spargo, a 66-year-old employee with the Department of Agriculture in Florida, pled no contest to 20 felony child pornography counts and was sentenced, February 2015, to 10 years in prison. Spargo was arrested when investigators found child sex abuse images/videos on his government computer. Most of the children in the images/videos were infants and toddlers. "The activity we uncovered here was just horrible," said Florida Department of Agriculture and Consumer Services spokesperson Erin Gillespie. "It was horrifying, it was disgusting, and we gathered all the evidence we could to make sure that this arrest was going to happen.[106]

• William Shaffer, a Child Protection Services (CPS) staffer was arrested, July 2013, after he purchased nearly $7,000 of child rape and torture videos/images. According to Shaffer's criminal complaint "a 1987 police report alleged Shaffer sexually molested a boy between the ages of 8 and 9. The police report alleged the incident happened while Shafer was a Child Protective Services employee." Investigators also seized "sexual stories" from Shaffer's home. "One of them describes a seventh-grade boy being abducted, molested and sodomized."[107]

• Robert Singer, 49-year-old father of two and Chief Operating Officer for Washington D.C.'s National Children's Museum, was arrested November 6, 2007, and charged on five child pornography distribution counts. He pled guilty and was sentenced July 16, 2009, to five years in prison. Singer was caught sending child sex abuse images of children as young as five, including from his work computer, to an undercover New York Police Detective who was posing as a 12-year-old girl and her 33-year-old mother. Singer was pretending to be a 15-year-old boy. He was using the online handle badboy2.[108]

• Stanley Dorozynski, a 53-year-old Child Protective Services (CPS) employee, was arrested December 21, 2010, and charged with two counts, one each, of possessing and receiving child pornography. Upon his arrest, Dorozynski possessed more than 2,400 child sex abuse images/videos including the abuse of children as young as four. Investigators also recovered 11 zip discs of child porn in a locked trunk, among other CDs. Dorozynski had been trading in child rape and torture since 1990. Dorozynski pled guilty July 27, 2012, and was sentenced to six years in federal prison. His girlfriend found the child sex abuse images/videos and notified law enforcement. He had been a police officer in Utica, New York, before he went to work for Health and Human Services.[109]

• Jasper Neil Blair, a 27-year-old civil engineer with the Bureau of Indian Affairs, was arrested for child pornography possession and pled guilty May 31, 2012, "to knowingly possessing an image of a six-year-old girl being sexually abused," and was sentenced October 4, 2012, to two-and-half years in federal prison. Blair was using his government computer to trade in child rape.[110]

CHILD PORNOGRAPHY IS A NATIONAL SECURITY THREAT

The Director of the Pentagon's Defense Security Service, Daniel Payne, verified the "amount of child porn" on government computers is just "unbelievable." My research establishes that the U.S. government, at all levels, has a considerable child pornography problem; one that is a serious threat to our personal and national security. Pedophiles have infiltrated government service and cultivated positions of power to protect their crimes and access children. Children are not being protected. Pedophiles are. Too many pedophiles are government employees. This kind of criminal behavior makes employees prime targets for organized criminal networks and foreign espionage operations. A U.S. government employee, trading in child rape, particularly with Russian sources, makes him/herself vulnerable to blackmail maneuvers to leak secure information and other acts designed to undermine the U.S. government.[111] This vulnerability to blackmail as well as the opening of government computer networks compromises many aspects of the national security apparatus and all of our personal day-to-day security.

In a democratic system, as America is meant to be, oversight and accountability is built into our structure of governance. There is supposed to be legislative, executive and judicial separation of powers and rule of law. The trade in child rape appears to have broken down institutionalized checks and balances. Pedophiles can, and do, easily provide cover to each other from various powerful positions they hold inside and outside of government. Pedophiles are extensive networkers. Networking is one of their defining behaviors. This is not a crime done alone, with no one watching. Pedophiles want the world to watch them rape children. They obsessively video themselves violently abusing children and broadcast these crimes on the Internet. They brag about the crimes

Jonathan Adleta was sentenced to two life terms for the sex abuse of his own infant children along with his wife, Sarah Adleta, who was sentenced to 54 years. Adleta had made "daddy-daughter sex" part of a pre-nuptial agreement. When they divorced she continued to rape her children on Skype and he distributed this on the Internet. He also raped his girlfriend's Samantha Bryant's four-year-old daughter. Bryant participated in and filmed the abuse. Adleta had served two tours with the Marine Corps in Afghanistan.

84

they commit. A police chief trading in child rape is very likely to know local judges, state legislators, teachers and prosecutors also engaged in the crime. Pedophiles not only network online, they also meet in person to share children for rape. They know each other and they protect each other.

The fact that this is occurring in what appears to be epidemic-scale numbers should outrage and frighten us. Funded research is needed to adequately document the scope of this crime by U.S. government employees so that effective public policy can be created to address this serious national security issue. As journalist Aliya Sternstein, of *The Christian Science Monitor,* said, "pornographic images of children on government computers present a profound national security risk that if left unresolved could endanger American lives at home and abroad."[112]

This is America's wake-up call. The child rape industry is no longer a Russian, Asian, or Eastern European problem. The illegal trade in child rape is an American problem. Far too many local, state and federal government employees in sensitive positions of trust within our communities and national security structures are involved. Too often these criminals are exposing our most sensitive government computer networks to organized crime as they trade in child rape while at work. This is an acute security problem. The media isn't reporting on it. Public policy institutes are not focusing on it. Academic researchers are ignoring it.

One has to wonder why.

Endnotes

1. United Nations, "United Nations, "Report of the Special Rapporteur on the Sale of Children," 11. *See also* Special Rapporteur on the sale and sexual exploitation of children http://www.ohchr.org/EN/Issues/Children/Pages/ChildrenIndex.aspx

2. DSS Public Affairs [DSSPA@dss.mil], e-mail message to author, May 4, 2016.

3. Aliya Sternstein, "Child porn on government devices: A hidden security threat," *Christian Science Monitor,* December 5, 2016, accessed July 15, 2017, http://www.csmonitor.com/World/Passcode/2016/1205/Child-porn-on-government-devices-A-hidden-security-threat

4. Bryan Bender, "Pentagon lagged on pursuing porn cases," *Boston Globe,* January 5, 2011, accessed July 16, 2017, http://www.boston.com/news/nation/washington/articles/2011/01/05/pentagon_lagged_on_pursuing_porn_cases; Robert Beckhusen, "Child Porn, Coke Smuggling: Hundreds of DHS Employees Arrested Last Year," *Wired Magazine,* August 22, 2012, accessed July 16, 2017, http://www.wired.com/dangerroom/2012/08/employees; United States Senate Senator Charles Grassley, "Justice Department Silent on Pornography Found on Assistant U.S. Attorney's Computer," October 14, 2011, accessed July 15, 2017, https://www.grassley.senate.gov/news/news-releases/justice-department-silent-pornography-found-assistant-us-attorney%E2%80%99s-computer; "South Florida ICE official arrested on child porn charges," Cable News Network (CNN), September 29, 2011, accessed July 16, 2017, http://www.cnn.com/2011/09/28/justice/florida-ice-arrest/index.html; Office of the Inspector General Department of Transportation, "Air Traffic Control Specialist Sentenced to 78 Months Imprisonment for Charges of Child Pornography," (Washington D.C.: United States Government) November 14, 2008, accessed July 16, 2017, http://www.oig.dot.gov/library-item/3663; Joce Sterman,

"Former TSA agent from Baltimore County indicted on federal porn charges," ABC News 2, March 18, 2012, accessed July 16, 2017, http://www.abc2news.com/dpp/news/crime_checker/baltimore_county_crime/former-tsa-agent-from-baltimore-county-indicted-on-federal-porn-charges; "Donald Sachtleben, former FBI agent, arrested on child pornography charges," CBS News, May 15, 2012, accessed July 16, 2017, http://www.cbsnews.com/news/donald-sacht-leben-former-fbi-agent-arrested-on-child-pornography-charges; Jim McElhatton, "CIA able to keep its secrets on budgets, bad apples IG documents reveal porn, fraud, other misconduct," The Washington Times, November 13, 2012, accessed July 16, 2017, http://www.washingtontimes.com/news/2012/nov/13/cia-able-to-keep-its-secrets-on-budgets-bad-apples/?page=2; The Cato Institute's National Police Misconduct Reporting Project, http://www.policemisconduct.net maintains a running tally of police misconduct.

5. Sternstein, "Child porn on government devices," 2016.

6. "West Point Army Officer," 2011.

7. Desiree Stennett, "Patrick Air Force Base: Chief scientist held on $250K bond after child-porn arrest," Orlando Sentinel, May 10, 2013, accessed July 16, 2017, http://articles.orlandosentinel.com/2013-05-10/news/os-air-force-child-porn-arrest-20130510_1_patrick-air-force-base-mel-bourne-home-brevard-deputies

8. "Navy revokes imprisoned Vietnam veteran's Silver Star," Stars & Stripes, July 27, 2011, accessed July 18, 2017, https://www.stripes.com/news/navy/navy-revokes-imprisoned-vietnam-veter-an-s-silver-star-1.150372

9. Samantha Greenaway, "4 Disturbing Ways Child Molesters Use Tech To Commit Crimes," Business Insider, March 15, 2014, accessed July 16, 2017, http://www.businessinsider.com/child-mo-lesters-technology-2014-3

10. Bender, "Pentagon lagged," 2011. Bender has since left the Boston Globe and is now with Politico http://www.politico.com/staff/bryan-bender

11. United States Senate Senator Charles Grassley, "Q&A: Holding the Pentagon Accountable," (Washington D.C.: United States Government) November 24, 2010, accessed July 16, 2017, http://www.grassley.senate.gov/news/Article.cfm?customel_dataPageID_1502=30081

12. Tony Capaccio, "Missile Defense Staff Warned to Stop Surfing Porn Sites," Bloomberg News, August 2, 2012, accessed July 16, 2017, http://www.bloomberg.com/news/2012-08-01/missile-defense-staff-warned-to-stop-surfing-porn-sites.html

13. Capaccio, "Missile Defense Staff Warned," 2012.

14. Daintry Duffy, "Inside the DoD's Computer Forensics Lab: Searching for the Truth," CSO On-Line, May 1, 2004, accessed July 16, 2017, http://www.csoonline.com/article/2117173/investigations-forensics/inside-the-dod-s-computer-forensics-lab--searching-for-the-truth.html

15. Merritt Baer, "Two-Thirds Of Military Supreme Court Cases Are About Child Pornography," Talking Points Memo, December 3, 2013, accessed July 16, 2017, http://talkingpointsmemo.com/cafe/two-thirds-of-military-supreme-court-cases-are-about-child-pornography

16. David Cloud, "Child abuse in the military: Failing those most in need," Los Angeles Times, December 29, 2016, accessed July 16, 2017, http://www.latimes.com/nation/la-na-child-abuse-mil-itary-20161229-htmlstory.html

17. Phillip O'Connor, "Oklahoma airman found guilty of possessing child pornography," News OK, November 26, 2012, accessed July 16, 2017, http://newsok.com/oklahoma-air-man-found-guilty-of-possessing-child-pornography/article/3731487

18. Terri Moon Cronk, "Sexual Assaults in Military Drop, Reporting Goes Up, Annual Report Reveals," U.S. Department of Defense, May 1, 2017, accessed July 16, 2017, https://www.defense.

gov/News/Article/Article/1167971/sexual-assaults-in-military-drop-reporting-goes-up-annu-al-report-reveals

19. Richard Lardner and Eileen Sullivan, "Opaque military justice system shields child sex abuse cases," Associated Press (AP), November 24, 2015, accessed July 16, 2017, http://bigstory. ap.org/article/c7c2772ba05c4241a9bcebcf745d1c71/opaque-military-justice-system-shields-child-sex-abuse

20. "March courts-martial results announced," *Navy Times*, April 15, 2015, accessed July 16, 2017, https://www.navytimes.com/story/military/2015/04/15/special-general-courts-martial-re-sults-march/25832281 and U.S. Navy, "Results of Trial - Special and General Court-Martial con-vened within the United States Navy," accessed July 16, 2017, http://www.jag.navy.mil/news/ROT.htm

21. "Army releases verdicts of March courts-martial," *Army Times*, May 12, 2017, accessed July 16, 2017, https://www.armytimes.com/articles/army-releases-verdicts-of-march-2017-courts-martial

22. Jared Keller, "A Disturbing Portion Of Marine Corps' Courts-Martial In 2017 Are For Child Sexual Abuse," *Task & Purpose*, June 13, 2017, accessed July 16, 2017, http://taskandpurpose. com/marine-corps-child-sex-abuse/?utm_content=bufferca0c7&utm_medium=social&utm_source=twitter&utm_campaign=tp-buffer

23. "The Army's hidden child abuse epidemic," *Military Times*, July 29, 2013, accessed July 16, 2017, http://www.militarytimes.com/story/military/archives/2013/07/29/the-army-s-hid-den-child-abuse-epidemic/78540504

24. "The Army's hidden," 2013.

25. Editorial Staff, "Editorial: Save the children," *Military Times*, accessed July 16, 2017, https://www.militarytimes.com/story/military/archives/2013/08/13/editorial-save-the-chil-dren/78541482

26. Jen Fifield, "One Major Reason Why Child Abuse In Military Families Goes Unreport-ed," *Task & Purpose*, June 12, 2017, accessed July 16, 2017, http://taskandpurpose.com/mili-tary-child-abuse-unreported and "President Obama signs 'Talia's law,' aimed at protecting children on military bases," *Hawaii News Now*, December 27, 2016, accessed July 16, 2017, http://www.hawaiinewsnow.com/story/34135848/president-obama-signs-talias-law-aimed-at-protecting-children-on-military-bases

27. Richard Lardner, Eileen Sullivan and Meghan Hoyer, "Pentagon: Hundreds of military kids sexually abused annually," Associated Press (AP), January 4, 2016, accessed July 16, 2017, https://apnews.com/e3089b0ab5444ea38bd2e0a0aeeeaf06/military-kids-sexually-abused-hundreds-times-each-year

28. Richard Lardner, Eileen Sullivan and Meghan Hoyer, "Military Children Sexual Assault Num-bers Released," *U.S. News & World Report*, January 4, 2016, accessed July 16, 2017, https://www.usnews.com/news/articles/2016-01-04/military-children-sexual-assault-numbers-released

29. Lardner, Sullivan and Hoyer, "Pentagon: Hundreds of military kids," 2016.

30. Lardner, Sullivan and Hoyer, "Pentagon: Hundreds of military kids," 2016.

31. Fifield, "One Major Reason," 2017.

32. Marisa Taylor, "National Reconnaissance Office hasn't told police of crime confessions," Mc-Clatchy Newspapers, July 10, 2012, accessed July 16, 2017, http://www.mcclatchydc.com/news/special-reports/article24732604.html

33. Taylor, "National Reconnaissance Office," 2012.

34. Justin Wm. Moyer, "Army lieutenant colonel gets 20 years in child pornography case," *Washington Post*, November 8, 2016, accessed July 16, 2017, https://www.washingtonpost.com/local/public-safety/army-lieutenant-colonel-gets-20-years-in-child-pornography-case/2016/11/08/5b-420c9a-a5dd-11e6-ba59-a7d93165c6d4_story.html?utm_term=.763470964237

35. "Army colonel sentenced to 12 years in child pornography case," CBS News, Crimesider Staff, December 28, 2016, accessed July 16, 2017, http://www.cbsnews.com/news/army-colonel-robert-rice-sentenced-to-12-years-in-child-pornography-case

36. Immigration and Customs Enforcement (ICE), "Child predator sentenced to life imprisonment in Louisiana," (Louisiana, United States Government) July 18, 2012, accessed July 16, 2017, https://www.ice.gov/news/releases/child-predator-sentenced-life-imprisonment-louisiana

37. "Air Force sergeant sentenced to 10 years for child porn," Lincoln Journal Star, May 4, 2006, accessed July 16, 2017, http://journalstar.com/news/state-and-regional/air-force-sergeant-sentenced-to-years-for-child-porn/article_ea66de28-7032-5e8e-bbba-17b18b354623.html

38. William R. Levesque, "MacDill officer sought out 'pervs,' records in child porn case show," Tampa Bay Times, February 4, 2014, accessed July 16, 2017, http://www.tampabay.com/news/military/macdill/macdill-officer-charged-with-distributing-child-porn/2164159

39. "Silver Star revoked for former Clinton defense official now in prison," Los Angeles Times, July 28, 2011, accessed July 16, 2017, http://latimesblogs.latimes.com/lanow/2011/07/wade-sanders-silver-star-revoked.html

40. Lardner, Sullivan and Hoyer, "Military Children Sexual Assault," 2016.

41. E.H. "Why does liberal Iceland want to ban online pornography?" The Economist, April 24, 2013, accessed July 16, 2017, http://www.economist.com/blogs/economist-explains/2013/04/economist-explains-why-iceland-ban-pornography

42. "Online pornography to be blocked by default, PM announces," British Broadcasting Corporation (BBC), July 22, 2013, accessed July 16, 2017, http://www.bbc.com/news/uk-23401076

43. Andy Wagner, "Lawmakers Want Digital Devices to Block "Obscene" Websites Including Some Social Media Platforms," Multi-State, April 4, 2017, accessed July 15, 2017, https://www.multistate.us/blog/lawmakers-want-digital-devices-to-block-obscene-websites-including-some-social-media-platforms and Dave Maass, "States Introduce Dubious Anti-Pornography Legislation to Ransom the Internet," Electronic Freedom Foundation (EFF), April 12, 2017, accessed July 15, 2017, https://www.eff.org/deeplinks/2017/04/states-introduce-dubious-legislation-ransom-Internet

44. National Conference of State Legislatures, "Children and the Internet Laws Relating to Filtering, Blocking and Usage Policies in Schools and Libraries," November 16, 2016, accessed July 16, 2017, http://www.ncsl.org/research/telecommunications-and-information-technology/state-Internet-filtering-laws.aspx

45. Lardner and Sullivan, "Opaque military justice system," 2015.

46. Lardner, Sullivan and Hoyer, "Military Children Sexual Assault," 2016.

47. *See also* "Lori Handrahan's Medium profile," accessed July 17, 2017, https://medium.com/@LoriHandrahan2 and "Lori Handrahan's website," accessed July 17, 2017, www.LoriHandrahan.com

48. Cato Institute, "National Police Misconduct Reporting Project (NPMRP) website," accessed July 17, 2017, https://www.policemisconduct.net/about/npmsrp-faq

49. *See also* Cato Institute, "National Police Misconduct," 2017.

50. Shelley Hyland, Lynn Langton, and Elizabeth Davis, "Police Use of Nonfatal Force, 2002–11 NCJ 249216," (Washington D.C.: United States Government) November 2015, accessed July 16, 2017, https://www.bjs.gov/content/pub/pdf/punf0211.pdf

51. Matthew J. Hickman, "Citizen Complaints about Police Use of Force," NCJ 210296 (Washington D.C.: United States Government) June 2006, accessed July 16, 2017, https://www.bjs.gov/content/pub/pdf/ccpuf.pdf and see also Department of Justice's Bureau of Justice Statistics webpage https://web.archive.org/web/20070808080406/http:/www.ojp.usdoj.gov/bjs/abstract/ccpuf.htm

52. "A look inside AP's investigation on officer sex misconduct," Associated Press (AP), November 1, 2015, accessed July 14, 2017, https://apnews.com/2e9a520557f649ddb5a68f16c7eb07ed/look-inside-aps-investigation-officer-sex-misconduct and "Hundreds of officers lose licenses over sex misconduct," Associated Press (AP), November 1, 2015, accessed July 14, 2017, https://apnews.com/fd1d4d05e561462a85abe50e7eaed4ec/ap-hundreds-officers-lose-licenses-over-sex-misconduct.

53. https://apnews.com/2e9a520557f649ddb5a68f16c7eb07ed/look-inside-aps-investigation-officer-sex-misconduct

54. "Lori Handrahan's Medium profile," accessed July 17, 2017, https://medium.com/@Lori-Handrahan2 Cite: Police Trading in Child Rape & Torture and When Law Enforcement is the Perpetrator, and Law Enforcement Arrested for Trading in Child Rape

55. Tom Cleary, "Michael Harding: 5 Fast Facts You Need to Know," Heavy.com, May 24, 2016, accessed July 16, 2017, www.heavy.com/news/2015/09/michael-harding-port-st-lucie-florida-police-officer-of-the-year-child-pornography-porn-federal-charges-documents-arrested-photos-wife-children

56. Tracy Jordan, "Child pornography charges filed against former police chief," The Morning Call, December 12, 2013, accessed July 16, 2017, http://articles.mcall.com/2013-12-12/news/mc-c-pennsylvania-police-chief-arrested-on-child-p-20131212_1_police-chief-police-detective-peer-to-peer-file-sharing-program and Bob Keeler, "Bedminster resident Robert Geist sentenced for possessing child pornography," Montgomery News, September 29, 2014, accessed July 16, 2017, www.montgomerynews.com/perkasienewsherald/news/bedminster-resident-robert-geist-sentenced-for-possessing-child-pornography/article_5666c593-2794-5857-9cb8-68d6a445dd7d.html

57. Federal Bureau of Investigations (FBI), "Former Bakersfield Police Detective Pleads Guilty to Possession of Child Pornography," (Eastern District of California: United States Government) February 19, 2013, accessed July 16, 2017, https://archives.fbi.gov/archives/sacramento/press-releases/2013/former-bakersfield-police-detective-pleads-guilty-to-possession-of-child-pornography

58. Brogan, "Former Maine State Police chief," 2014.

59. Joseph Berger, "Ex-Police Chief in Westchester County Pleads Guilty to Child Pornography Charge," New York Times, July 27, 2015, accessed July 17, 2017, https://www.nytimes.com/2015/07/28/nyregion/ex-police-chief-in-westchester-county-pleads-guilty-to-child-pornography-charge.html?_r=0

60. Robert Gearty and Bill Hutchinson, "'Cannibal Cop' partner Michael Van Hise wanted to keep children as sex slaves: prosecutors," New York Daily News, January 7, 2013, accessed July 16, 2017, http://www.nydailynews.com/new-york/cannibal-partner-wanted-children-sex-slaves-prosecutors-article-1.1235343; Liz Goff, "Cannibal Cop Seeking New Trial," Queens Gazette, June 26, 2013, accessed July 16, 2017, www.qgazette.com/news/2013-06-26/Front_Page/Cannibal_Cop_Seeking_New_Trial.html and "NYPD officer accused of plot to kill and eat women has conviction overturned," The Guardian, July 1, 2014, accessed July 16, 2017, https://www.theguardian.com/world/2014/jul/01/new-york-cannibal-cop-conviction-overturned

61. "Accused NYPD 'cannibal cop' Gilberto Valle: Facebook postings, instant messages paint picture of twisted mind," New York Daily News, October 25, 2012, accessed July 17, 2017, www.nydailynews.com/new-york/mind-accused-cannibal-article-1.1192701 and "Accused NYPD 'cannibal cop' Gilberto Valle: Facebook postings, instant messages paint picture of twisted mind," New York

Daily News, October 25, 2012, accessed July 16, 2017, http://www.nydailynews.com/new-york/mind-accused-cannibal-article-1.1192701

62. Rebecca Davis O'Brien, "Former Police Officer Accused of Cannibal Plot Goes Free," *Wall Street Journal*, November 12, 2014, accessed July 16, 2017, https://www.wsj.com/articles/former-police-officer-accused-of-cannibal-plot-goes-free-1415811639

63. Brian Reaves, "Federal Law Enforcement Officers, 2008," Bureau of Justice Statistics, June 26, 2012, accessed July 16, 2017, https://www.bjs.gov/index.cfm?ty=pbdetail&iid=4372

64. Sternstein, "Child porn on government devices," 2016.

65. Julian Sher, "Child porn bust: The U.S. postal investigator who helped Toronto police," The Star, November 14, 2013, accessed July 16, 2017, https://www.thestar.com/news/world/2013/11/14/child_porn_bust_the_us_postal_investigator_who_helped_toronto_police.html

66. Office of the Inspector General (OIG), Department of Justice, *The Handling of Sexual Harassment and Misconduct by the Department's Law Enforcement Components*, (Washington D.C.: United States Government, 2015) accessed July 16, 2017, https://oig.justice.gov/reports/2015/e1504.pdf

67. *See also*: Elyssa Pachico, "Putting Salacious DEA Sex Party Report in Perspective," *Insight Crime*, March 27, 2015, accessed July 16, 2017, http://www.insightcrime.org/news-analysis/putting-salacious-dea-sex-party-report-in-perspective

68. OIG, *The Handling of Sexual Harassment and Misconduct*, i-ii.

69. OIG, *The Handling of Sexual Harassment and Misconduct*, 51.

70. Other federal law enforcement include: (1) Department of State's Bureau of Diplomatic Security and Diplomatic Security Service (DSS); (2) Department of Treasury's Internal Revenue Service Criminal Investigations Division (IRS-CID) and Treasury Inspector General for Tax Administration (TIGTA); (3) Mint Police (USMP); (4) Department of Defense's Defense Criminal Investigative Service (DCIS) and Pentagon Force Protection Agency; (5) Army Criminal Investigation Division (Army CID) and Military Police Corps; (6) Air Force Office of Special Investigations (Airforce OSI), Air Force Security Forces and Department of the Air Force Police; (7) Naval Criminal Investigative Service (NCIS), Office of Naval Intelligence Police (ONI Police), Marine Corps Provost Marshal's Office and Marine Corps Criminal Investigation Division (USMC CID); (8) National Security Agency's National Security Agency Police (NSA Police); (9) Department of the Interior's Bureau of Indian Affairs Police, Bureau of Land Management Office of Law Enforcement & Security, National Park Service, National Park Rangers, United States Park Police and Fish & Wildlife Service Office of Law Enforcement; (10) Department of Agriculture's Forest Service Law Enforcement and Investigations; (11) Department of Commerce's National Oceanic and Atmospheric Administration Fisheries Office for Law Enforcement; (12) Department of Health and Human Services Food and Drug Administration (FDA), Office of Criminal Investigations; (13) Department of Veterans Affairs Police; (14) United States Postal Inspection Service (USPIS); (15) Congress' Sergeant at Arms of the House of Representatives, Sergeant at Arms of the Senate, United States Capitol Police, and Government Printing Office Police; (16) Central Intelligence Agency's Security Protective Service (SPS); (17) Federal Reserve Police; (18) Library of Congress Police; (19) United States Probation Service (USPO); (20) United States Supreme Court Police (21) and the Amtrack Police among others.

71. Carol Leonnig, "Homeland Security inspector general who was under probe steps down," *Washington Post*, December 16, 2013, accessed July 15, 2017, http://www.washingtonpost.com/politics/homeland-security-inspector-general-who-was-under-probe-steps-down/2013/12/16/0aeac5ae-66c8-11e3-8b5b-a77187b716a3_story.html

72. Levi Pulkkinen, "Judge: FBI-tied child porn collector 'not a danger' to school," SeattlePI, April 8, 2016, accessed July 15, 2017, http://www.seattlepi.com/local/crime/article/Seattle-child-

porn-collector-with-FBI-ties-7236986.php and Kevin Krause, "The FBI ran a huge child porn site to catch predators. The accused are crying foul," *Miami Herald,* January 22, 2017, accessed July 15, 2017, http://www.miamiherald.com/news/nation-world/national/article128081009.html

73. Federal Bureau of Investigations (FBI), "Carmel Man Petitions to Plead Guilty to Charges of Possession, Distribution of Child Pornography," (Southern District of Indiana: United States Government) May 14, 2013, accessed July 16, 2017, https://archives.fbi.gov/archives/india-napolis/press-releases/2013/carmel-man-petitions-to-plead-guilty-to-charges-of-possession-distribution-of-child-pornography; Bill Mears, "Former top FBI agent charged with child porn distribution," Cable News Network (CNN), May 15, 2012, accessed July 17, 2017, http://www.cnn.com/2012/05/15/justice/ex-fbi-agent-pornography/index.html and Evan West, "Explosive Charges: The Donald Sachtleben Case," *Indianapolis Monthly,* July 11, 2014, accessed July 16, 2017, http://www.indianapolismonthly.com/news-opinion/explosive-charges-the-don-ald-sachtleben-case/

74. Department of Justice, "FBI Employee Sentenced 46 Months for Possessing Child Pornography," (Eastern District of Virginia: United States Government), August 27, 2010, accessed July 16, 2017, https://oig.justice.gov/reports/press/2010/2010_08_27.pdf

75. Scott McCabe, "FBI analyst busted in online child porn sting," *Washington Examiner,* December 4, 2012, accessed July 16, 2017, http://www.washingtonexaminer.com/fbi-analyst-busted-in-online-child-porn-sting/article/2515088 and Ann E. Marimow, "Former FBI analyst sentenced to more than three years in prison in child pornography case," *Washington Post,* September 9, 2013, accessed July 16, 2017, https://www.washingtonpost.com/local/former-fbi-analyst-sentenced-to-more-than-three-years-in-prison-in-child-pornography-case/2013/09/09/e9163076-197e-11e3-82ef-a059e54c49d0_story.html

76. Jonathan Dienst, "DEA Agent Brought Child Porn to Work: Feds," NBC 4 New York, March 4, 2011, accessed July 16, 2017, http://www.nbcnewyork.com/news/local/DEA-Agent-Brought-Child-Porn-To-Work-99953384.html and "Darren Argento Registered Sex Offender," Homefacts.com accessed July 16, 2017, http://www.homefacts.com/offender-detail/NY38277/Darren-Ar-gento.html

77. Department of Justice, "Former DEA Agent Pleads Guilty to Child Pornography Charges," (Southern District of Texas: United States Government) June 2, 2016, accessed July 16, 2017, https://www.justice.gov/usao-sdtx/pr/former-dea-agent-pleads-guilty-child-pornography-charges

78. Julia Davis, National Security Expert, comment in response to question from author about Homeland Security employees arrested for misconduct, "Just the way #DHS protects itself from infamy. Often news of convictions appear, then disappear. Very tricky," March 6, 2014, accessed July 15, 2017, https://twitter.com/JuliaDavisNews

79. In 2012, overwhelmed with cases, Homeland's then Inspector General, Charles Edwards, transferred 360 corruption and misconduct cases at Immigration and Customs Enforcement (ICE) and Customs and Border Protection (CBP) to internal affairs of the two agencies. At the time Homeland's OIG had a back log of some 750 cases in ICE and CBP alone. *See also* Andrew Becker, "Homeland security office to unload hundreds of corruption probes," *Reveal News,* May 7, 2010, accessed July 15, 2017, https://www.revealnews.org/article/homeland-security-of-fice-to-unload-hundreds-of-corruption-probes; Andrew Becker, "Homeland Security Office to Unload Hundreds of Corruption Probes," Huffington Post, July 7, 2012, accessed July 15, 2017, http://www.huffingtonpost.com/andrew-becker/homeland-security-office-_1_b_1497538.html and Office of the Inspector General Department of Homeland Security, "Statement of Charles K. Edwards Acting Inspector General U.S. Department of Homeland Security Before the Subcommittee on Oversight, Investigations and Management, U.S. House of Representatives," (Washington D.C.: United States Government), May 17, 2012, accessed July 15, 2017, https://www.oig.dhs.gov/assets/TM/OIGtm_CKE_051712.pdf

80. Julia Davis, "Department of Homeland Security's untouchables: shielded by the badge," Julia Davis Blog, accessed July 15, 2017, http://www.juliadavisnews.com/articles-about-corruption/department-of-homeland-securitys-untouchables-shielded-by-the-badge/

81. Julia Davis, "Department of Homeland Security's untouchables: shielded by the badge," *The Examiner*, September 2, 2012, accessed July 15, 2017, http://cdn.optmd.com/V2/101676/277799/index.html?g=Af////8=&r=www.examiner.com/article/department-of-homeland-security-s-untouchables-shielded-by-the-badge

82. Ron Nixon, "Claims of Corrupt Immigration Contractors Go Unexamined, Investigators Say," The New York Times, January 23, 2017, accessed July 15, 2017, https://www.nytimes.com/2017/01/23/us/politics/immigration-contractors-corruption-dhs.html?_r=0

83. "Federal-Air-Marshal-Misconduct-Database," *Pro Publica*, accessed July 15, 2017, https://www.propublica.org/documents/item/2716034-Federal-Air-Marshal-Misconduct-Database.html

84. Becker, "Homeland Security Office to Unload," 2012.

85. Tia Ghose, "On Polygraph Tests, Would-Be Border Patrol Agents Confess to Crimes," *The Daily Beast*, March 4, 2013, accessed July 15, 2017, http://www.thedailybeast.com/articles/2013/04/04/on-polygraph-tests-would-be-border-patrol-agents-confess-to-crimes.html

86. "Anthony Mangione," CBS Miami, 2011-2012, accessed July 15, 2017, http://miami.cbslocal.com/tag/anthony-mangione and Peter Franceschina, Linda Trischitta and Jon Burstein, "Leader of ICE in South Florida pleads not guilty to child porn charges," *South Florida Sun-Sentinel*, September 28, 2011, accessed July 15, 2017, http://articles.sun-sentinel.com/2011-09-28/news/fl-anthony-mangione-arrest-20110927_1_mangione-ice-official-psychological-evaluation

87. John Shiffman, "Airport passenger screener charged in distributing child pornography," *The Inquirer*, April 23, 2011, accessed July 15, 2017, http://www.philly.com/philly/news/year-in-review/20110423_Airport_passenger_screener_charged_in_distributing_child_pornography.html

88. *Ben Simmoneau, "I-Team: Priest Removed From Ministry Due To Sex Abuse Allegations Now Works At PHL," CBS Philly, May 24, 2012, accessed July 15, 2017,* http://philadelphia.cbslocal.com/2012/05/24/i-team-priest-removed-from-ministry-due-to-sex-abuse-allegations-works-at-phl/

89. Marc Fortier, "Ex-TSA Employee Indicted on Child Porn Charges," *Patch.com*, September 17, 2013, accessed July 15, 2017, https://patch.com/new-hampshire/londonderry/extsa-employee-indicted-on-child-porn-charges

90. Sternstein, "Child porn on government devices," 2016.

91. Sternstein, "Child porn on government devices," 2016.

92. Paul Farrell, "Daniel Rosen: 5 Fast Facts You Need to Know," *Heavy.com*, April 17, 2015, accessed July 15, 2017, http://heavy.com/news/2015/02/daniel-dan-rosen-arrested-charges-child-sex-scandal-state-department-terrorism/ and Shane Harris, "3rd U.S. Official Hit With Child Sex and Porn Charges," *The Daily Beast*, February 25, 2015, accessed July 15, 2017, www.thedailybeast.com/3rd-us-official-hit-with-child-sex-and-porn-charges

93. Julie Jennings, "Federal Workforce Statistics Sources: OPM and OMB," Congressional Research Service, December 7, 2016, accessed July 15, 2017, https://fas.org/sgp/crs/misc/R43590.pdf and Stephen Dinan, "Federal workers hit record number, but growth slows under Obama," *Washington Times*, February 9, 2016, accessed July 15, 2017, http://www.washingtontimes.com/news/2016/feb/9/federal-workers-hit-record-number-but-growth-slows/

94. Bureau of Labor Statistics, "Data Retrieval," 2017, and Terence Jeffrey, "21,995,000 to

12,329,000: Government Employees Outnumber Manufacturing Employees 1.8 to 1," CNS News, September 8, 2015, accessed July 15, 2017, http://www.cnsnews.com/news/article/terence-p-jeffrey/21955000-12329000-government-employees-outnumber-manufacturing

95. Among others: "12 arrested in largest child pornography case in Puerto Rico," Fox News, April 9, 2015, accessed July 15, 2017, http://www.foxnews.com/world/2015/04/09/12-arrested-in-largest-federal-child-pornography-crackdown-in-puerto-rico.html and Bill Bird, "EPA employee from Naperville charged in child porn case," Chicago Tribune, June 9, 2016, accessed July 15, 2017, http://www.chicagotribune.com/suburbs/naperville-sun/crime/ct-nvs-naperville-epa-employee-arrested-st-0610-20160609-story.html

96. U.S. Congress, "H.R.680 - Eliminating Pornography from Agencies Act 115th Congress (2017-2018)," Congress.gov, accessed July 15, 2017, https://www.congress.gov/bill/115th-congress/house-bill/680

97. Zach Carter, "A Pointless Anti-Porn Rider Is Congress' Latest Obsession," Huffington Post, September 9, 2014, accessed July 15, 2017, http://www.huffingtonpost.com/2014/09/08/porn-congress_n_5785030.html

98. U.S. Congress, "H.R.244 - Consolidated Appropriations Act, 2017," Congress.gov, accessed July 15, 2017, https://www.congress.gov/bill/115th-congress/house-bill/244

99. Kevin Bogardus, "Committee passes anti-porn bill," E&E News, March 9, 2017, accessed July 15, 2017, https://www.eenews.net/eedaily/2017/03/09/stories/1060051183 and U.S. Congress, "Eliminating Pornography from Agencies," 2017.

100. "LePage issues order prohibiting state workers from viewing porn," Portland Press Herald, February 20, 2015, accessed July 15, 2017, http://www.pressherald.com/2015/02/20/lepage-issues-order-prohibiting-state-workers-from-viewing-porn and State of Maine, "An Order Clarifying State Management's Response to Certain Prohibited Misconduct," No. 2015-002, February 5, 2015, accessed July 15, 2017, http://www.maine.gov/tools/whatsnew/index.php?topic=Gov_Executive_Orders&id=638259&v=article2011

101. Wagner, "Lawmakers Want Digital Devices," 2017 and Maass, "States Introduce Dubious Anti-Pornography," 2017.

102. Department of Justice, "Former Acting HHS Cyber Security Director Sentenced to 25 Years in Prison for Engaging in Child Pornography Enterprise," (Washington D.C.: United States Government), January 5, 2015, accessed July 15, 2017, https://www.justice.gov/opa/pr/former-acting-hhs-cyber-security-director-sentenced-25-years-prison-engaging-child

103. Department of Justice, "U.S. Postal Employee Charged with Viewing Child Pornography on Work Computers," (District of Massachusetts: United States Government), September 22, 2016, accessed July 15, 2017, https://www.justice.gov/usao-ma/pr/us-postal-employee-charged-viewing-child-pornography-work-computers

104. Department of Justice, "Former U.S. Army Corps of Engineers Employee Sentenced to 30 Years in Prison for Transportation and Possession of Child Pornography," (Washington D.C.: United States Government) April 14, 2016, accessed July 15, 2017, https://www.justice.gov/opa/pr/former-us-army-corps-engineers-employee-sentenced-30-years-prison-transportation-and

105. Matthew Barakat, "Ex-U.S. diplomat gets 20 years for child porn," USA Today, August 22, 2008, accessed July 15, 2017, http://usatoday30.usatoday.com/news/nation/2008-08-22-1129567526_x.htm

106. Julie Montanaro, "Former Department of Agriculture Worker Sentenced for Child Porn," WCTV.TV, February 10, 2015, accessed July 15, 2017, http://www.wctv.tv/home/headlines/Tallahassee-Man-Arrested-For-Child-Porn-Charges-253386421.html

107. "Feds say former Child Protective Services employee purchased nearly $7K in child porn," ABC News 7 WXYZ Staff, July 2, 2013, accessed July 15, 2017, http://www.wxyz.com/news/region/oakland-county/feds-say-former-child-protective-services-employee-purchased-nearly-7k-in-child-porn

108. Mary Beth Sheridan and Jerry Markon, "Official at Children's Museum Is Charged in Child Pornography Case," *Washington Post*, November 7, 2007, accessed July 15, 2017, http://www.washingtonpost.com/wp-dyn/content/article/2007/11/06/AR2007110601973.html

109. Jeremy Ryan, "Former cop, child caseworker accused of possessing child porn," *CNY Central.com*, December 21, 2010, accessed July 15, 2017, http://cnycentral.com/news/local/former-cop-child-caseworker-accused-of-possessing-child-porn?id=557874#.VPr9wuGFEtI

110. "Former Ore. man gets 30 mos. for child porn on gov't computer, NBC News Portland KGW Staff, October 4, 2012, accessed July 15, 2017, http://www.kgw.com/news/former-ore-man-gets-30-mos-for-child-porn-on-govt-computer/73118310

111. So many U.S. government employees, often at senior levels, caught trading in Russian sourced child pornography on U.S. government computers ought to raise alarms, particularly given the common knowledge that the line between Russian government agencies and Russian organized crime to non-existent. It is beyond the scope of this book to explore Russia's new cyber-warfare but it appears child pornography may be a tool underdevelopment in Russia's arsenal. For more details on Russia's cyber-ware fare *see also*: Andy Greenberg, "How An Entire Nation Became Russia's Test Lab for Cyberwar," *Wired*, June 20, 2017, accessed July 15, 2017, https://www.wired.com/story/russian-hackers-attack-ukraine

112. Sternstein, "Child porn on government devices," 2016.

6

The Legal Profession

The justice system is supposed to be a noble pursuit, built upon objectivity and fairness. But the scandal has instead revealed an immature fraternity, a place where everyone is in on the joke – except for Pennsylvania's 12 million residents.

– David Gambacorta, February 24, 2016.[1]

JUDGES AND PROSECUTORS

Judges and prosecutors are also, of course, government employees; ones with significant power. They can provide justice and uphold the rule of law or cause significant harm to innocent lives through abuse of their position. While prosecutors and judges are supposed to be held accountable, too often oversight is weak or non-existent. More than a few judges and prosecutors have been caught trading in child rape. This creates a fundamental problem for child survivors and those who advocate for them. Pedophiles are deviants prepared to fight for their continued access to children, child rape images/videos and impunity for their crimes. When pedophiles are employed in powerful governmental positions as judges or prosecutors the perversion of justice is substantial.

As mentioned in Chapter One, the crime of trading in child rape in America occurs within the context of a broken, sexist and racist justice system dominated by white men.[2] This is relevant to the crime because child pornography appears to be overwhelmingly committed by white men. The U.S. Sentencing Commission has documented more than 85 percent of child pornography convictions have been of white men. Since pedophiles are highly networked and help protect each other a criminal justice system dominated and controlled by white men is relevant to a discussion of child pornography prosecution and sentencing. While black men are arrested for "obstructing the sidewalk" and receive harsh jail sentences for using marijuana, too often white, wealthy men trading in child rape receive light sentences or no jail time at all.[3]

JUDGES

As previously mentioned, what and how much a pedophile is sentenced to is inconsistent.[4] It depends on the judge in the district and the person being prosecuted. Although there are federally mandated minimum sentencing guidelines, judges are routinely ignoring these; judges like Jack Weinstein in Brooklyn, New York, who sentenced a father, identified only by his initials R.V., to five days in jail in 2016.[5] R.V. had been trading in the rape of children as young as three-years-old. Weinstein issued a 98-page decision denouncing child pornography mandatory minimum sentencing and refusing to comply. He told the *New York Times* that he "doesn't believe in 'destroying lives unnecessarily' over a crime that harms nobody."[6] Pietro Polizzi, owner of Tony's Pizzeria, was another pedophile Weinstein attempted to protect. Upon his arrest Polizzi possessed more than 5,000 images of child rape including the rape of toddlers. He was convicted on 23 counts and eventually sentenced to five years in federal prison. Polizzi said "I don't see Judge Weinstein as a judge… I see him as my father. He helps people. He doesn't destroy lives the way the prosecutor has. He's the one who is going to set me free from the court."[7]

A pedophile convicted on 23 counts of trading in child rape, including of toddlers, sees a federal judge as his "father" who will set him "free?" As discussed throughout this book, pedophiles network. They know each other. They protect each other. A judge trading in child rape himself is unlikely to sentence another pedophile to jail. A judge networked with other pedophiles is likely to engage in case-rigging and ensure friends who need protection come before his court. Judges also use their position to traffic children – as is happening in family and juvenile courts across the country. Family and juvenile courts expose vulnerable children. A judge occupies the ideal observation point to identify children that can easily be trafficked.

home, pursuant to Boeckmann's desires. The "work" usually consisted of picking up cans either alongside city roads in Wynne, or actually picking up cans at Boeckmann's residence, wherein Beockmann would photograph the buttocks of the men as they were bending to retrieve the garbage. Multiple male litigants have been photographed by Boeckmann during these "community service" type sentences. Boeckmann maintained these photographs of male litigants' buttocks in his home for his own personal use. In addition to the illegal sentences, Boeckmann has used his judicial status to form relationships, personal and sexual, with certain male litigants. Boeckmann has engaged in a consistent pattern of seeking out young Caucasian male litigants before Cross County District Court for the purpose of forming personal, sexual relations with the litigants, thus creating a self-imposed conflict of interest for himself in his role as Cross County District Court Judge. Boeckmann's method of

Statement of Allegations against Joseph Boeckmann's

Judges like Tim Nolan, a District Judge in Campbell County, Kentucky arrested in May 2017, on human trafficking and unlawful transaction with a minor.[8] Or Joseph Boeckmann in Arkansas who case-rigged male defendants, including teenagers, into his court and traded sex and child pornography for reduced sentences. Boeckmann paid attorneys to help him channel vulnerable boys and men into his court. The defendants would then be sentenced to "community service" at Boeckmann's home while he photographed their body parts and demanded sex. Arkansas' Judicial Discipline and Disability Commission said that Boeckmann gave "preferential court treatment to 'young Caucasian male litigants' that he had sexual relations with."[9]

The Kids for Cash scandal in Pennsylvania was not explicitly for trafficking children into sex abuse (although children may have been sexually abused in juvenile detention); however, it is another example of judges trafficking children for money.[10] Judges Mark Ciavarella and Michael Conahan organized a racketeering scheme with the builder/owner of for-profit juvenile detention centers. The judges made sure the centers were full and the builder/owner paid the judges. The more children sentenced to juvenile detention, the more money the judges were paid, totaling some $2.6 million before they were caught. Judicial oversight and monitoring in Pennsylvania failed to investigate complaints filed against the judges. The local legal community of lawyers and prosecutors were aware of the trafficking but also failed to alert authorities. Eventually, the FBI and IRS opened investigations resulting in prosecution and sentencing of the judges.[11]

Pennsylvania judges have also been in the news for trading in graphic adult pornography, encouraging violence against women and exhibiting disturbing racist attitudes. As I have argued, the domination of white, racist, sexist men over our legal system presents a real barrier to efforts to halt America's child rape epidemic. Pennsylvania's former Attorney General (AG) Kathleen Kane exposed these attitudes and behaviors that seem rampant in our legal system. As a former child sex abuse prosecutor, Kane ran for the office of Attorney General with the intention of cleaning up the justice system and holding those who harm children to account. She was thwarted from the very start.

KATHLEEN KANE: TENS OF THOUSANDS OF EMAILS

Further, our analysis identified 38 individuals who sent 50 or more e-mails containing sexually explicit or offensive language or pictures. These individuals included current and former OAG agents, a Supreme Court Justice, a Senior Deputy Attorney General in the OAG, high-ranking officials of Commonwealth executive branch agencies, a judicial employee, city and county detectives, a parole agent, and other state and county employees. In light of available

Gansler Report on Misuse of Commonwealth E-Mail Systems, pg. 6

When Kane became Pennsylvania's AG she immediately threatened pedophile power-structures. First, she opened a state-wide hotline for tips on Catholic priests who sexual abused children. Calls to the hotline resulted in 250 cases. Kane established a state-wide grand jury to investigate and prosecute pedophiles protected by the Catholic Church. Then she appointed a former federal prosecutor to investigate how the previous governor had interacted with the Penn State child sex abuse investigation involving Jerry Sandusky and former Penn State President Graham Spanier among others. Sandusky and Spanier were convicted in 2012 and 2017 respectively. Sandusky is serving 30-60 years in prison for sexually abusing at least ten boys. Spanier was sentenced, in June 2017, to two months in jail and two months of house arrest on child endangerment charges. Prosecutors said Spanier showed a "stunning lack of remorse" for the victims.[12] Kathleen Kane used her position as AG to investigate if attempts had been made to protect Pennsylvania's powerful white men, rather than children.

We identified more than 45 senders holding the following positions[62] and sending inappropriate e-mails in the following volumes:

Type of Position	Number of Sent E-Mails
Judges	More than 160
Assistant District Attorneys	More than 35
Senior Executive Branch Officials	More than 30
Members of the General Assembly	Approximately 5

Gansler Report on Misuse of Commonwealth E-Mail Systems, pg. 23

Kane's investigation into the Penn State scandal yielded tens of thousands of emails sent among judges, prosecutors, law enforcement and other government employees exposing a dangerous racist and sexist culture. The emails included "loads of pornography littered the exchanges between government officials. ... Office-secretary porn. Sarah Palin-photoshopped porn. Hardcore, objects-stuck-in-a-woman's-every-orifice porn ... Fat jokes. Gay jokes. Racist jokes. Domestic-violence jokes. The bulk of which were sent on state computers, on state time, from one state employee to another."[13] The emails were "a spiderweb, stretching out in every possible direction, connecting small-town attorneys to big-name prosecutors to State Supreme Court Justices."[14] Thirteen judges or senior government officials were described as 'offenders' with judges, overwhelmingly, being the worst offenders.

These thousands of emails evidence a culture of racism and extreme misogyny among "a who's who of Pennsylvania elite." One local paper reported, "you may have an easier time figuring out who in the criminal justice community *didn't* receive the emails" rather than who did.[15] Almost exclusively, white, male judges, prosecutors, law enforcement and senior government employees were trading, at work, images such as: "Blonde Banana Split" with women inserting bananas into orifices; a woman performing oral sex on a white man with the words "making your boss happy is your only job;" a white man carrying a bucket of fried chicken fending off two African American men with the caption "BRAVERY At Its Finest."[16] Bruce Ledewitz, Associate Dean of Academic Affairs and Law Professor at Duquesne University, said "When you see these emails… it's just a swamp of misogyny, racism, homophobia and white privilege. It taints everybody, especially in the judicial branch.… You get the impression that every white male office holder in the state is a creep."[17]

Kathleen Kane hired a law firm to conduct a full analysis of the emails and release a public report.[18] Long before the report was released, Kane held press conferences and released the emails in small batches including more than 1,500 emails sent by a Supreme Court judge. The white men in power hit back hard. Kane was arrested. Her law license was revoked by the very men she was exposing. Eventually she was sentenced in October 2016, to 10-23 months in jail followed by eight years of probation for her "political ego," convicted on two felony counts of perjury and seven charges of lying and abusing the power of her office. Although two Supreme Court Judges lost their positions, none of the men involved in undermining America's justice system by displaying blatantly threatening behavior towards women and minorities on government computers were criminally charged.

> Kane referenced those emails again on Thursday, claiming she delivered this week more than 1,500 emails from a Supreme Court justice to the state Ethics Commission, the Judicial Conduct Board and the Disciplinary Board. "Those emails contained both sent and received emails from a present Supreme Court justice. They contained racial, misogynistic pornography," Kane claimed without naming the justice. "There's other emails regarding 30 percent of women are killed or murdered by their husbands or boyfriends and the punchline is 'well 30 percent of them should have just shut the expletive up.' "I'm not the woman to shut up. It is my job as attorney general to make sure that this commonwealth is run properly and the people of this commonwealth are protected. The images themselves aren't the only story. The problem is the network that's involved and the breadth of this network is incredible," Kane added.[19]

Not only did those involved, with what the local media dubbed porngate, enjoy impunity, there was not even a sense of wrong-doing on display by these powerful white male judges and prosecutors. The only thing that was evident was a determination to silence and punish Kathleen

Kane for exposing these men and how they behave among each other. Her story became a cautionary tale, with white male judges and prosecutors sending a public warning to anyone who might attempt to hold them accountable. She was made an example of what could be done to those who dare to expose corrupt judges and prosecutors. Through it all Kane retained her faith in the rule of law and determination to accomplish what she was elected to do: hold people to account even if they were judges, prosecutors and police. When she was arrested she said:

> You can arrest me two times, you can arrest me 10 times. I'm sure this isn't the end of the game, but I will not stop until the truth comes out, and I will not stop until the system operates the way it's supposed to be.... And what does this mean to the public? ... That means that your system, your criminal justice system that you think you have and you think you deserve is not working properly.[20]

PENIS PUMP AND CHILD PORNOGRAPHY

The pattern of behavior Kane exposed of judges and prosecutors reinforcing and making acceptable violence against women is similar to how pedophiles encourage each other and normalize a cultural of violence against children. This kind of conduct occurring in judges' chambers and prosecutors' offices is not limited to Pennsylvania. It is occurring across the country. Judges arrested on child pornography-related charges is, I fear, only the smallest hint of a much larger problem in the judiciary. With arrested judges, I have included cases that attest to overall sexual deviancy, misogynistic and racist behavior that appears to be widespread. It is critical that the American public know how many and which judges have been arrested for trading in child rape. Currently, the Department of Justice is failing to provide America with this information. A longer list of judges is available on my Medium profile. Similar to the demographics of other child pornography arrests, the arrests of judges are almost exclusively of white men.

A few recent examples include:

- Steven Vincent Smith, 52-year-old lawyer and substitute judge in Alabama, was arrested March 18, 2016, on four child pornography charges. In May 2016, additional charges of first-degree sodomy and sexual abuse of a child less than 12 years old. He was indicted in September 2016, on two counts. Smith was originally held on $1 million bond and remains in custody. Sentencing has not yet been set.[21]

- Louis M. Parry, a 61-year-old judge in Florida, was arrested, December 2004, on child pornography charges. He pled guilty and was sentenced in December 2005 to five years and months in prison followed by three years of supervised release. Parry was trading in child rape of children as young as six. At the time of his arrest he had hundreds of images/videos in his possession.[22]

• John P. Junke, a 70-year-old retired Walla Walla, Washington judge was arrested in December 2013, on child pornography charges. He told investigators he had been using pornography for a long time. Junke pled guilty in February 2014 to six child pornography counts and was sentenced to 90 days in jail and 15 years on the sex-offender registry. Junke was caught by information technology staff when he took his computer in for servicing. He had been reprimanded by the state's judicial conduct commission when he was a judge and some lawyers refused to let him preside over cases, forcing the court to pay for substitute judges. When he lost his re-election bid, Junke became a private practice lawyer. He was disbarred for ethics violations.[23]

• Ronald C. Kline, a 66-year-old Orange County, California judge, was charged in November 2001, on seven child pornography charges. In January 2002, he was charged with five counts of child molestation. Kline pled guilty in December 2005, and was sentenced February 2007, to 2.25 years in federal prison followed by three years of supervised release and a life-time on the sex offender registry. Kline was under home arrest with electronic monitoring pending sentencing. Kline was trading in child pornography from his work computer. At the time of his arrest, he had more than 1,500 child sexual abuse images of young boys. Kline served on the court's Technology Committee and help developed the policy warning employees their computers were not their private property and could be searched.[24]

• Michael Maggio, a 54-year-old Judge in Arkansas Circuit Court, was investigated by Arkansas Judicial Discipline and Disability Commission after posting comments about incest and bestiality as well as "racist, sexist and homophobic comments" to an online message board called TigerDroppings.com.[25] Maggio was using the online name GeauxJudge and was exposed by political reporter Matthew Campbell. Some of Maggio's posts included "What's the most used line in Arkansas: daddy get off me you are crushing my cigarettes" and "Sex with animals ... been there done that ... signed, Arkansas." Although Maggio was not, to public knowledge, investigated on child pornography charges, the argument could be made that his incest and bestiality posts were probable cause to open an investigation. In March 2016, Maggio was sentenced, in a separate case, to ten years in prison for accepting a payment for a judgment.[26]

• Donald Thompson, a 54-year-old Judge in Oklahoma, was convicted and sentenced in August 2006, to four felony counts of indecent exposure in his own courtroom. Thompson was masturbating and using a "penis pump" while presiding over trials. He was seen numerous times by various witnesses. One witness said the judge did this almost daily during a murder trial. An investigation revealed semen on the judge's chair, robe and carpet as well as a "penis pump" hidden beneath the bench. In 2011, the Oklahoma Supreme Court upheld the decision by the Oklahoma Public Employees Retirement System Board of Trustees that Thompson was not eligible for his $7,789 monthly state retirement pay because he had violated his oath of office. Thompson's pension had been suspended when he was sentenced. Thompson was again arrested in March 2011, for stalking his former girlfriend. While Thompson was not investigated for child pornography, there was certainly probable cause to do so. Thompson is a registered sex offender.[27]

PROSECUTORS

The failure in America to better tackle the crime of trading in child rape is due, in part, to corrupt prosecutors. A prosecutor, perhaps more than any other government employee, can arrange considerable protection for a pedophile. Even if many victims come forward, a prosecutor can choose not to bring charges. This was described, most vividly, in the documentary film *The Keepers*. In the middle of Baltimore's network of pedophile priests and police there was a prosecutor who simply refused to prosecute. Law enforcement often express frustration, as depicted in *The Keepers*, about cases they had spent considerable time and resources on only to be blocked by a prosecutor.[28] This is not uncommon.

How is this possible? Prosecutorial discretion – the two dirtiest words in the American legal system. In 2014, the *New York Times* editorial board called prosecutorial misconduct "rampant."[29] Prosecutors are not legally obliged to prosecute crimes. Prosecutors can choose which crimes they prosecute. Stunning, isn't it? The poor get prosecuted and the rich play golf, drink, sail and party with their favorite local or federal prosecutor, who simply declines to prosecute his/her friend's crimes.[30] In terms of child pornography, this means wealthy business men, priests, lawyers, politicians, judges, lawyers and prosecutors themselves are enjoying a great deal of impunity. Prosecutorial discretion too often provides a green light for powerful pedophiles in America to engage in the child-rape trade. More than a few prosecutors, themselves, have been caught trading in child rapes sometimes on their work computers. For example, at the Department of Justice (DOJ), the agency responsible for protecting America's children, an Assistant Attorney General (AAG) under former Attorney General Eric Holder was caught trading in child pornography at work. Holder refused to prosecute his own AAG and protected this criminal to the extent that his name was never made public.[31]

By many accounts, the Department of Justice was transformed, under Eric Holder's reign, into a revolving door for criminal defense lawyers.[32] Defense attorneys, like Holder and his Criminal Division Chief, Lanny Breuer, leave their private practice of protecting the wealthy and do a stint at the Department of Justice (DOJ) where they protect the wealthy from prosecution. Then, after refusing to prosecute the affluent, defense attorneys return to private practice with a new and improved client list of grateful criminals. It is a cozy little arrangement and one that is perverting our justice system in dangerous ways. For example, Breuer, when head of DOJ's criminal division, is infamous for telling *PBS Frontline* it was his job to protect criminal bankers from prosecution.[33] Breuer, back at the Washington DC law firm of Covington & Burling, along with Holder, now advertises he can help clients with "cybercrime incidents;" a euphemism for child pornography charges.

There is a great deal of well-researched material on the corruption of prosecutors, including Matt Taibbi's *The Divide: American Injustice in the Age of the Wealth Gap* and Jesse Eisinger's *The Chickenshit Club: Why the Justice Department Fails to Prosecute Executives*.[34] What has not yet been considered is how the perversion of America's prosecutors relates to child pornography. For example, there is a need to explore how prosecutors handle arrests of fellow lawyers, prosecutors and judges on child pornography charges versus the prosecution of non-lawyers. Many lawyers interact in tight professional and social circles of judges and prosecutors they know from law school or previous private or public practice. A law degree can provide considerable protection for a pedophile. Are pedophiles with a law degree receiving preferential treatment in our justice system?

As with my other data sets, a longer list of prosecutors arrested on child pornography related charges is available on my Medium profile. Similar to the demographics of other child pornography arrests, prosecutors who have been arrested are almost exclusively white men.

A few recent examples include:

- Patrick Michael Moran, a 39-year-old assistant attorney general (AAG) assigned to the juvenile division in Baltimore, Maryland, was arrested in October 2016, on child pornography charges. He pled guilty in April 2017, and was sentenced in May 2017, to ten years in jail with nine of those years suspended followed by five years of supervised release. He must register as a sex offender. Moran was free on $150,000 bail pending sentencing. He was trading in child rape that included children as young as three-year- old.[35]

- James Cameron, 51-year-old assistant attorney general (AAG) in Maine, was arrested and indicted on sixteen child pornography charges in 2009. He was sentenced in 2014, to nearly 16 years in jail followed by six years of supervised release.[36] Cameron distributed hundreds of child pornography images and videos, including children as young as four, and used "an ever-changing array of account names ... frequently posed as a teenage girl." He also traded in images "depicting patently sadistic conduct."[37] In 2016, he appealed his sentence and lost.[38] Cameron had been an assistant attorney general for 18 years and served as Maine's top drug prosecutor.

• Steve Giardini, a 50-year-old assistant district attorney in Mobile County, Alabama, who prosecuted sex crimes, was arrested in August 2010, and charged with enticement and solicitation with the intent to produce child pornography. Refusing a plea deal, his case went to trial and ended in a mistrial. The Attorney General re-submitted the case and a judge, in December 2012, refused to allow the charges to go to trial, claiming there was no "victim."[39] Giardini had been attempting to have sex with a fifteen-year-old, over a four-month period, who was in reality an undercover FBI agent. Giardini asked the "girl" to take off her clothes and masturbate.[40] He had at least twenty different screen names and false personae which he used to solicit sex and/or nude images from children and, upon his arrest, had hundreds of child sex abuse images/videos. Giardini worked as an assistant DA for 20 years prosecuting sex crime for the Child Advocacy Center and was in charge of handling allegations of sex abuse by the Catholic Church.

• George Richard Fox, a 68-year-old prosecutor and part-time municipal judge in St. Louis, Missouri, was arrested, August 2009, on child pornography charges. He pled guilty and was sentenced, May 2010, to two years in federal prison. Fox had been trading in the rape of infants and toddlers for at least a year and told investigators child pornography did not harm children. He was allowed to resign, rather than being terminated, from his position as a government prosecutor. Fox was disbarred and is a registered sex offender.[41]

As regarding Count I, the Defendant engaged in oral sex with [NAME REDACTED] (hereinafter the BOY) during a time frame that the BOY was 5 to 7 years of age. The BOY would have been age 5 to 7 during June 1, 2011, to January 29, 2014. The Defendant had sexual encounters with the BOY for approximately 2 years, and the Defendant indicates the last encounter was in 2013. The sexual encounters included the Defendant performing oral sex upon the BOY, as well as the BOY performing oral sex upon the Defendant. The

Christopher Jansen's Criminal Complaint

- Christopher Jansen, a 35-year-old former Walworth County, South Dakota State's Attorney was arrested in July 2014, on child pornography related charges. He pled guilty in November 2015, to federal charges and was sentenced in federal court in March 2016, to 40 years in jail and sentenced in state court, September 2015, to 50 years in jail. Starting when he was Walworth County State's Attorney and continuing in his capacity as a family law lawyer, when he left the State's Attorney office, Jansen sexually abused a five-year-old child of a client he was representing in a family law matter. Jansen spent overnights with the child and his family and sexually abused the boy, over a two-year period, producing and distributing child pornography of the abuse. Jansen used a picture of the boy as an avatar on a child pornography website. In addition to this abuse, Jansen sexually abused two other of his client's minor children. He had been trading in child rape since college. Jansen was disbarred and must register as a sex offender.[42]

LAWYERS

Lawyers do not necessarily lose their license after child pornography arrests and convictions. For a professional license to be removed a complaint must be filed with the state licensing board and then the board must vote to remove the license. In 2014, the California Overseers of the Bar issued a decision stating that lawyers convicted on child pornography charges will automatically be disbarred. To my knowledge, California is the first state to make this an automatic process. This policy improvement resulted when Gary Douglass Grant, a former Army lawyer, attempted to retain his law license after his child pornography conviction. A judge requested Grant be disbarred but the board of appeals recommended only a two-year suspension.[43] The California Supreme Court then ruled, from that point forward, all lawyers convicted of child pornography "charges will automatically be disbarred and prohibited from practicing law in the state.... (because) possessing or sharing sexual images of children necessarily constitutes an act of moral turpitude that makes an attorney unfit for the legal profession."[44] Every state should follow California's lead and make child pornography convictions cause for automatic disbarment.

Perhaps more than any other profession, pedophiles who are lawyers are in the best position to protect themselves and the crimes they commit against children. Many private practice lawyers know colleagues serving as prosecutors or judges. Lawyers cycle in and out of private practice and public service, using time in public service to enrich their private practice. There is no comprehensive data on how many lawyers have been arrested on child pornography related-charges and if arrested lawyers are receiving preferential treatment. If judges and prosecutors are protecting their colleagues, this would be important to the public interest and represents another example of why a child pornography database is needed.

In text-boxes through the book several examples of prominent attorneys arrested on child pornography charges and involvement in elite child sex rings are profiled. A longer list of lawyers arrested on child pornography related charges is available on my Medium profile; again, almost all white men.

A few recent examples include:

• Aaron Biber, a 48-year lawyer and treasurer of the Minnesota State Bar Association, was arrested, December 2009, on child pornography related charges. He pled guilty and was sentenced, October 2010, to 18 years in jail. Biber had groomed, since the child was 11, and raped his 15-year-old son's friend. Biber sent the child "explicit text messages and pornography" asked the child to "perform sexual acts" and anally raped the child.[45] In May 2011, Biber was ordered to pay $15 million, into a trust for the child victim, in punitive damages for assault, battery and emotional distress of the child.[46]

• Samuel Logan, 46-year-old lawyer in Kansas, was arrested and charged, July 2010, on child pornography charges. He pled guilty May 2011, and was sentenced in September 2011, to ten years in prison. Logan had been a partner at Foulston Siefkin; one of Kansas' most prestigious law firms. He distributed images/videos of "himself masturbating" in his law office to an undercover agent posing as a fourteen-year-old girl. Logan sent thirty-two images, two of which were child pornography, to the undercover investigator.[47] He was arrested when he arrived at the local mall, thinking he was meeting a 14-year-old girl for sex. Logan's father, James Logan, is a former federal appeals court judge and former dean of the University of Kansas School of Law. Samuel Logan has been disbarred.[48]

• Joseph Patrick Redd, a 32-year-old lawyer in Baltimore, Maryland, was arrested in 2009, and pled guilty in May 2011, to one count of child pornography possession. He was sentenced September 2011 to two years in jail followed by ten years of supervised release. The local newspaper described anger in the community that Redd was allowed to remain free and with his infant child, pending sentencing, "the delay allowed a suspected child sex offender to remain in a community full of children for more than two years before authorities filed criminal charges... (the neighbors) had seen the man push his baby carriage along the sidewalk and wave."[49] At the time of his arrest, Redd had hundreds of child rape images/videos in his possession. He was a married malpractice attorney and his wife was pregnant at the time of his arrest. Redd was disbarred by consent by the Maryland Attorney Grievance Commission prior to his guilty plea. Redd is a registered sex offender.[50]

• Leo Flynn, a 62-year-old criminal defense lawyer in South Dakota, was arrested, 2009, on child pornography charges. He was charged with two counts of distribution and one count each of receipt, possession and access with intent to view child pornography. In December 2010, a jury failed to convict Flynn on any charges. Flynn pled not guilty, claiming he had to trade in child rape, weekly, as research to help defend his clients and that trading in child rape was part of his "official duties." So many of his client-base are sex offenders, Flynn earned the nickname "perv attorney." In May 2017 Flynn was in the news again as the attorney for Sioux Falls Fire Chief Jim Sideras, who was arrested for trading in pre-teen hard core, the brutal rape and torture of very small children including infants.[51]

• Christopher G. Young, a 53-year-old prominent lawyer and lobbyist in Baton Rouge, Louisiana, was arrested on child pornography charges. He was indicted, 12 May 2016, on two counts. His federal trial is currently scheduled for October 2017. Young had been trading in child rape and bestiality of children under twelve-years-old and donkeys.[52]

• Joshua Jesse Robert Gessler, a 41-year-old lawyer with Arnold and Porter, one of Washington DC's most prestigious law firms, and an adjunct professor at George Mason University, was arrested twice in August and September 2010, on child pornography charges. He was indicted on ten child pornography counts. He pled guilty and was sentenced in May 2011, to three months in jail followed by two years of supervised release. Gessler had been preying upon and paying a 15-year-old run-away girl for sex. He also recorded and distributed the child sex abuse he produced of these encounters.[53] Gessler lost his Virginia and Pennsylvania law licenses. He is a registered sex offender.[54]

SOMETIMES IT'S FELLOW LAWYERS

As *JD Journal*, a popular legal magazine, writes, "sometimes it's fellow lawyers that harbor a dark secret or defend pedophile behavior."[55] Out of all the government employees trading in child rape, judges and prosecutors represent, perhaps, the most dangerous to the fabric of our democracy and rule of law. Are there more arrests of government-employed pedophiles among judges and prosecutors than among law enforcement and military? We do not know because there is no database. Are prosecutors and judges giving preferential treatment on child pornography sentencing to their legal colleagues? Again, absent the data, we do not know. The American public has a right to know how many lawyers, judges and prosecutors have been arrested for this crime. The data must be gathered.

Of course, the criminals caught represent only a fraction of the population engaged in the crime. As with other professional categories, enhanced oversight is needed of all judges and prosecutors' workplace electronic devices and networks. Robust monitoring of the electronic networks of all DA and AG offices should be instituted. Because judges and prosecutors wield great, and too often unchecked, power in the communities in which they serve, such monitoring cannot be left in the hands of local law enforcement, given the conflicts of interest and the difficulty local level law enforcement often have investigating judges and prosecutors. A federal law enforcement agency, perhaps the U.S. Postal inspectors, could be mandated to provide routine monitoring of prosecution and judicial offices across the country.

Not one judge or prosecutor should be trading in child rape. Ever. We must do more to investigate and prosecute those who do.

Endnotes

1. David Gambacorta, "The Great Pennsylvania Government Porn Caper," Esquire, February 24, 2016, accessed July 15, 2017, http://www.esquire.com/news-politics/a42234/porngate-pennsylvania-kathleen-kane.

2. United States Sentencing Commission, "2012 Report to the Congress: Federal Child Pornography Offenses," (Washington DC: United States Government), p. 142, March 8, 2017, accessed July 01, 2017, http://www.ussc.gov/research/congressional-reports/2012-report-congress-federal-child-pornography-offenses.

3. Nicole Flatow, "Rochester Teens Arrested For Obstructing The Sidewalk While Waiting For School Bus," Think Progress, December 2, 2013, accessed July 15, 2017, https://thinkprogress.org/rochester-teens-arrested-for-obstructing-the-sidewalk-while-waiting-for-school-bus-deb4049ee831 and Will Sommer, "Where the Sidewalk Ends," Washington City Paper, May 22, 2015, accessed July 15, 2017, http://www.washingtoncitypaper.com/news/article/13046861/where-the-sidewalk-ends-dcs-law-against-blocking-the-sidewalk.

4. "Perverted justice? Child pornography sentences vary widely in federal, state courts." Naples Daily News, May 18, 2013, accessed July 15, 2017, http://archive.naplesnews.com/news/state/perverted-justice-child-pornography-sentences-vary-widely-in-federal-state-courts-ep-512862682-342098901.html.

5. Tracy Connor, "Judge Gives Man 5 Days for Child Porn, Rails Against Harsh Sentences," NBC News, February 1, 2016, accessed July 15, 2017, http://www.nbcnews.com/news/us-news/judge-gives-man-5-days-child-porn-rails-against-harsh-n507406

6. A.G. Sulzberger, "Defiant Judge Takes On Child Pornography Law," The New York Times, May 21, 2010, accessed July 15, 2017, http://www.nytimes.com/2010/05/22/nyregion/22judge.html and Dahlia Lithwick, "Jack Weinstein," The Atlantic, November 2010, accessed July 15, 2017, https://www.theatlantic.com/magazine/archive/2010/11/jack-weinstein/308273.

7. Sulzberger, "Defiant Judge Takes on Child Pornography Law," 2010.

8. "Former Campbell County judge indicted on rape, human trafficking charges," FOX 19 News, Digital Media Staff, May 4, 2017, accessed July 15, 2017, http://www.fox19.com/story/35345653/former-campbell-county-judge-indicted-by-ky-attorney-general.

9. Andy Campbell, "Arkansas Judge Accused Of Trading Sentence Reductions For Sex," *The Huffington Post*, November 18, 2015, accessed July 15, 2017, http://www.huffingtonpost.com/entry/arkansas-judge-accused-of-trading-sentence-reductions-for-sex_us_564bb5ade4b045bf3df198a9.

10. William Ecenbarger, *Kids for Cash: Two Judges, Thousands of Children, and a $2.8 Million Kickback Scheme,* (New York: The New Press, 2014) and Robert May, Kids for Cash (SenArt Films), 2014, accessed on July 15, 2017, http://kidsforcashthemovie.com.

11. "Mark A. Ciavarella," *The New York Times,* 2009-2013, accessed July 15, 2017, https://www.nytimes.com/topic/person/mark-a-ciavarella and John Schuppe, "Pennsylvania Seeks to Close Books on "Kids for Cash" Scandal," *NBC News*, August 12, 2015, accessed July 15, 2017, http://www.nbcnews.com/news/us-news/pennsylvania-seeks-close-books-kids-cash-scandal-n408666.

12. Schuppe, "Pennsylvania Seeks to Close Books," 2015.

13. Gambacorta, "The Great Pennsylvania Government Porn Caper," 2017.

14. Gambacorta, "The Great Pennsylvania Government Porn Caper," 2017.

15. Wallace McKelvey, "Kathleen Kane's porn report: 5 things you need to know as AG's office releases email probe," *PennLive.com,* November 22, 2016, accessed July 15, 2017, http://www.pennlive.com/politics/index.ssf/2016/11/ags_office_to_release_porn_ema.html

16. Gambacorta, "The Great Pennsylvania Government Porn Caper," 2017.

17. Natalie Pompilio, "Pornographic email scandal roils Pennsylvania politics," *The Washington Post*, December 26, 2015, accessed July 15, 2017, https://www.washingtonpost.com/politics/pornographic-email-scandal-ripples-through-pennsylvania-politics/2015/12/26/fc411a76-a374-11e5-b53d-972e2751f433_story.html?utm_term=.03511b1a886a.

18. Gansler, *Gansler Report,* 2016.

19. Carl Hessler Jr., "Kane: 'I will not stop until the truth comes out'," *The Delaware County Daily Times*, October 2, 2015, accessed July 15, 2017, http://www.delcotimes.com/article/DC/20151002/NEWS/151009930.

20. "Kane defiant after latest arrest, vows to expose officials," *Lehigh Valley Live*, October 2, 2015, accessed July 15, 2017, http://www.lehighvalleylive.com/news/index.ssf/2015/10/kane_defiant_after_latest_arre.html.

21. Department of Justice, "Federal Grand Jury Indicts Jefferson County and Marshall County Men in Separate Child Pornography Cases," (Northern District of Alabama: United States Government), September 29, 2016, accessed July 15, 2017, https://www.justice.gov/usao-ndal/pr/federal-grand-jury-indicts-jefferson-county-and-marshall-county-men-separate-child.

22. Teresa Stepzinski, "Ex-judge gets jail for child porn," *Florida Times-Union*, December 17, 2005, accessed July 15, 2017, http://jacksonville.com/tu-online/stories/121705/geo_20589347.shtml.

23. Terry, McConn, "Ex-Walla Walla judge, former minister sentenced in child porn case," *Tri-City Herald,* February 27, 2014, accessed July 15, 2017, http://www.tri-cityherald.com/news/local/crime/article32168667.html.

24. Larry Welborn, "Ex-judge Kline gets prison," *Orange County Register*, February 20, 2007, accessed July 15, 2017, http://www.ocregister.com/2007/02/20/ex-judge-kline-gets-prison and "Ronald C. Kline," 2001-2007, *Los Angeles Times*, accessed July 15, 2017, http://articles.latimes.com/keyword/ronald-c-kline.

25. Albert Lin, "Arkansas Judge's Shocking Racist, Sexist, Homophobic Comments," *Diversity Inc*, March 10, 2014, accessed July 15, 2017, http://www.diversityinc.com/news/arkansas-judges-shocking-racist-sexist-homophobic-comments.

26. Max Brantley and Benjamin Hardy, "Mike Maggio gets maximum 10-year sentence for taking bribe as judge," *Arkansas Times*, March 24, 2016, accessed July 15, 2017, https://www.arktimes.com/ArkansasBlog/archives/2016/03/24/maggio-sentencing-in-federal-court-today.

27. "Penis pump judge gets 4-year jail term," *USA Today*, August 18, 2006, accessed July 15, 2017, http://usatoday30.usatoday.com/news/nation/2006-08-18-judge-sentenced_x.htm.

28. Ryan White, "The Keepers," Netflix, May 2017, accessed July 15, 2017, https://www.netflix.com/title/80122179 and Joaquin Sapien and Sergio Hernandez, "Who Polices Prosecutors Who Abuse Their Authority? Usually Nobody," *ProPublica*, April 3, 2013, accessed July 15, 2017, https://www.propublica.org/article/who-polices-prosecutors-who-abuse-their-authority-usually-nobody.

29. The Editorial Board, "Rampant Prosecutorial Misconduct," *The New York Times*, January 4, 2014, accessed July 15, 2017, https://www.nytimes.com/2014/01/05/opinion/sunday/rampant-prosecutorial-misconduct.html?nl=todaysheadlines&emc=edit_th_20140105&_r=1.

30. Glenn Harlan Reynolds, "Our criminal justice system has become a crime," *USA Today*, March 19, 2014, accessed July 15, 2017, https://www.usatoday.com/story/opinion/2014/03/19/law-enforcement-clue-jury-criminal-column/6490641; and Radley Balko, "Exposing corrupt prosecutors," *The Washington Post*, January 9, 2014, accessed July 15, 2017, https://www.washingtonpost.com/news/opinions/wp/2014/01/09/exposing-corrupt-prosecutors.

31. United States Senate Senator Charles Grassley, "Justice Department Silent," 2011.

32. Jesse Eisinger, *The Chickenshit Club: Why the Justice Department Fails to Prosecute Executives*, (New York: Simon & Schuster, 2017).

33. "The Untouchables," *Frontline: Public Broadcasting Service (PBS)*, January 22, 2013, accessed July 15, 2017, http://www.pbs.org/wgbh/frontline/film/untouchables and Sarah Childress, "DOJ Criminal Chief Lanny Breuer Stepping Down," *Frontline: Public Broadcasting Service (PBS)*, January 23, 2013, accessed July 03, 2017, http://www.pbs.org/wgbh/frontline/article/report-doj-criminal-chief-lanny-breuer-stepping-down.

34. Matt Taibbi, *The Divide, American Injustice in the Age of the Wealth Gap*, (New York: Spiegel & Grau, 2014) and Eisinger, *The Chickenshit Club*, 2017.

35. "Former Baltimore prosecutor gets jail for child porn," *Maryland Daily Record, Daily Record Staff*, June 1, 2017, accessed July 15, 2017, http://thedailyrecord.com/2017/06/01/maryland-baltimore-patrick-michael-moran.

36. Department of Justice, "James Cameron Sentenced to 15 and 3/4 Years on Child Pornography and Contempt Charges," (District of Maine: The United States Government) December 17, 2014, accessed July 15, 2017, https://www.justice.gov/usao-me/pr/james-cameron-sentenced-15-and-34-years-child-pornography-and-contempt-charges.

37. Betty Adams, "Lawyers seek sentencing range in Maine child porn case," *Portland Press Herald*, August 30, 2013, accessed July 15, 2017, http://www.pressherald.com/news/lawyers-seek-sentencing-range-in-child-porn-case_2013-08-31.html

38. Betty Adams, "Ex-Maine prosecutor loses appeal of child pornography sentence," *Portland Press Herald*, August 23, 2016, accessed July 15, 2017, http://www.pressherald.com/2016/08/23/ex-maine-prosecutor-loses-appeal-of-sentence-on-child-pornography-charges.

39. Brendan Kirby, "No actual victim, judge rules in dismissing former Mobile prosecutor's enticement charges," *AL.com*, December 5, 2012, accessed July 15, 2017, http://blog.al.com/live/2012/12/no_actual_victim_judge_rules_i.html

40. Jonathan Turley, "Charges Dismissed Against Former Child Sex Crimes Prosecutor For Lack Of Actual Minor In FBI Sting," *Jonathan Turley Blog*, December 7, 2012, accessed July 15, 2017,

http://jonathanturley.org/2012/12/07/charges-dismissed-against-former-child-sex-crimes-prosecutor-for-lack-of-actual-minor-in-fbi-sting.

41. Robert Patrick, "Former prosecutor gets two years in child porn case," *St. Louis Post-Dispatch*, May 12, 2010, accessed July 15, 2017, http://www.stltoday.com/news/local/metro/former-prosecutor-gets-two-years-in-child-porn-case/article_e12fc278-c103-5b9f-ba5b-35c8b6a7bbb6.html.

42. Bob Mercer, "Accused of child sex and porn, Former state's attorney gives up his law license," *Black Hills Pioneer*, August 19, 2014, accessed July 15, 2017, http://www.bhpioneer.com/local_news/accused-of-child-sex-and-porn-former-state-s-attorney/article_7d38702c-27f0-11e4-98bd-0019bb2963f4.html and "Former prosecutor gets more prison time for child rape," *Huron Daily Tribune*, March 22, 2016, accessed July 15, 2017, http://www.michigansthumb.com/news/article/Former-prosecutor-gets-more-prison-time-for-child-7278423.php.

43. "Court: Calif. Lawyers Will Be Disbarred Over Child Porn" CBS Sacramento, January 23, 2014, accessed July 15, 2017, http://sacramento.cbslocal.com/2014/01/23/court-calif-lawyers-will-be-disbarred-over-child-porn

44. "Court: Calif. Lawyers Will Be Disbarred," 2014.

45. Abby Simons, "Disgraced attorney owes $15 million to teenager he raped," Star Tribune, May 25, 2011, accessed July 15, 2017, http://www.startribune.com/disgraced-attorney-owes-15-million-to-teenager-he-raped/122544694

46. Simons, "Disgraced attorney owes $15 million," 2011.

47. Justin Kendall, "Samuel Logan, disbarred JoCo lawyer, pleads guilty to trying to sex a teen girl over the Internet," *The Pitch*, May 26, 2011, accessed July 15, 2017, http://www.pitch.com/news/article/20574542/samuel-logan-disbarred-joco-lawyer-pleads-guilty-to-trying-to-sex-a-teen-girl-over-the-internet

48. Kendall, "Samuel Logan, disbarred," 2011.

49. Peter Hermann, "Crime Scenes: Neighbors angry at delay in child porn arrests," *The Baltimore Sun*, April 9, 2011, accessed July 15, 2017, http://articles.baltimoresun.com/2011-04-09/news/bs-md-hermann-porn-charges-20110406_1_patrick-joseph-redd-undercover-fbi-agent-rodgers-forge.

50. Martha Neil, "Former Attorney Takes Plea in Child Porn Case, Will Get 24 to 37 Months," *ABA Journal*, May 24, 2011, accessed July 15, 2017, http://www.abajournal.com/news/article/ex-attorney_takes_plea_in_child_porn_case_will_get_24_to_37_months

51. "Flynn Child Porn Trial Day 2," *Keloland Media Group*, December 15, 2010, accessed July 15, 2017, http://www.keloland.com/news/article/other/flynn-child-porn-trial-day-2-; "Sideras' attorney was previously acquitted on multiple child pornography charges," *ABC News KSFY*, May 25, 2017, accessed July 15, 2017, http://www.ksfy.com/content/news/Sideras-attorney-was-previously-acquitted-on-multiple-child-pornography-charges-424350754.html and "South Dakota lawyer acquitted of child porn charges," *Sioux City Journal*, December 18, 2010, accessed July 10, 2017, http://siouxcityjournal.com/news/state-and-regional/south-dakota/south-dakota-lawyer-acquitted-of-child-porn-charges/article_cfffefc2-0aaa-11e0-8773-001cc4c03286.html.

52. Joe Gyan Jr., "Baton Rouge lawyer says 'crude joke' led to child porn charges," *The Advocate*, September 15, 2016, accessed July 15, 2017, http://www.theadvocate.com/baton_rouge/news/courts/article_8aeeea4e-7b8a-11e6-958c-7b6d630f139e.html; Joe Gyan Jr., "More to story than Christopher Young allegedly distributing child porn, ex-Jefferson Parish president's brother argues," *The Advocate*, December 26, 2016, accessed July 15, 2017, http://www.theadvocate.com/baton_rouge/news/courts/article_43d6d082-c6d4-11e6-ab83-c35e57a66980.html and Department of Justice, "Baton Rouge Attorney Charged With Distribution And Possession Of Child

Pornography," (Middle District of Louisiana: United States Government) May 12, 2016, accessed July 15, 2017, https://www.justice.gov/usao-mdla/pr/baton-rouge-attorney-charged-distribution-and-possession-child-pornography.

53. Debra Cassens Weiss, "Ex-Arnold & Porter Lawyer Loses Law License After Child Porn Guilty Plea," *ABA Journal*, June 22, 2011, accessed July 15, 2017, http://www.abajournal.com/news/article/ex-arnold_porter_lawyer_loses_license_after_child_porn_guilty_plea.

54. Wiess, "Ex-Arnold & Porter Lawyer," 2011.

55. Teresa, Lo, "9 Lawyers Associated with Child Pornography," *JD Journal*, January 1, 2016, accessed July 15, 2017, http://www.jdjournal.com/2016/01/01/9-lawyers-associated-with-child-pornography.

Educators

Filename	Depiction
PTHC Ultra Hard Pedo Child Porn Pedofilia (New) 058 childfugga darkcollection kidzilla hussyfan lolitaguy childlover.1.jpg	Image of an adult male inserting his penis into a young female's vagina
SHX GAY BOYS PEDO YOUNG PRETEENS JUST TEEN KIDS 359.jpg	Image of a nude, young male masturbating while lying on a bed
Carl David Hyman Jr - KIDDIE PORN 701 - nude witch penis expose genitals gay black cock virgin little girls panties pedo 8yo sex preteen - persephone01@comcast,net(1).jpg	Image of a young female's vagina
Cp Tvg 13 Bond 10-11-12Yo Childlover Little Collection Video 0039 Girl - Vicky String Bikini Pthc 11Yo Pedofilia(1).mpg	Partial download of a video file of a young prepubescent female engaging in sex

SA Evans determined that the subscriber for IP address

68.204.195.254 was Clyde Fant in Deland, Florida. SA Lathrop verified the

– Clyde Fant's Plea Agreement. Fant was Dean of the Chapel and professor of Christian Studies at the Institute for Christian Ethics, Stetson University.

GOVERNMENT EMPLOYEES IN EDUCATION

In addition to government employees in our national security agencies, military, law enforcement and judiciary and prosecution offices, there is a problem with pedophiles in the educator sector. Most state and local level government employees, 48% and 55% respectively, work in the public education sector.[1] How many government employees in our public schools and universities have been arrested on child pornography related charges? No one knows because our government is not maintaining a public record.

As explained in the introduction of this book, my research on professors and staff went viral in mid-February of 2017. "Professors & Staff Arrested for Trading in Child Rape" received over 400,000 shares within weeks. I am not sure why this touched an emotional hot-spot for so many people but it did. In addition

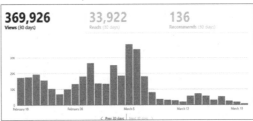

to shares, many people wrote expressing anger about the silence on this subject and gratitude for the work. This research clearly fills a gap that people recognize mainstream media and our nation's research institutes are neglecting.

Higher Education

Who holds government employees accountable, particularly when oversight seems to be failing? In a democracy, such as we are meant to have, citizens, journalists and intellectual leaders are supposed to hold government to account. Institutes of higher education were conceived to mentor the next generation of leaders and create knowledge on issues of importance to society. Intellectuals, primarily academics with tenured positions, are intended to be our nation's brain-trust; conducting difficult and controversial research that enables future generations to enjoy a better quality of life.

The child pornography epidemic in America today is a critical community and national security issue threatening the fabric of our society. As described throughout the book, our government is failing to gather data on this epidemic. Academic research centers, public policy institutes and investigative journalism programs are also failing to document America's trade in child rape. Detailed data is needed to implement public policies that will halt the crime. In the absence of good governance, America's intellectual leadership should be invested in making our democracy work to protect our most vulnerable citizens: our children. Yet, higher education institutions, where knowledge on critical social issues is generated, have been almost totally silent.

> **Action Item**
> Contact Secretary of Education,
> Betsy DeVos
> 🐦 @BetsyDeVosED
> Ask her to create a public database, maintained by the Department of Education, listing child pornography related arrests for all employees in public education.

Higher education may be failing on this issue due to the number of professors and staff themselves engaged in this crime. No one knows how many in higher education are participating in America's child pornography epidemic. Based on my research, it appears extensive. From University of Virginia's assistant dean, Michael Morris downloading the anal rape of infants, to Kirk Nesset, Allegheny College professor with over 500,000 videos/images including folders called "kidsfuck," far too many in higher education, both public and private, seem to be in involved. Every time an image or video of a child being raped is shared, that child is trafficked again. This kind of child trafficking is occurring on college and university campuses across America.

When pedophiles are in significant positions of power, as they appear to be in higher education, the ability to build a knowledge-base on the crime is hampered. If a university president claims to have a child pornography collection in his office that he masturbates to, would this president support efforts by his faculty to document the scope and damage of the crime? If a university dean is trading in a 6-year-old child sexually abused while held at knife point, would this dean support professors, under his supervision, to build a database on this crime? In both cases, not likely. Those engaged in the crime, most often white male campus leaders, are often in positions of power that allow them to create barriers and chilling environments for other academics who may attempt to document America's trade in child rape.

Over the past few years I have been monitoring reports of professors and staff, in the public and private sector, arrested on child pornography related charges. My research posted on Medium profiles nearly 100 cases and is far from comprehensive. Pedophiles often tell investigators that they have been trading in child rape and molesting children for years. Those who are arrested are frequently caught by chance rather than systematic monitoring of institutional networks. If higher education pro-actively scrutinized their electronic networks, many more arrests would occur. As with other professional categories the pattern appears to be consistent in the education sector – white men in leadership positions often trading in infant and toddler rape.

Some examples of recent arrests include:

Video #1:
File Name: Casey Abduction.avi
Description: a video file in the AVI format running for approximately 46 minutes. The video file depicts a prepubescent girl approximately 9-13 years old. The prepubescent girl enters a residence and takes off her coat. A subject dressed completely in black grabs the prepubescent girl from behind and holds a cloth over her mouth until she passes out. The prepubescent girl is then seen bound and tied. The subject forces the prepubescent girl to strip with a knife in hand and to suck on a dildo. The subject spanks the prepubescent girl with his hand and then with a whip. The subject inserts a dildo into the prepubescent girls vagina and anus. The subject then whips the prepubescent girl all over her body.

Christopher DeZutter's Criminal Complaint

- Christopher DeZutter, a chemistry professor at the University of Minnesota, was arrested in September 2016, for the second time on four new counts of child pornography possession. He was sentenced February 2016, to four years in jail. DeZutter was first arrested in February 2015, and charged with ten possession and one distribution child pornography counts. Despite the volume and type of child rape and torture, including infant rape, DeZutter was trading in, he was sentenced September 2015, to only 4 months in jail with five years of probation. He was free, for the first conviction, on conditional release, without monetary surety, until his sentencing.[2]

- Mark Ranzenberger, a 61-year-old professor of journalism at Central Michigan University (CMU), was arrested and charged May 2016, and pled guilty September 2016, to one federal count of child pornography possession and four (of which three were dropped in a plea deal) state counts of first-degree criminal sexual conduct for repeatedly raping a girl younger than 13 over a 7-year period. On January 19, 2017, Ranzenberger was sentenced in federal court to 14 years in prison followed by 5 years of supervised release. On January 26, 2017, he was sentenced to 14 to 45 years in prison in Michigan's Isabella County Court to be served concurrently with his federal sentencing. Ranzenberger was caught when he mistakenly showed child pornography to his students. A student reported the crime, triggering university police to open an investigation. At the time of his arrest, Ranzenberger was in possession of over 1,000 images/videos of child sex abuse, including the rape of infants. He also had a "grooming" document instructing pedophiles how to manipulate children from birth to age 11 "to participate in sexual acts." The girl whom Ranzenberger raped for years, testified at his sentencing calling him a "psychopath, monster." She said "He's smooth, charming, and manipulative. . . . He was able to hide the monster he was in every word he spoke. His coworkers and family didn't know he was a child molester." The victim described Ranzenberger as "a slug of man" and "a pathological liar."[3]

A video that depicted, in part, a prepubescent minor male, approximately 3-6 years old, performing oral sex on an adult male. The video then depicted the prepubescent minor male straddling the male's upper chest (F4, F12);

Justin Carroll's Indictment

• Justin Carroll, 67-year-old Associate Vice Chancellor for Student Affairs and interim athletic director at Washington University, was indicted January 30, 2017, on one federal charge of access with intent to view child pornography. Carroll had been using university computers to trade in child rape with the handle "MOperv." His twitter account was @WashUDeanoFun. Carroll was trading in the rape and torture of boys between three and six. He had videos of children as young as three years old forced to handle adult erect penises and subjected to anal rape. One video was called "boy-bending," a how-to guide for child sex abuse and grooming, "the art of remotely directing a boy on webcam, through typing text and displaying videos, to achieve a desired pose or behavior." Carroll submitted his resignation after his arrest. He had been at the university for 36 years.[4]

undercover downloaded and viewed was named "!NEW! (pthc) Nata-Cumshot.avi." This video depicts a prepubescent girl, approximately 10 years of age, performing oral sex on an adult male.

within his collection images depicting the anal penetration of an infant girl, a prepubescent minor girl engaged in oral copulation on an adult while held at knifepoint, a prepubescent minor girl bound, gagged, and locked in a dog cage, and a prepubescent girl and boy engaged in vaginal intercourse.

Michael Morris' Sentencing Memo

- Michael Morris, a 50-year-old Assistant Dean at University of Virginia (UVA) and father of two teenage daughters, was arrested and charged November 2013. Morris was an "ultimate" member of Gigatribe a peer-to-peer (P2P) program he used to trade pre-teen hard core (PTHC), the brutal torture of young children. His online name was "funshooter2006." At the time of his arrest he had over 4,000 images/videos of child sex abuse including of toddlers. Morris pled guilty in April 2014, and was sentenced in July 2014, to 8.8 years in federal jail and 20 years of supervised release. Morris also posed as a teenage boy or girl, and coerced children to perform sex acts for him live-streamed on web cameras. He had been trading in child sex rape and torture for 15 years. In the few months he was under investigation, Morris accessed over 192 times child rape videos/images from home and office computers. UVA suspended Morris pending investigation and he was later allowed to resign.[5]

PRIMARY AND SECONDARY EDUCATION

Unfortunately, educators engaged in the trade in child rape are not limited to higher education. Among public and private primary and secondary education there appear to be many involved in the crime. No one knows how many arrests and prosecutions have occurred because the U.S. government is failing to maintain a database. Dr. Charol Shakeshaft, the leading expert on sex abuse by educators, estimated in 2006, "the physical sexual abuse of students in schools is likely more than 100 times the abuse by priests."[6] A report by the Association of University Women, in 2000, estimated one in ten children are sexually abused by teachers and/or staff.[7] The Department of Education reported, in 2002, that six to ten percent of all public school students have been sexually abused by a teacher or staff.[8] A 2004 report, "Educator Sexual Misconduct: A Synthesis of Existing Literature," details a staggering number of teachers arrested for child sex abuse. In 2014 the U.S. Government Accountability Office (GAO) released a report detailing how public schools are failing to protect children from sex abuse by staff and teachers.[9] In 2016, *The Boston Globe's* Spotlight team released, "Private Schools, Painful Secrets," detailing sex abuse in New England's private schools.[10]

In 2016, *USA Today* released a year-long investigation into child sex abuse and child pornography among teachers. Journalists obtained and analyzed "millions of teachers' records from all 50 states, pored over documents in state buildings, schoolhouses and police stations."[11] In total *USA Today* compiled 10 million individual records. The resulting series of publications, including, "Teachers who sexually abuse students still find classroom jobs," details how teachers are often "let go from one school, with school administrators failing to report that teacher to law enforcement, and the teacher is employed around children, elsewhere, going on to harm more children and continue committing more crimes."[12] Similar to an attitude pervasive in higher education there is a widespread practice in primary and secondary schools that "the institution" should be protected not the children. Predators are provided "a graceful exit" and passed along to "become someone else's problem."

The comprehensive *USA Today* investigation documents how pedophiles are routinely protected in America's public schools. School administrators, who are government employees, cover up evidence of abuse, keep allegations secret and help pedophile teachers stay employed. Teachers flaunting red flag behavior are not reported to police; their computers and electronic devices are not searched for child pornography. Although child sex abuse and the production of child pornography are almost always synonymous, teachers caught sexually abusing children are not routinely investigated for child pornography. This hampers investigations and prosecutions, as critical electronic evidence of the child sex abuse is absent.

USA Today's investigation also describes how the federal ban, passed in December 2015, on secrecy deals, called "passing the trash," is routinely ignored. In secrecy deals sexual crimes and inappropriate behavior are hidden, teachers are given "hush money" and asked to quietly leave and find work in another school. In the rare cases when teachers are re-

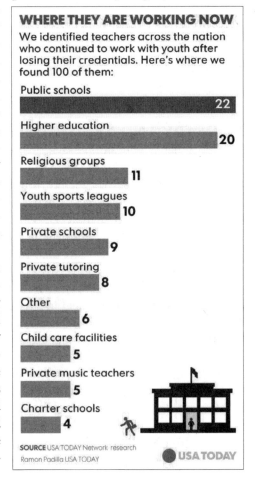

WHERE THEY ARE WORKING NOW

We identified teachers across the nation who continued to work with youth after losing their credentials. Here's where we found 100 of them:

Public schools
22

Higher education
20

Religious groups
11

Youth sports leagues
10

Private schools
9

Private tutoring
8

Other
6

Child care facilities
5

Private music teachers
5

Charter schools
4

SOURCE USA TODAY Network research
Ramon Padilla USA TODAY

USA TODAY

ported, and their teaching credentials revoked, many are still re-employed elsewhere. Similar to the national law enforcement decertification database, the National Association of State Directors of Teacher Education and Certification is voluntary and does not include information on why the teacher was decertified. In one case, a school in Louisiana hired a registered sex offender. The students discovered this through a simple online search.

Consistent with the pattern of pedophile arrests in America, many primary and secondary educators arrested are white men in leadership positions; principals, vice principals, school board members and union representatives. Type into a Google or Twitter search "principal" or "school board" and "child pornography" and see how many have been arrested. Both the number of arrests in policy-making positions as well as the type of child rape, very often infant and toddler, demands attention. A longer list of primary and secondary school educators arrested on child pornography related charges is located on my Medium account.

Some recent examples of principals, school board members and teachers' union representative arrests include:

- Donald Clippinger, a Vice Principal at Fienberg-Fisher K-8 Center in Miami, Florida, was arrested January 31, 2017. He pled guilty and was sentenced in July 2017, to nearly five years in jail followed by 25 years of supervised release. Clippinger was trading in pre-teen hard core (PTHC) the brutal rape and torture of very small children. Some of his files were called "diaz 2010-pthc baby raaamat 10.mp4," indicating baby-rape. His online name was "666prv." Prv is short for pervert, a term pedophiles, apparently proudly, call themselves. In pedophile chats he also called himself a "pedo," short for pedophile. Clippinger live-streamed video of himself masturbating to child rape. He had been trading in child rape for at least four years and was employed at Miami-Dade County Public Schools for 23 years.[13]

- James Uphoff, a 76-year-old Ohio Education Association Union President and Oakwood, Ohio School Board President, was arrested in August 2013. In October 2013, Uphoff pled guilty and was sentenced in September 2014, to 1.2 years in federal prison. He had been trading in child sex abuse for at least a decade. While on bail Uphoff was caught, again, with child pornography. No additional charges were brought. During his first arrest investigators found hundreds of images and videos including children in bondage. Uphoff was caught when he left child pornography on a university printer/copier which was discovered and reported to university police. This triggered a search of Uphoff's university computer. Uphoff had cultivated a reputation as a leading expert on early childhood education. He was a retired early childhood education professor from Wright State University and also volunteered for the Court Appointed Special Advocates (CASA) of Montgomery County Juvenile Court.[14]

• Timothy Dorway, a 44-year-old Principal at Chanhassen High School in Chanhassen, Minnesota, was arrested in December 2016, on 17 child pornography charges. Dorway had been trading in child rape from his work computer. He told investigators his "primary interest" is the sexual abuse of children aged 11-13 years old. He had been trading in child rape for at least the past decade. The school district terminated Dorway after his arrest.[15]

• Ricky Delano Sheppard, a 59-year-old Principal at Spessard Holland Elementary School in Florida, was arrested in June 2016. He pled guilty in August 2016, and was sentenced in December 2016, to 6.5 years in jail followed by ten years of supervised release. Investigators found more than a thousand images/video of child rape, including children being bound, in Sheppard's possession. Sheppard had been given a reprimand in 1999, when he was a teacher at Gemini Elementary School for "inappropriate professional behavior and poor judgment" related to his conduct with a 6-year-old boy in his classroom. He had been giving "excessive gifts" to the child and discussed "taking students home" with him. Sheppard was employed with Brevard Public Schools since 1981. He is now a registered sex offender.1[6]

• Phillip Heiney, a 67-year-old President of the Dunellen Board of Education in Middlesex County, New Jersey, was arrested in August 2016. Investigators seized more than one hundred pieces of computer equipment from Heiney's home. Heiney was trading in child rape that included an adult male raping a young girl who was blindfolded and bound with rope and a dog raping another bound child. As of July 2017, his case is still pending, with no current court date set.[17]

• Stephen Goodlett, a 36-year-old Principal at LaRue County High School in Kentucky, was arrested in October 2016, on 63 child pornography charges at the state level and two child pornography related counts at the federal level. Goodlett has been free, pending sentencing, on a $25,000 unsecured bond for the federal charges and $75,000 bond for the state charges. He is scheduled to enter a guilty plea in the federal charges and the State charges are set for trial on October 23, 2017. Goodlett would confiscate students' cell phones with the intention of obtaining nude photographs that he traded online. One 15-year-old student's nude photographs were on her cellphone which Goodlett confiscated. He uploaded these images to a Russia-based child pornography website. Goodlett's employment was terminated after his arrest. Goodlett is a married father of three children.[18]

• Warren Nelson Anderson, a 55-year-old principal at Sterling Education School's Pembina Campus (managed by the Plymouth Brethren Christian Church) in St. Vincent, Minnesota, was arrested in March 2017, and charged on ten child pornography related counts. At the time of his arrest he had over 3,000 images/videos of children as young as five being abused. He told investigators he had been trading in child rape for ten years. Anderson had previously worked at international schools in Albania and Pakistan and was a Boy Scout leader for 23 years. In 1987, he received a Congressional Award Gold Medal for his work with youth. Anderson is under electronic surveillance pending his next court date set for August 28, 2017.[19]

• Michael Scott Hatfield, a 58-year-old middle school teacher at American Preparatory Academy in West Valley City, Utah, was arrested in April 2017, on seven felony counts of sexual exploitation of a minor and three misdemeanor counts of accessing pornographic material on school property. Hatfield maintained his child pornography collection in his classroom and was masturbating to images of child rape in school.[20] He had pages of child pornography some of which he labeled "Carnal Cravings of the Cute and Cuddly." American Preparatory Academy terminated Hatfield upon his arrest.[21]

SPECIAL EDUCATION TEACHERS

The first image depicts a female child's anus and vagina. The child appears to be an infant based on her relative size and lack of body or pubic hair. There is an adult hand on the infant's right buttock and there is an adult erect penis penetrating the infant's anus.

The second image appears to have been made using night vision and depicts a nude male child lying on his back. The child appears to be of infant or toddler age based on his relative size, lack of body hair and undeveloped penis. There is an adult penis penetrating the child's anus.

The third image depicts a female child lying flat on her back. The child appears to be prepubescent based on her relative size and total lack of body or pubic hair. The child is not wearing pants and her shirt is pulled up to her chest, covering her breasts. There is an adult penis penetrating the child's vagina.

Jay Michaud's Criminal Complaint. Michaud was a special education teacher at Gaiser Middle School in Vancouver, Washington.

The movie *Spotlight*, about *The Boston Globe's* investigation of child rape in the Catholic Church, has been lauded for raising awareness about how pedophiles within influential institutions, like the Catholic Church, enjoy impunity for so long. Pedophiles are able to rape children for decades because many in the community protect the pedophile and not the children. Of all the complex issues related to child-trafficking rings and criminal conspiracies, *Spotlight* highlighted one of the most important. Pedophiles target vulnerable children. Vulnerable children make the perfect victim; offering easy access over many years and, often, total impunity. Pedophiles know few adults will choose to protect a child if that entails challenging a powerful predator. Pedophiles know that most people are cowards. They count on it.

The Catholic priests in Boston, as the film depicts, went after poor children, children who had lost their parents, children struggling with identity issues; children vulnerable in all the ways humans can be vulnerable. This is standard operating procedure for pedophiles. Child rapists are always on the hunt for defenseless children; pre-verbal children like newborns, infants and toddlers, foster children trapped in a broken system, sick children in cancer-wards, minority children, single-parent children in after-school programs and special-needs children. Those least able to protect themselves are the highest risk for rape. Pedophiles wait, watch and prey on the most vulnerable. Always.

Special-needs children, in particular, are easy and ideal prey for pedophiles. Why? Because special-needs children make terrible witnesses. A Down's Syndrome child is unlikely to be a witness that prosecutors consider "credible." No credible witness, no crime. No crime, no prosecution. When I started researching child pornography arrests I was horrified to see report after report of special education teachers and care-providers. Because the Department of Justice is not maintaining comprehensive statistics on child pornography arrests, no one knows how many special education teachers and caregivers have been arrested. There appear to be many.

Pedophiles are documented, as of 2016, to be strategically targeting special-needs children. The UN reported a key development in child sex trafficking networks is an increasing trend of adopting of "children with special needs" with the intention of trafficking these children. The UN reports "illicit practices in this context mostly concern cases of intercountry adoptions in which States prioritize the adoption of children because they do not have appropriate childcare policies. Moreover, there have been cases of false documentation being used to classify children as

Peter Flynn, a 61-year-old special education teacher at Bethesda-Chevy Chase High School in Maryland, was arrested in September 2014. He pled guilty and was sentenced in November 2015, to nearly four years in prison. Flynn had some 30,000 child rape images/videos including bondage and violence against young children. He had worked at Bethesda-Chevy Chase High School since 1978.

having "special needs" to render them adoptable abroad when such adoptions are prioritized or facilitated."[22]

A longer list of special education teachers arrested for this crime is located on my Medium profile. As with other professional categories profiled in this book, almost all of the special education teachers arrested have been white men. These arrests do not represent one-off cases of individual special education teachers. This crime is not about "sexual attraction" to certain children. As discussed, throughout this book, pedophiles are highly networked and strategize about child rape in teams online. They cultivate positions of power and access to children. They share the children they have access to. Special-needs children are being tactically pursued by pedophiles.

A few recent examples of arrests include:

> 13.   While continuing his forensic examination, CFA Chace found a short essay on McGlothlin's laptop computer in which McGlothlin graphically relives the sexual abuse of the infant depicted in the video described above.   McGlothin finishes the essay by expressing his desire to escalate the sexual abuse of the infant, observing, "[s]he is using more words so my window is closing fast."

James McGlothlin's Criminal Complain

- James McGlothlin, a 39-year-old physical education instructional assistant for disabled children with the Oregon City School District in Portland, Oregon, was arrested on February 19, 2016. As of July 2017, his trial was set for September 12, 2017. McGlothlin was trading images of child rape including infants and had raped a disable child in his care during swimming lessons. He made plans to baby-sit children with the intention of drugging and raping them and had photos of children who were relatives or children of friends, children's underwear and "sexually explicit videos of a baby girl and a man believed to be McGlothlin." He admitted he had already raped a friend's two-year-old daughter while baby-sitting the child. McGlothin was married and lived with his wife and their two-year-old son.[23]

- Bruce Omlor, a 49-year-old special education teacher with Riverside Elementary School in Toledo, Ohio, was indicted in December 2012, on one count each of child pornography receipt, distribution, and possession. In a plea agreement two charges were dismissed and Omlor was sentenced September 9, 2013, to more than six years in jail. At the time of his arrest he had more than 17,000 images of child sex abuse. He was suspended without pay and his Ohio teaching license has been revoked. Omlor is a retired Marine.[24]

• John David Yoder, 43-year-old special education teacher's assistant at Desert Hot Springs High School in Riverside, California, was convicted in February 2016, on ten felony counts and sentenced in May 2016, to 24 years in state prison. Yoder was part of a "significant ring of human traffickers and child pornographers" targeting young boys. Prosecutors said Yoder "provided a 'safe haven' for pedophiles." A registered foster parent, with two adopted sons, Yoder used his sons as bait to lure other children including at least one special-needs child. Yoder posted more than 10,000 times on a "boy lover" website where he was a member. He was held in lieu of $1 million bail. From jail Yoder attempted to have a witness murdered for $8,000. Prior to his arrest, Child Protective Services (CPS) had received a tip that Yoder was raping children and had child pornography. CPS took no action. Yoder previously worked as a special education assistant in Fairfax County, Virginia from 2005 to 2007.[25]

• Timothy Cheatwood, a 44-year-old, foster care worker in Oklahoma who cared for Christian special-needs children in Health and Human Services custody, was arrested in September 2015, on two counts of aggravated possession of child pornography, manufacturing child pornography, distributing child pornography and violating Oklahoma's Computer Crimes Act. Cheatwood's sentencing is currently scheduled for September 18, 2017. At least one local child victim was identified. One of the files in Cheatwood's possession was titled "7yo Blond Boy Play With Dady (with sound)." Cheatwood worked for the Bair Foundation, an organization contracted by Health and Human Services. His LinkedIn profile says he currently works for GDH Consulting.[26]

> hours between the dates of October 31, 2014, and March 2, 2015. Pewter viewed 187 different threads on "Website A" including threads with the titles, "10yo teen with anal front with his father", "2012, Lolita Cat Goddess 4, alicia 10 yo little girl loves adult sex (cum in mouth)", "7yo APRIL hj bj finger pencil in ass vib cum" and "Lauri ~8yo 3 videos, tasting cum". Most of the threads viewed by Pewter included links to view files and comments regarding child pornography. Pewter was observed accessing "Website

Jay Michaud's Criminal Complaint

• Jay Michaud, a 62-year-old special education teacher, at Gaiser Middle School in Vancouver, Washington, was arrested July 13, 2015, on child pornography charges. Michaud had been using a site called Playpen and trading in video/images of "child rape and some images that showed infants being raped." At his indictment hearing in January 2016, Michaud entered a not guilty plea and in March 2017, federal prosecutors were forced to drop charges after a judge ordered federal investigators must disclose the "network investigative technique" used in obtaining information on Michaud's trade in child rape. Michaud had worked for the Vancouver School District for more than 20 years.[27]

Michaud's case represents the importance of FBI investigators taking over websites, like Playpen, and gathering all the IP addresses of those trading in child rape. Judges across the country affirmed the federal search warrant was valid and sentenced many caught in Playpen. In May 2017, the creator and administrator of Playpen, Steven Chase, a 58-year-old man in Naples, Florida, was sentence to 30 years in prison followed by a lifetime of supervised release. The FBI's critical work obtaining all the IP addresses using Playpen, rather than only arresting the site owner, resulted, so far, in the arrests of 350 pedophiles in America and 548 international arrests.[28] If similar investigations were conducted on every child pornography website hosted in the US, we could shut down America's trade in child rape.

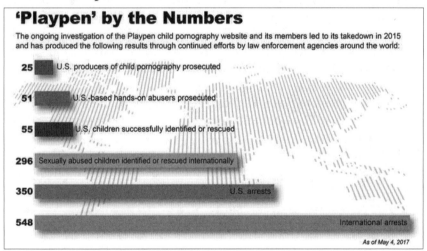

FBI Press Release on Playpen

That a judge protected Michaud, claiming the warrant was not valid, means a dangerous child predator has been set free. As described in Chapter Six of this book on the legal profession, too many judges are protecting pedophiles and, it appears, participating in the crime itself. The Michaud case is an example where law enforcement worked long, difficult hours to investigate and arrest a child predator only to have a judge provide impunity. Michaud is now free to become a special education teacher in another state. Perhaps, he will be arrested again, as so many pedophiles are, and will finally be held to justice for the crimes he has committed against children. How many lives may be destroyed before that might occur?

Day Cares and Pre-Schools

> A.   This image depicts a prepubescent naked female. The child is tied upside down to a chair that is sitting right-side up. She is bound at the hands and ankles to the chair. Her genitals are fully exposed.
>
> B.   This image depicts a prepubescent naked female, of about 8-9 years old, with an erect adult penis in her mouth. The child's face is covered in ejaculate.

Carl McBride's Criminal Complaint

Pedophile Magnets

Child pornography is an organized crime driven by a demand for images and videos of children being raped and tortured. Pedophiles require, to commit this crime, a secure and constant supply of children to abuse. Preschools and day cares are magnets for pedophiles. In some cases, day cares are established as a mechanism for unfettered access to children with the intention of producing and distributing child pornography. Infant and toddler rape is considered high-value in online pedophile networks. As discussed in previous chapters, children under four-years-old are targets because they do not make credible witnesses. Children under two-years-old are considered pre-verbal and, often, cannot explain what has happened to them. Day care and pre-school children are at real risk of being abused by teachers and caregivers, often without the parents ever knowing.

Longer lists of arrests are located on my Medium profile. These are, by no means, comprehensive. A few examples of recent arrests include:

> **(3) "2012 Rosemary 8yo sucks dad - SDC10676.avi"**— This video depicts a prepubescent, minor girl who is nude from the waist up and lying on her side. An adult male is standing in front of her; he inserts his erect penis in her mouth. While he continues to hold the head of his penis in the minor girl's mouth, he masturbates himself with his hand. The male then ejaculates on the minor girl's chest, face, and arm. This video is approximately 47 seconds in length. This video was distributed on the P2P network by the defendant on at least one occasion.
>
> **(4) "2012-05 Predator.AVI"**— This video appears to be two different videos spliced together. The video begins with a banner described as a black background with a white square. An animated picture of a girl with her head facing down and her hands over her nose and mouth appears within the white square. In large pink letters the word "PREDATOR" is written across the picture of the girl. The words "A predator edit" appears above the square and "torchat: ayjsfrpmcels6n6f" is written underneath. The video depicts a nude, minor girl who is blindfolded and performing oral sex on an adult male. The minor has been previously identified by law enforcement. The

David Moe's Plea Agreement

- David Moe, a 45-year-old pre-school teacher at Denver, Colorado's elite Paddington Station Preschool (annual tuition is

$12,000), was arrested July 24, 2012 for "one of the largest" child pornography collections in America. Moe pled guilty May 30, 2013, and was sentenced, September 2013, to eight years in prison. Investigators estimated he possessed six terabytes of child sex abuse files and had been trading in child rape for at least a decade. Just one, of more than 500 CDs, included 4,100 videos/images of child sex abuse including pre-teen hard core; the torture of small children. At the time of his arrest, he had some 800,000 images and 13,000 videos of child sex abuse. In 2001, parents reported their 3-year-old daughter, enrolled at the preschool, said that Moe had touched her vagina. No action was taken against Moe by the school, child protection or law enforcement. Moe had been a respected teacher at Paddington for 18 years.[29]

> D.   This movie is entitled "I ass fuck my stepdaughter." The movie depicts a prepubescent female, of about 6 years old, who is bound round the neck. An adult male bends the bound child over a table and anally sodomizes her.

Carl McBride's Criminal Complaint

• Carl McBride, a 48-year-old man who lived at a home-based day care, Little Tykes Day Care, in Claymont, Delaware was arrested on November 5, 2013, on child pornography charges. He pled guilty in September 2015, and was sentenced to ten years in jail followed by ten years of supervised release. McBride was distributing pre-teen hard core, child porn from the day care. Investigators "seized a laptop computer found next to a diaper-changing table in a room used for daycare services" and found "hundreds of images and movies of child pornography depicting prepubescent females engaged in sex acts. Young children were bound and violently assaulted.[30]

• Erik Dean Rabes, a 44-year-old Air Force Computer Security Specialist who had been assigned to the U.S. Strategic Command, a joint service unit that oversees the nation's nuclear arsenal, was sentenced to ten years in federal prison for child pornography production. Rabes' now former wife operated a home-based day care in Colorado Springs from December 1998 until December 2004. Unbeknownst to his ex-wife, Rabes was sexually abusing children, as young as 4-years-old, at the day care and filming and distributing the abuse. In September 2007, Rabes was also sentenced to an additional 34 years in state prison on related charges. Upon his arrest, Rabes had more than 30,000 child sex abuse images and/or videos. The military refused to confirm if Rabes had used military computers. Rabes had served in South Korea.[31]

In all, the videos show MANRING performing sex acts on at least five boys and two girls. In the scenes in which the children are running around naked, there are at least ten children participating. All of the children are approximately 5 years of age.

7 seconds MANRING is seen giving fellatio to an unresponsive pre-pubescent boy. At approximately 8 minutes and 50 seconds MANRING is

James Douglas Manring's Statement of Facts

- James Douglas Manring, a 54-year-old pre-school teacher from Fredericksburg, Virginia, was arrested November 13, 2012. He pled guilty on January 28, 2013, and was sentenced May 24, 2013, to 14 years in jail. His arrest was part of the U.S. Postal Inspection Service's Project Spade. Manring produced child pornography from 1996 to 1999, by sexually abusing the children in his care as a pre-school teacher at Remei Hoikuen School in Japan. Manring was caught when he returned from Japan with at least eight DVDs documenting the rape and sexual abuse of the pre-school children. In America Manring taught music lessons in his home and at local music stores and organized "a rock band geared toward offering extra encouragement to special-needs children."[32]

PROTECT THE INSTITUTION NOT THE CHILDREN

Both the volume and type of crime should raise alarm bells across educational institutions. Yet educators have remained, collectively, silent. Education communities, institutes and associations are not taking necessary preventative measures to stop child sex trafficking among their ranks. Instead, institutions with an arrest typically attempt to minimize media exposure rather than focus on protecting children and holding perpetrator accountable. This short-sighted response of "protect the institution" is collective denial that enables protection of criminals and not children – much like the ill-advised strategy the Catholic Church has adopted. Denial and inaction by America's educators to prevent this crime in our schools is turning educational institutions into organizations harboring criminals of the worst kind; those who prey on children.

While American consumers may purchase dolphin-safe tuna fish, we do not have the option of enrolling our children in certified child-pornography-free schools. Shouldn't we insist our schools become verified child-pornography-free institutions? Education organizations, from day cares to universities, could and should require all employees sign Codes of Conduct including consent agreements for monitoring work-based networks and electronics. As a matter of standard practice, child pornography blocking and reporting software should be installed. Law enforcement, like the Internet Crimes Against Children (ICAC) Task Forces, should be invited to search institutional networks, on a regular and random basis, for child pornography. Educational institutions could work with organizations like the Anti-Predator Project, Christopher Hadnagy of Social-Engineer.com, the Child Rescue Coalition or NetClean to certify their networks are child-pornography-free.

Pedophiles seek out professions that place them in positions of authority and trust over children. They cultivate leadership positions within institutions that allow them to perpetrate their crime and silence those who attempt to expose the crime and protect children. No pedophile should ever be employed at any institution of education and care for our children, let alone as a government employee at public schools. It is time parents, educational institutions and care-providers started taking pro-active measures to protect our children, particularly our most vulnerable.

This is possible.

We simply must demand these changes occur and protect our children.

Endnotes

1. Bureau of Labor Statistics, "Data Retrieval: Employment, Hours, and Earnings (CES)," (Washington DC: United States Government), accessed July 14, 2017, https://www.bls.gov/webapps/legacy/cesbtab1.htm and Terence Jeffrey, "21,995,000 to 12,329,000: Government Employees Outnumber Manufacturing Employees 1.8 to 1," CNS News, September 8, 2015, accessed July 14, 2017, http://www.cnsnews.com/news/article/terence-p-jeffrey/21955000-12329000-government-employees-outnumber-manufacturing.

2. Kim David, "UPDATED – UMR Professor Nabbed in Rochester Child Porn Bust; 7th Arrest," KROC AM 1340, February 6, 2015, accessed July 15, 2017, http://krocam.com/updated-umr-professor-nabbed-in-rochester-child-porn-bust-7th-arrest/ and "Former UMR Professor Sentenced to Prison for 2nd Child Porn Conviction," ABC News 6 KAALTV, March 3, 2017, accessed July 15, 2017, http://www.kaaltv.com/news/christopher-dezutter-child-pornography-sentencing/4415835/#.WLq39czEWTt.twitter.

3. John Hogan, "Former CMU faculty member arrested, charged with possession of child pornography," Central Michigan Life, May 20, 2016, accessed July 15, 2017, http://www.cm-life.com/article/2016/05/ranzenberger-arrested-for-child-pornography; Cole Waterman, "Victim calls CMU pedophile professor a psychopath, monster at sentencing," MLive, January 20, 2017, accessed July 15, 2017, http://www.mlive.com/news/bay-city/index.ssf/2017/01/victim_calls_cmu_pedophile_pro.html and Susan Field, "Mt. Pleasant child rapist gets 14 to 45 years in prison," The News Herald, January 26, 2017, accessed July 15, 2017, http://www.thenewsherald.com/news/mt-pleasant-child-rapist-gets-to-years-in-prison/article_ea666290-b3d0-5091-a255-15a33a84ffff.html.

4. Robert Patrick and Ashley Jost, "Washington University dean of students indicted on child pornography charge," St. Louis Post-Dispatch, January 30, 2017, accessed July 15, 2017, http://www.stltoday.com/news/local/crime-and-courts/washington-university-dean-of-students-indicted-on-child-pornography-charge/article_ff18ebf8-eed7-53a5-b698-b7fb-c7b427f3.html?utm_content=buffer24dd5&utm_medium=social&utm_source=facebook.com&utm_campaign=LEEDCC and "Washington University administrator faces federal

child porn charges," *Crime Watch Daily*, January 30, 2017, accessed July 15, 2017, https://crimewatchdaily.com/2017/01/30/washington-university-administrator-faces-federal-child-porn-charges/?utm_content=buffer90bb9&utm_medium=social&utm_source=twitter.com&utm_campaign=buffer.

5. Courteney Stuart, "Former UVA associate dean Michael Morris pleads guilty to child porn charges," C-Ville, April 22, 2014, accessed July 15, 2017, http://www.c-ville.com/former-uva-associate-dean-michael-morris-pleads-guilty-to-child-porn-charges and Department of Justice, "Former University of Virginia Dean Sentenced on Child Pornography Charges: Michael G. Morris Will Spend 106 Months in Prison," (Washington DC: United States Government) July 14, 2014, accessed July 15, 2017, https://www.justice.gov/opa/pr/former-university-virginia-dean-sentenced-child-pornography-charges.

6. Hillary Profita, "Has Media Ignored Sex Abuse In School?" CBS News, August 24, 2006, accessed July 15, 2017, http://www.cbsnews.com/news/has-media-ignored-sex-abuse-in-school.

7. Brian Palmer, "How Many Kids Are Sexually Abused by Their Teachers?" *Slate*, February 8, 2012, accessed July 15, 2017, www.slate.com/articles/news_and_politics/explainer/2012/02/is_sexual_abuse_in_schools_very_common_.html.

8. Profita, "Has Media Ignored," 2006.

9. Jane Meredith Adams, "Schools failing to protect students from sexual abuse by school personnel, federal report says," *Ed Source*, February 5, 2014, accessed July 15, 2017, https://edsource.org/2014/schools-failing-to-protect-students-from-sexual-abuse-by-school-personnel-federal-report-says/57023.

10. "Private Schools, Painful Secrets," *Boston Globe Spotlight Team*, 2016, accessed July 15, 2017, http://www.bostonglobe.com/metro/2016/05/06/private-schools-painful-secrets/OaRI9PF-pRnCTJxCzko5hkN/story.html.

11. Steve Reilly and John Kelly, "How USA TODAY audited the country's broken systems for tracking teacher discipline," *USA Today*, February 14, 2016, accessed July 15, 2017, https://www.usatoday.com/story/news/2016/02/14/how-usa-today-audited-countrys-broken-systems-tracking-teacher-discipline/80357584.

12. Reilly and Kelly, "How USA TODAY audited," 2016, and Steve Reilly, "Broken discipline tracking systems let teachers flee troubled pasts," *USA Today*, 2017, accessed July 15, 2917, https://www.usatoday.com/story/news/2016/02/14/broken-discipline-tracking-system-lets-teachers-with-misconduct-records-back-in-classroom/79999634 and Steve Reilly, "Teachers who sexually abuse students still find classroom jobs: Despite decades of scandals, America's schools still hide actions of dangerous educators," *USA Today*, 2017, accessed July 15, 2017, https://www.usatoday.com/story/news/2016/12/22/teachers-who-sexually-abuse-students-still-find-classroom-jobs/95346790.

13. David Neal, "Child-porn arrest of a Miami Beach educator started with a 'room' flagged in Arizona," *Miami Herald*, February 6, 2017, accessed July 15, 2017, http://www.miamiherald.com/news/local/crime/article130975354.html and Alex Harris, "Ex-Miami Beach assistant principal gets nearly 5 years in prison for child porn," *Miami Herald*, July 17, 2017, accessed July 24, 2017, http://www.miamiherald.com/news/local/crime/article161855528.html#storylink=cpy.

14. "James Uphoff sentenced in child porn case," WHIO News 7 Breaking News Staff, September 10, 2014, accessed July 15, 2017, http://www.whio.com/news/crime--law/james-uphoff-sentenced-child-porn-case/DqHVchXU2yWNaJW16MnWlM.

15. Haley Hansen, "Former Chanhassen High principal charged with 10 more counts of child porn," *Star Tribune*, March 30, 2017, accessed July 15, 2017, http://www.startribune.com/former-chanhassen-hs-principal-charged-with-10-additional-counts-child-pornography/417710633.

16. "Former Brevard County Principal, Ricky Sheppard To Plead Guilty To Child Porn Charges," *Space Coast Daily*, August 9, 2016, accessed July 15, 2017, http://spacecoastdaily.com/2016/08/former-brevard-county-principal-ricky-sheppard-to-plead-guilty-to-child-porn-charges.

17. Carlos Ramirez, "Dunellen Board Of Education President Arrested on Charges Of Child Pornography," *New Brunswick Today*, August 25, 2016, accessed July 15, 2017,http://newbrunswick-today.com/article/dunellen-board-education-president-arrested-charges-child-pornography.

18. Doug Ponder, "Child porn trial set for principal accused of taking students' phone photos," *LaRue County Herald-News*, March 29, 2017, accessed July 15, 2017, http://www.kentucky.com/news/state/article141450594.html.

19. Andrew Hazzard, "Former principal charged with child porn had many roles close to children," *Grand Forks Herald*, April 13, 2017, accessed July 15, 2017, http://www.grandforksherald.com/news/4250527-former-principal-charged-child-porn-had-many-roles-close-children.

20. Chris Harris, "Utah Teacher Allegedly Brought 'Meticulous' Child Porn Scrapbooks to His Middle School," *People Magazine*, May 2, 2017, accessed July 15, 2017, http://people.com/crime/utah-middle-school-teacher-kept-child-porn-scrapbooks.

21. Pat Reavy, "West Valley teacher had 'meticulous' child porn scrapbook in class, police say," *Desert News*, May 1, 2017, accessed July 15, 2017,http://www.deseretnews.com/article/865678980/West-Valley-teacher-had-meticulous-child-porn-scrapbook-in-class-police-say.html.

22. UN, "Report of the Special Rapporteur on the Sale of Children," 2015, 9.

23. Everton Bailey, "Child porn, written plans to abuse kids seized from Oregon City teaching aide's home, police say," *Oregon Live*, February 20, 2016, accessed July 22, 2017, http://www.oregonlive.com/oregon-city/index.ssf/2016/02/child_porn_written_plans_to_ab.html

24. Jennifer Feehan, "TPS teacher gets 75 months for child porn: Bruce Omlor had pled guilty in May to receiving the material on his home computer," *Toledo Blade*, September 9, 2013, accessed July 22, 2017, http://www.toledoblade.com/Courts/2013/09/09/TPS-teacher-gets-75-months-for-child-porn.html

25. Joseph Serna and Christine Mai-Duc, "Special education aide arrested in alleged Riverside child porn ring," *Los Angeles Times*, February 15, 2015, accessed July 22, 2017, http://www.latimes.com/local/lanow/la-me-ln-foster-care-provider-special-ed-teachers-aid-child-porn-ring-20150217-story.html

26. "Undercover sting results in child pornography arrest," September 3, 2015, accessed July 22, 2017, KRMG News 102.3, http://www.krmg.com/news/local/undercover-sting-results-child-pornography-arrest/aPCHWjk8mwBQJRDMwZVHpO

27. "Middle school special ed teacher allegedly caught with child pornography," *Q13 Fox News*, July 15, 2015, accessed July 22, 2017, http://q13fox.com/2015/07/15/middle-school-special-ed-teacher-caught-with-child-pornography

28. FBI, "'Playpen' Creator," 2017.

29. Alex Johnson, "Former Denver preschool teacher pleads guilty in horrifying child porn case," NBC News, May 30, 2013, accessed July 22, 2017, https://usnews.newsvine.com/_news/2013/05/30/18634877-former-denver-preschool-teacher-pleads-guilty-in-horrifying-child-porn-case?chromedomain=openchannel

30. Department of Justice, "Claymont Man Charged With Distributing Child Pornography From Residence Used For In-Home Daycare," (District of Delaware: U.S. Government), November 5, 2013, accessed July 22, 2017, https://www.justice.gov/usao-de/pr/claymont-man-charged-distributing-child-pornography-residence-used-home-daycare

31. "Strategic Air Command Computer Specialist Admits Child Porn: AF Sergeant Took Photos Of Himself, 4-Year-Old Girl," The *Denver Channel*, February 1, 2006, accessed July 22, 2017, http://www.thedenverchannel.com/news/strategic-air-command-computer-specialist-admits-child-porn

32. Pamela Gould, "Child porn convictions worry area parents," *Fredericksburg.com*, February 2, 2013, accessed July 22, 2017, http://www.fredericksburg.com/news/child-porn-convictions-worry-area-parents/article_de0b3104-96b5-5bd7-8f86-b6a31df554d4.html

8

The Way Forward

> • *Offender Communities.* In closed and highly protected online spaces, online communities dedicated to the sexual abuse of children have proliferated. Hand-picked members normalize each other's sexual interest in children and encourage each other to act on their deviant sexual interests.

U.S. Department of Justice's 2016
National Strategy for Child Exploitation Prevention and Interdiction[1]

TACKLING THE CRIME

As explained in the introduction, this book is the result of a difficult journey. One I did not wish to take but have been compelled to continue. The research has been painful. Reading criminal complaints often left me reeling with anger and anguish. The descriptions of what is being done to children seared my memory and caused jarring pain. This book is the beginning of documenting America's child pornography epidemic, demonstrating the need for comprehensive, demographic data on the crime. It is my hope a donor and an institution may provide support to make a national child pornography arrest database possible.

I struggle to forget what I now know. But there is no erase function to knowledge of this crime. Once you know, you cannot "unknow." I wish I could. I wish I knew nothing about how many seemingly "respectable" men are raping infants and toddlers and trading in this with enthusiasm, calling it "hot" and expressing pleasure and excitement at what can only be described as revolting evil. I cannot imagine how difficult it must be for investigators and prosecutors to view the videos and images and bear witness to the brutal torture and rape of so many children. Then, I think of the children. I cannot image how children are surviving the horror being inflicted upon them. I realize that so many children do *not* survive.

Interacting with this crime is incredibly destructive. The trauma from exposure to the malevolence is tremendous. There is no way to fight this crime, and defend our children, without it taking an indelible toll on the psyche and personal lives of those who dare to confront it. Most people are not prepared to battle this inexplicable evil. The few who are, cannot do it for long. Dedicated law enforcement officers and prosecutors, responsible for putting those who trade in child rape behind bars, often leave child exploitation units, requesting transfers to crimes psychologically easier to tackle, explaining they need to protect themselves and their own families. Investigators and prosecutors battling this crime need our support and gratitude. Without them there would be no arrests, no prosecutions and total impunity for pedophiles.

I would have preferred not to have known about this crime, but I was not given that choice. Like many mothers I was totally unaware of this epidemic and how many fathers are engaged in it until it touched my family. This research is dedicated to survivors of sexual abuse, America's children and the adults who love and protect them. I've written this book so children, and those who protect them, are verified. So

> Marine Sergeant, Jarod Barry, had hundreds of videos of children under twelve-years-old "being raped and strangled and bondage."

that pedophiles can no longer win in court claiming the child, or those defending the child, "made it up." This book documents the scope and severity of America's child rape crisis. It is real and it is destroying children, families and communities across America.

I am asking you, the reader and every American, to challenge what is happening to our children. Stop hiding because it is too painful. Stop being silent because you are afraid of what you might lose. What about America's children? What about your children? I hope people will read this book and act. Fund and create public policies needed to halt this crime. Get involved. Spread the word. End the silence that is destroying a generation of American children.

IMPROVED INVESTIGATIONS AND PROSECUTIONS

In the past decade, or so, since broadband Internet, public Wi-Fi and inexpensive smart-phones with cameras and video recorders all became widely available in America, the trade in child rape exploded. We were not prepared. Law enforcement and prosecutors were, for the most part, blind-sided. This epidemic exploded into an American criminal justice system that is broken, racist, sexist and favors the wealthy while preying on the poor. Since most pedophiles arrested in America appear to be white men in leadership positions, the weaknesses in our criminal justice system favor the pedophiles. While there are many noble prosecutors and investigators who have dedicated their lives to justice, they are extremely overworked and critically under-resourced. Pedophiles have better technical skills, more advanced electronic equipment and more expensive software. At every point, from the way our criminal justice system is organized, to the flaws in it, to the lack of substantial financial resources and staff to tackle this crime, pedophiles are in a vastly superior position to those seeking to protect our children.

The offense also defies the way our legal system is organized. Because child pornography explodes all over the world the instant the rape of a child is posted online, the criminality does not occur in a single physical location. The idea of boundaries, based on lines on a map, makes no sense when the server distributing child rape may be based in Australia – and thousands of IP addresses all over America are trading through that location. Unfortunately, law enforcement and prosecutors are still bound by traditional geo-political jurisdictions, although this is starting to change. To halt the global epidemic, child pornography cases demand creative investigative and legal solutions. For example, if the political will were generated, child pornography kingpins could be prosecuted by the International Criminal Court (ICC) in The Hague. The jurisdiction is the Internet. We must police and prosecute the Internet as if it were its own physical location.

Canadian investigators are doing some of the most innovative investigations by "going after companies that host the online files and profit from the data sharing."[2] In other words, Canadians are shutting down the servers hosting child rape. Journalist Bruce Campion-Smith details this new practice and quotes Deputy Commissioner Scott Tod, who says, "rather than the peer-to-peer, one-to-one, we now want to look at ... how do corporations actually profit and benefit from trading in child sexual exploitation.... This is the first investigation of the scale in my knowledge in North America, if not worldwide."[3] In this manner, Canadian investigators closed a file service owned by several web hosting companies and seized 1,250 terabytes of data. Terabytes. Estimated profits, in this one investigation, were $18 million in just three months. Of those trading in child rape through this one server, 2,200 IP addresses were located in the United States.

> Rocco Martino, a 43-year-old New Jersey doctor, pled guilty to receiving and distributing "sadistic and violent" videos and images of very young children being restrained and raped including one image of a toddler bound and gagged. Martino is graduate of Columbia and Princeton Universities; his medical residency was completed at Brown University.

Haven't American investigators, like the Canadians, been shutting down the servers? Surprisingly, no. As detailed in Chapter One, half of the world's servers hosting child pornography were, until 2016, located in the United States. Why are these servers allowed to proliferate? Why hasn't U.S. law enforcement shut them down? Rather than cutting off the trade in child rape at the source, standard operating procedure in American investigations has been trolling online venues, peer-to-peer (P2P) networks, posing as a pedophile and catching criminals one by one. Imagine throwing your hand into an Alaskan spring salmon run, mid-stream, and pulling out whatever you catch. Not a very effective strategy. So dense is the trade in child rape, the flow so rapid and the volume so large, pedophiles know chances of being caught are small so long as law enforcement continues this hand-fished method. America must change procedures. Our top priority should be shutting down servers that host, store and distribute child rape. The owners and all the users, every single IP address, must be prosecuted. The trade in child rape must be cut off at the source.

Additionally, child pornography investigations must become more focused on known supply-side sources to which pedophiles flock. Wherever there are children, particularly vulnerable children, pedophiles are in business. For example, the amount of arrests related to day cares, preschools, baby-sitters and special education teachers is significant enough for investigators to obtain search warrants to randomly search institutionally affiliated IP addresses. State licensing agencies should require a Code of Conduct and consent for random electronic searches as a component of granting a license to day cares and to all teachers. Likewise, all government employees, particularly those working in child protection units, should sign a Code of Conduct agreeing to random electronic searches of their work and personal electronic devises. This public policy change would allow law enforcement systematic monitoring without the need to obtain individual search warrants.

> Charles Church, a 41-year-old Marine veteran and Richmond, Virginia Police Officer who once received commendation for duty at Camp David, the presidential retreat, was sentenced, July 2017, to life in prison for the rape of a child. The young girl, "just tall enough to peer over the witness box," testified. She was raped and sodomized. Church's DNA was found in her Barbie underwear. Church told the girl if she told anyone "one of them would die."

Pedophiles who have infiltrated our government agencies know there is almost no institutional oversight. They are aware they can abuse their positions of power to commit this crime with little chance of getting caught. Pedophiles understand how, across the board, systems of monitoring and accountability in America are flimsy or non-existent from schools, to police departments to our most elite federal law enforcement agencies. Pedophiles realize a little bit of cash or the threat of a lawsuit can easily make people look the other way. Few have the courage to challenge those who trade in child rape, in part because most people find the crime so repulsive they either do not believe "that nice man" would "ever hurt a child" or they fear harm done to themselves or their children if they oppose the pedophile in public and demand justice.

Who do you call for help when you discover your police chief is trading in child rape? How do you leave your child at school after learning a popular kindergarten teacher has been raping children for decades and been quietly protected and passed along from one school to the next? What security do you have when you learn the FBI agent based in your town was raping a ten-year-old girl for years and will only spend six months in the county jail? How does the average citizen even begin to challenge a pedophile who happens to be a judge, prosecutor or police chief? Especially when so many of these pedophiles in powerful positions protect each other.

The answer is greater public awareness. Strength in numbers. Decent adults who care about protecting children vastly outnumber those who harm children. But we have become the silent majority. We must gather and make the data public. We must study, investigate and prosecute the crime. We must support and fund those willing to face this crime and dedicate their lives to researching, investigating and prosecuting individuals who trade in child rape.

We can win this war being waged against our children. To do so, we must generate a public revolution to protect our children and take back our communities, institutions and nation from those who trade in child rape.

We must stop being silent and afraid.

BETTER MEDIA COVERAGE OF THE EPIDEMIC

Greater public awareness depends on comprehensive reporting. In the introduction to this book, I explained how a grassroots movement, using the hashtag #PedoGate on Twitter, took my research viral. This happened, in part, because various media personalities were claiming people trying to expose America's child rape epidemic were producing "fake" news. To be dismissed with such callousness by journalists who are supposed to be asking the tough questions and exposing the corruption, felt like betrayal and made people angry. When activists discovered my research, they shared it widely saying things like, "this is not 'fake.' This is real. Look at all these arrests." My research validated America's child rape crisis, often committed by government employees, is real. It is not 'fake' news, as some journalists have claimed.

Journalists are meant to expose government employees who use the system to benefit themselves and fail to act in the public service. This kind of reporting provides awareness and leverage to citizens and intellectual leaders to advocate and demand accountability. These past years, as the trade in child rape exploded, journalism, as a profession, has been in a free-fall. Media outlets are struggling to survive. There is a sense of frustration, expressed by the American public, with mainstream media. More people are engaging in "citizen-journalism" believing professional journalism is worthless. Those who earn their living as journalists, by and large, are rejecting the idea that they have failed the public. Yet, circulation numbers and profit-loss tell a different story. At a time when journalists are searching for ways to have a meaningful and relevant impact on people's lives, the child pornography epidemic has been largely ignored.

There are a few journalists doing valuable reporting on this crime. Their work has been featured throughout this book. Steve Reilly and his team at USA Today have done ground-breaking reporting on child sex abuse in public schools. Richard Lardner and Eileen Sullivan of the Associated Press (AP) have done incredible reporting on child sex abuse within the military.[4] Likewise, Matt Sedensky and Nomaan Merchant, also with AP, published comprehensive reporting on sexual misconduct by law enforcement.[5] Levi Pulkkinen, with the *Seattle PI*, in Washington state, has been covering this crime in-depth for years now. His work is outstanding.[6] Lex Talamo, a young journalist with the *Shreveport Times* in Louisiana, just published an excellent series called The Sinister Web, examining various elements of the crime.[7] Aliya Sternstein, of *The Christian Science Monitor*, conducted an important investigation into child pornography on government computers.[8] Canadian journalist Julian Sher's work and his book, *Caught in the Web: Inside the Police Hunt to Rescue Children from Online Predators*, are essential reading.

We need more journalists better engaged, conducting more in-depth reporting of this epidemic. Crime-beat reporters in our communities should obtain and report on information in the criminal complaints when describing child pornography arrests. Reporting a man had 30,000 images and videos of child sex abuse is meaningless. Only pedophiles, and those investigating them, have any idea what that means. In contrast, reporting the university dean was masturbating to a child held in a dog cage being raped at knife point, or an Army prosecutor was raping infants who were bound and gagged, provides an understanding the American public needs to comprehend about what is happening to our children.

> c. "(Premature Sexual) 2yo pedo 1yo 3yo 4yo.mpg" – This video, approximately 2 minutes and 19 seconds in duration, displays an adult male attempting insert his penis into the vagina of a minor female. During the video, a male voice is heard stating "good baby" following the cry of the minor female. That cry was consistent with the cry of an infant. At the conclusion of the video, the male ejaculates on the minor female.

Andrew Cheever's Criminal Complaint

For example, consider Andrew Cheever's arrest. Journalists reported that a 33-year-old TSA agent in Boston was arrested on September 1, 2011, on child pornography charges and sentenced, in 2012, to nearly three-and-half-a-years in prison. Media reports said Cheever had more than 2,000 images/videos of child sex abuse. There were no links to his criminal complaint and no descriptions of what "child pornography"

Cheever was trading. A section from Cheever's criminal complaint is included above. "Premature Sexual 2yo pedo 1yo 3yo 4yo." Yo is short for year. 1, 2, 3 and 4 refers to the ages of the children being raped in the video. "Premature sexual," refers to infant and toddler rape. The video describes a man saying, "good baby" as he rapes an infant crying in pain.

Do you think the criminal complaint describing what this government employee was engaged in changes the story? I certainly do.

We need journalists to accurately report on this crime. The public needs to be aware of precisely what pedophiles are doing to our children. As detailed in Chapter Three, on infant and toddler rape, the public must understand how many men, and some women, are being arrested for trading in the rape of very small children. Journalists are, largely, failing to report the details and the context of America's trade in child rape. We depend upon journalists to provide accurate reporting of issues that affect our towns, communities and country. Without wide-spread public understanding of the videos and images pedophiles are producing and sharing, America has little hope of winning this war being waged against our children.

At the moment, pedophiles are far more informed about this crime than the public. This must change. Contact your local journalists. Ask them to report on the criminal complaints. Ask them to post links to the court documents in their stories so the public may learn exactly what the man in the local community "no one could ever believe would hurt a child" was doing; the kinds of crimes he was committing against our children all too often on government computers. Ask journalists in your town to fully report on all child pornography arrests so Americans can begin to understand, and fight against, what pedophiles are doing to our children and our country.

UNMASKING AND DOCUMENTING

Before this crime destroyed my life and the lives of those I love, I never thought I would struggle to recognize evil. The problem, I've since learned, is that evil does not present itself as vile but rather as "the nice guy, who adores children." I never thought it would be difficult to differentiate good from evil. Pedophiles caused me, and I suspect many others, to lose that certainty. The security that middle and upper-middle class white Americans believe, as if it were our birth-right, that our world is okay. Our children are safe. We are good people. If we wish each other "to have a nice day" it will really be a nice day. Bad things don't happen to good people and other such naïve myths the white, privileged American psyche has been built upon. The American epidemic of trading in child rape, blows all these false narratives apart.

This book is about unmasking the evil. Showing that nice, white professor who married the poor single mother with two small children, is actually malevolence embodied as he rapes his own six-year-old step-daughter, unbeknownst to her mother – his wife, and shares this rape online to gain increased status among pedophiles. This is what evil looks like. The pedophile grooms the parents first, even his own wife or adult children, to gain access to the child or grandchild. Grooming is about gaining trust so children are left with the pedophile. Acting evil does not obtain children. Acting like the kindest man dedicated to children obtains unfettered access to children.

> Earl Bradley a pediatrician in Pennsylvania and Delaware who "specialized in welfare patient," was allowed to become one of the "nation's most prolific" child rapist. For 15 years those, often mothers, who reported he was raping children were called "not credible." Bradley raped at least 1,200 children, average age three-years old with the youngest three-months, and recorded his crimes on video. His rapes were so violent he sometimes "had to resuscitate" the children. Bradley was finally arrested in 2009 and sentenced, in 2011, to life in prison.

Ask yourself, are you being groomed? Question, most particularly, male relatives or friends who exhibit concerning behavior in the form of extreme and inappropriate generosity towards your children. Any man who wants to spend an inordinate amount of time with your children should be watched closely.

Protect your children.

The material reviewed in this book provides an introduction to a critically needed, and largely absent, American research agenda. So much has not been included. The medical and mental health profession, the sports world, non-profit charities, international humanitarian sector, corporate America, religious communities, among others, have not been touched upon. In these sectors there have also been many arrests. I focused my research primarily on government employees because these pedophiles are in the most powerful position to undermine our national and personal security and our democracy and rule of law. They are also in the best position to commit and cover up their crimes.

In the areas I examined, military, law enforcement, the legal profession and educators, I have only been able to provide a dip-analysis much like law enforcement are forced to perform on the overwhelming data. I am a data-nerd. I would like to be able to say that I have reviewed every arrest record from the past ten years and provide detailed statistics about all these arrests. I would like to be able to conduct a series of analyses on all the data of all the child pornography arrests in America. Unfortunately, without the funding to build a comprehensive child pornography arrest database, I have only been able to provide an overview lacking in the kind of extensive quantitative data that is needed. What is important about the qualitative data I have gathered and reviewed, is that it is consistent with the few other studies on child pornography trends. White men in leadership positions, often fathers, frequently involved in infant and toddler rape – this appears to be the average pedophile profile.

I have attempted to demonstrate that is there is a child pornography epidemic in America and an urgent need to document this crime through credible social science research conducted by academics with institutional support and funding so that a national database can be built. The data must be gathered and made public so that we can create better laws and public policy to halt this crime. We must mandate that oversight and accountability, including random electronic monitoring, be built into employment sectors where people have access to children. In order to obtain that mandate, we need to document, for example, how many special educations teachers have been arrested allowing the argument to be made, with

> David Turkos, a 44-year-old police officer in Dupont, Pennsylvania, pled guilty, July 2017, to raping two boys, aged 4 and 6, over a seven-year period. Turkos zip-tied the children to a railing as he raped them, pointed his gun at the children, sometimes while on duty, and said he would harm their pets and their mother if they told anyone what he was doing to them.

solid data, that signed code of conduct consent agreements for random electronic monitoring of cell phone and computer networks should be a standard part of the hiring package and a requirement for state licensing.

We need the data so we can demand that the White House hold their executive branch employees accountable. Not one government employee, ever, should be trading in child rape from government computers. We have the technical ability to prevent this. Now we need the political will. The political will depends on evidence-based data demonstrating that this is, undisputedly, a critical national security issue. Data that explains why action must be taken now, at the very highest levels of our government, to address this issue and stop pedophiles from infiltrating our government. Right now, pedophiles are winning. They know our system of governance is weak and they are exploiting all of America's vulnerabilities in order to facilitate their crimes. This comes at the cost of tremendous pain and destruction of thousands of America's children and their families as well as our national and community-level security.

REFUSE TO BE SILENT

If all of this sounds depressing, it is. But there is hope. One area of optimism is the Internet – the same vehicle that has allowed child pornography to expand beyond anything conceivable pre-Internet. It is also the tool anti-child abuse activists are using to demand an end to the cover-up of the crime. Twitter, for example, is filled with anti-child abuse activists: dedicated people in Australia, the United Kingdom, Ireland, the Netherlands, Canada and across America. Just as pedophiles network and information-share, so does the growing, global community of anti-child abuse activists. This community knows and supports each other, shares news articles, court transcripts, strategies for holding pedophiles accountable and moral outrage for the global child pornography crisis. That's the good news.

There is hope.

If you find all the research in this book difficult to believe, I don't blame you. I was in shock and denial for a long time. Read the articles I reference. Don't believe me. Check it out for yourself. Start to see the scope of the crisis. Notice how many times another trusted member in your community is arrested. Connect the dots. Start to see the pattern. Do a search for child pornography arrests. Observe how many arrests there are every week. Yet another police officer, teacher, coach, youth church leader, professor or lawyer? Be a volunteer researcher and help build the database. Document the crime and end the silence.

> Meinrad Kopp, a 55-year-old tourist from Germany, was arrested July 16, 2017, when he traveled to Orlando, Florida to have sex with a 13-year-old child – in reality an undercover detective posing as a father offering his daughter for sex. Kopp told the "father" he wanted "to treat the girl like a dog, humiliate her and cause her pain." He bragged of raping other children, including an 11-year-old girl he said he "beat with the help of her father." Kopp said beating children is "fun, fantastic" and "better than sex."

You can do something.

Get online. Get involved. Organize and hold public meetings in your community. Demand servers distributing child pornography be shut down. Contact your local court house. Get the criminal complaints of the child pornography arrests in your community. Learn what these pedophiles are doing. Contact local journalists and ask them to report on the information in the criminal complaints. Ask your local media to cover anti-child sex abuse meetings that you organize and host. Contact the Internet Crimes Against Children (ICAC) Taskforce and ask them to provide a presentation of their work. Ask how you can support their work.

Spread the word. Get involved.

Take our country back. Protect our children.

Pedophiles count on our silence.

Refuse to be silent.

(Endnotes)

1. Department of Justice, "The National Strategy 2016," 9.

2. Bruce Campion-Smith, "OPP probe targets firms that host child porn images: In change of tactics, an ambitious OPP probe goes after companies that host the online files and profit from the data sharing," *The Star*, April 19, 2015, accessed July 14, 2017, https://www.thestar.com/news/queenspark/2015/02/19/opp-probe-targets-firms-that-host-child-porn-images.html.

3. Campion-Smith, "OPP probe targets."

4. Lardner and Sullivan, "Opaque military justice system," 2015.

5. "A look inside AP's investigation," 2015 and "Hundreds of officers lose licenses," 2015.

6. Levi Pulkkinen's Twitter account is @levipulk. Please also see: "About SeattlePI," Settle PI, accessed July 14, 2017, http://www.seattlepi.com/facts.

7. "Sinister Web Series," The Shreveport Times, 2017, accessed July 14, 2017, http://www.shreveporttimes.com/series/sinisterweb.

8. Sternstein, "Child porn on government devices," 2016.

###

Bibliography

ABC News 6 KAALTV. "Former UMR Professor Sentenced to Prison for 2nd Child Porn Conviction." March 3, 2017.

ABC News 6 WPVI-TV. "Former Berks Co. police chief faces child porn charges." December 12, 2013.

ABC News 7 WXYZ. "Feds say former Child Protective Services employee purchased nearly $7K in child porn." July 2, 2013.

ABC News KSFY. "Sideras' attorney was previously acquitted on multiple child pornography charges." May 25, 2017.

ABC News. "Investigators: Berkeley County man asked for pics of infant rape." December 20, 2012.

Adams, Betty. "Ex-Maine prosecutor loses appeal of child pornography sentence." *Portland Press Herald*, August 23, 2016.

Adams, Betty. "Lawyers seek sentencing range in Maine child porn case." *Portland Press Herald*, August 30, 2013.

Akdeniz, Yaman. *Internet Child Pornography and the Law.* New York, Routledge, 2008.

Altamura, Alessia. "Understanding demand for CSEC and the related gender dimensions: A review of the research." *ECPAT Journal Series,* No. 7: 2013.

Altimari, Dave. "Former Granby Police Captain Pleads Guilty to Child Pornography Charges." *The Hartford Courant,* July 21, 2011.

Andrews, Travis. "Your weekend watch: 'Call Me Lucky,' a difficult profile of comedian and crusader against child abuse, Barry Crimmins." *Washington Post,* February 10, 2017.

Anti-Slavery Australia. Interpol Chart International Child Sexual Exploitation (ICSE) image database. *Behind the Screen: On-Line Child Exploitation in Australia.* Broadway: Anti-Slavery Australia, 2017.

Army Times. "Army releases verdicts of March courts-martial." May 12, 2017.

Associated Press (AP). "A look inside AP's investigation on officer sex misconduct." November 1, 2015.

Associated Press (AP). "Hundreds of officers lose licenses over sex misconduct." November 1, 2015.

Baer, Merritt. "Two-Thirds of Military Supreme Court Cases Are About Child Pornography." Talking Points Memo, December 3, 2013.

Bailey, Everton. "Child porn, written plans to abuse kids seized from Oregon City teaching aide's home, police say." *Oregon Live,* February 20, 2016.

Baldwin, James. *Going to Meet the Man.* New York: Vintage International, 1995.

Balko, Radley. "Exposing corrupt prosecutors." *The Washington Post,* January 9, 2014.

Barakat, Matthew. "Ex-US diplomat gets 20 years for child porn." *USA Today,* August 22, 2008.

Barrett, David. "Child sex abuse: 'Police guarded paedophile ring', claims victim: Esther Baker, 32, waives right to anonymity to highlight alleged sexual abuse by prominent figures and police in the Eighties and Nineties." *The Telegraph,* May 26, 2015.

Bay City News. "Former USF dean sentenced for child porn." March 28, 2007.

Becker, Andrew. "Homeland Security Office to Unload Hundreds of Corruption Probes." *Huffington Post,* July 7, 2012.

Beckhusen, Robert. "Child Porn, Coke Smuggling: Hundreds of DHS Employees Arrested Last Year." *Wired Magazine,* August 22, 2012.

Bender, Bryan. "Pentagon lagged on pursuing porn cases." *Boston Globe,* January 5, 2011.

Berger, Joseph. "Ex-Police Chief in Westchester County Pleads Guilty to Child Pornography Charge." *New York Times,* July 27, 2015.

Bialik, Carl. "Measuring the Child Porn Trade." *Wall Street Journal,* April 18, 2006.

Bird, Bill. "EPA employee from Naperville charged in child porn case." *Chicago Tribune,* June 9, 2016.

Bogardus, Kevin. "Committee passes anti-porn bill." *E&E News,* March 9, 2017.

Boston Globe, Spotlight Team. "Private Schools, Painful Secrets." 2016.

Box, Dan. "Abuse whistleblower Peter Fox admits secretly contacting journalist in wife's name." *The Australian,* January 17, 2014.

Brantley, Max and Benjamin Hardy, "Mike Maggio gets maximum 10-year sentence for taking bribe as judge." *Arkansas Times,* March 24, 2016.

British Broadcasting Corporation (BBC). "North Wales child abuse scandal: The road to Macur." March 17, 2016.

British Broadcasting Corporation (BBC). "Online pornography to be blocked by default, PM announces." July 22, 2013.

British Broadcasting Corporations (BBC). "Human trafficking: FBI warns of 'epidemic,." 28 July 2015.

Bronskill, Jim. "Canadian police unable to keep up with child porn 'epidemic': memo." *Globe and Mail,* July,4, 2016.

Bronskill, Jim. "Ralph Goodale warned more resources needed to fight online child exploitation: Briefing notes say online child pornography a growing challenge for justice agencies." Canadian Broadcasting Corporation (CBC), July 4, 2016.

Bryant, Nick. *The Franklin Scandal: A Story of Powerbrokers, Child Abuse & Betrayal.* Oregon: Trine Day, 2009.

Bureau of Justice Statistics (BJS). E-mail message to author, May 15, 2017.

Bureau of Labor Statistics. "Data Retrieval: Employment, Hours, and Earnings (CES)." Washington DC: United States Government.

Burke, Jason and Amelia Gentleman, and Philip Willan, "British link to 'snuff' videos." *The Guardian,* September 30, 2000.

Burrows, Thomas. "Former child sex slave sold into Belgian aristocratic paedophile ring where boys and girls were tortured and killed reveals the horrors of her five years of abuse." *Daily Mail,* January 19, 2017.

Byrne Hessick, Carissa. Ed., *Refining Child Pornography Law: Crime, Language, and Social Consequences*. Michigan: University of Michigan Press, 2016.

Byrne, Ciara. *"How Video Forensics Are Changing the Way Cops Find Criminals." Fast Company, June 28, 2013.*

Cable News Network (CNN). "South Florida ICE official arrested on child porn charges." September 29, 2011.

Campbell, Andy. "Arkansas Judge Accused of Trading Sentence Reductions for Sex." *Huffington Post*, November 18, 2015.

Campion-Smith, Bruce. "OPP probe targets firms that host child porn images: In change of tactics, an ambitious OPP probe goes after companies that host the online files and profit from the data sharing." *The Star*, April 19, 2015.

Canadian Centre for Child Protection. "Canadian Centre for Child Protection's survey speaks to damaging impacts of the sharing of child sexual abuse material." January 17, 2017.

Canadian Television (CTV). "Can the IRS Prevent Child Porn?" September 21, 2012.

Capaccio, Tony. "Missile Defense Staff Warned to Stop Surfing Porn Sites." Bloomberg News, August 2, 2012.

Carey, Julie. "Search Warrants in Case of State Dept. Official Charged with Soliciting Minor." NBC News 4 Washington, March 2, 2015.

Carter, Zach. "A Pointless Anti-Porn Rider Is Congress' Latest Obsession." *Huffington Post*, September 9, 2014.

Casiano, Louis. "Former Marine sergeant from Spring sentenced for child porn." *Houston Chronicle,* March 19, 2012.

Cassens Weiss, Debra. "Ex-Arnold & Porter Lawyer Loses Law License After Child Porn Guilty Plea." *ABA Journal,* June 22, 2011.

CBS News Connecticut. "Ex-Granby Police Captain Gets 10-year Child Porn Sentence." *February 10, 2012.*

CBS News Crimesider Staff. "Army colonel sentenced to 12 years in child pornography case." December 28, 2016.

CBS News Crimesider Staff. "International child-porn network busted, aided by clue of toy bunny, say feds." August 6, 2012.

CBS News. "Donald Sachtleben, former FBI agent, arrested on child pornography charges." May 15, 2012.

CBS Philly. "Former Police Chief in Berks County Pleads Guilty To Child Porn." April 8, 2014.

CBS Sacramento. "Court: Calif. Lawyers Will Be Disbarred Over Child Porn." January 23, 2014.

Central Michigan Life. "Ranzenberger admits sexual abuse of minor, pleads guilty to child porn possession." September 27, 2017.

Chappell, Bill. "Arizona Radio Station Stops Airing Advice on Hiding Child Pornography." National Public Radio (NPR), May 11, 2017.

Chen, Stephanie. "Pennsylvania rocked by 'jailing kids for cash' scandal." Cable News Network (CNN), February 24, 2009.

Child Exploitation and Online Protection Centre (CEOP). "Threat Assessment of Child Sexual Exploitation and Abuse," June 2013.

Child Exploitation and Online Protection Centre (CEOP). *A Picture of Abuse: A Thematic Assessment of the Risk of Contact Child Sex Abuse Posed by Those Who Possess Indecent Images of Children.* United Kingdom, June 2012.

Childress, Sarah. "DOJ Criminal Chief Lanny Breuer Stepping Down." *Frontline*: Public Broadcasting Service (PBS), January 23, 2013.

Clarke, Liam. "Richard Kerr: I was trafficked from Kincora boys home to be abused by a ring of VIPs in London." *Belfast Telegraph*, April 7, 2015.

Clark-Flory, Tracy. "Meet Pedophiles who mean well." *Salon*, July 1, 2012.

Cleary, Tom. "Michael Harding: 5 Fast Facts You Need to Know." Heavy.com, May 24, 2016.

Cloud, David. "Child abuse in the military: Failing those most in need." *Los Angeles Times*, December 29, 2016.

Connor, Terry. "Former West Point Cadet Ricky Hester Gets 8 Years for Child Porn." NBC News, January 6, 2016.

Connor, Tracy. "Judge Gives Man 5 Days for Child Porn, Rails Against Harsh Sentences." NBC News, February 1, 2016.

Crib, Robert. "Chilling evidence of organized child sex abuse revealed in survey." *The Star*, January 17, 2017.

Crime Watch Daily. "Washington University administrator faces federal child porn charges." January 30, 2017.

Davis O'Brien, Rebecca. "Former Police Officer Accused of Cannibal Plot Goes Free." *Wall Street Journal*, November 12, 2014.

Davis, Julie. "Department of Homeland Security's untouchables: shielded by the badge." *The Examiner*, September 2, 2012.

Davis, Julie. National Security Expert, comment in response to question from author about Homeland Security employees arrested for misconduct, "Just the way #**DHS** protects itself from infamy. Often *news of convictions* appear, then disappear. Very tricky." March 6, 2014.

DeCamp, John. *The Franklin Cover-up: Child Abuse, Satanism, and Murder in Nebraska.* AWT, Inc., 1992.

Delmonico David and Elizabeth Griffin. *Illegal Images: Critical Issues and Strategies for Addressing Child Pornography Use.* NEARI Press, 2013.

Denver Channel, The. "Strategic Air Command Computer Specialist Admits Child Porn: AF Sergeant Took Photos of Himself, 4-Year-Old Girl." February 1, 2006.

Department of Justice. *David O'Brien Plea Agreement.* Case 6:13-cr-00194-RBD-GJK Document 59. United States District Court Middle District of Florida Orlando Division: United States Government, May 30, 2014.

Department of Justice. "Baton Rouge Attorney Charged with Distribution and Possession of Child Pornography." Middle District of Louisiana: United States Government, May 12, 2016.

Department of Justice. "Federal Grand Jury Indicts Jefferson County and Marshall County Men in Separate Child Pornography Cases." Northern District of Alabama: United States Government, September 29, 2016.

Department of Justice. "James Cameron Sentenced to 15 and 3/4 Years on Child Pornography and Contempt Charges." District of Maine: The United States Government, December 17, 2014.

Department of Justice. "Air Force NCO Indicted for Sexually Exploiting Toddlers and Children to Produce Child Pornography." United States Government, September 12, 2013.

Department of Justice. "Claymont Man Charged with Distributing Child Pornography from Residence Used for In-Home Daycare." District of Delaware: US Government, November 5, 2013.

Department of Justice. "FBI Employee Sentenced 46 Months for Possessing Child Pornography." Eastern District of Virginia: United States Government, August 27, 2010.

Department of Justice. "Former Acting HHS Cyber Security Director Sentenced to 25 Years in Prison for Engaging in Child Pornography Enterprise." Washington DC: United States Government, January 5, 2015.

Department of Justice. "Former DEA Agent Pleads Guilty to Child Pornography Charges." Southern District of Texas: United States Government, June 2, 2016.

Department of Justice. "Former High School Teacher Pleads Guilty to Possessing Child Pornography." United States Government, June 29, 2015.

Department of Justice. "Former U.S. Army Corps of Engineers Employee Sentenced to 30 Years in Prison for Transportation and Possession of Child Pornography." Washington DC: United States Government, April 14, 2016.

Department of Justice. "Former University of Virginia Dean Sentenced on Child Pornography Charges: Michael G. Morris Will Spend 106 Months in Prison." Washington DC: United States Government, July 14, 2014.

Department of Justice. "U.S. Postal Employee Charged with Viewing Child Pornography on Work Computers." District of Massachusetts: United States Government, September 22, 2016.

Department of Justice. "West Point Cadet Convicted in White Plains Federal Court Of Distributing, Receiving, And Possessing Child Pornography." Southern District of New York: United States Government, June 23, 2015.

Department of Justice. *Brian Fanelli Criminal Complaint* 14MJ145. US District Court. Southern District of New York: United States Government, January 23, 2014.

Department of Justice. *Carl McBride Criminal Complaint* Case No. 13-195M,. US District Court for the District of Delaware. United States Government, November 5, 2013.

Department of Justice. *Christopher Craft Criminal Complaint* Case 1:16-cr-00047-TSE No. 1:16-CR-47 Document 9. US District Court Eastern District of Virginia. Alexandria Division: United States Government, April 21, 2016.

Department of Justice. *Christopher Jansen Criminal Complaint Case* 3:14-cr-30089-RAL Document 59. US District Court of South Dakota Central Division: United States Government, November 4, 2015.

Department of Justice. *Christopher McKee Criminal Complaint Case* 3:13-cr-00039-REP Document 16. US District Court. Eastern District of Virginia. Richmond Division: United States Government, March 30, 2013.

Department of Justice. *Clyde Fant Plea Agreement* Case 6:13-cr-00055-RBD-KRS Document 4. US District Court Middle District of Florida Orlando Division. United States Government, April 19, 2013.

Department of Justice. *David Moe Plea Agreement* Criminal Action No. 12-cr-00363-WJM. US District Court for the District of Colorado. United States Government, May 23, 2013.

Department of Justice. E-mail message to author in response to FOIA No. 15-00305 request February 3, 2017.

Department of Justice. *James Douglas Manring Statement of Facts* Case 1:13-cr-00013-CMH Document 22. US District Court for the Eastern District of Virginia Alexandria Division. United States Government, January 28, 2013.

Department of Justice. *James McGlothlin Criminal Complaint* Case 3:16-cr-00115-MO Document 1. US District Court for the District of Oregon. United States Government, February 19, 2016.

Department of Justice. *Jay Michaud Criminal Complaint* Case 3:15-cr-05351-RJB Document No. MJ15-5113. US District Court for the Western District of Washington at Tacoma. United States Government, July 10, 2105.

Department of Justice. *Justin Carroll Indictment* Case: 4:17-cr-00036-RWS-DDN Documenber 2. US District Court Eastern District of Missouri Eastern Division: United States Government, January 25, 2017.

Department of Justice. *Michael Morris Sentencing Memo* Case 3:13-cr-00021-NKM Document 48. US District Court for the Western District of Virgina Charlottesville Division. United States Government, July 10, 2014.

Department of Justice. *Nicholas Bolden Criminal Complaint* Case 1:13-cr-00033-WJG-RHW Document 1. US District Court Southern District of Mississippi Southern Division: United States Government, March 26, 2103.

Department of Justice. *Stephen Mantha Criminal Complaint* Case 4:16-cr-40033-TSH Document 1-3. Washington DC: United States Government, September 22, 2016.

Department of Justice. *Steven Jon Frederikson Criminal Complaint*. Case 1:16-cr-00096-GBL Document 2. US District Court for the Eastern District of Virginia, Alexandria Division: United States Government, March 28, 2016.

Department of Justice. *The National Strategy for Child Exploitation Prevention and Interdiction 2016*. Washington DC: United States Government, April 8, 2016.

Department of Justice. *The National Strategy for Child Exploitation Prevention and Interdiction 2010*. August 2010.

Dienst, Jonathan. "DEA Agent Brought Child Porn to Work: Feds." NBC 4 New York, March 4, 2011.

Dingle, Sarah. "Whistleblower Peter Fox says police should apologise now to abuse victims," Australian Broadcasting Corporation (ABC), January 17, 2017.

Dillon, Nancy and Bill Hutchinson, "Stephen Collins' estranged wife reached out to actor's first victim after receiving anonymous letter with child sex abuse warning." *New York Daily News*, October 9, 2014.

Dinan, Stephen. "Federal workers hit record number, but growth slows under Obama." *Washington Times*, February 9, 2016.

Dolinsky, Joe. "Former Dupont cop David Turkos pleads guilty in child sex assault case." *Times Leader*, June 12, 2017.

Dreger, Alice. "What Can Be Done About Pedophilia?" *The Atlantic*, August 26, 2013.

DSS Public Affairs [DSSPA@dss.mil]. E-mail message to author, May 4, 2016.

Duffy, Daintry. "Inside the DoD's Computer Forensics Lab: Searching for the Truth." *CSO On-Line,* May 1, 2004.

Dutch National Rapporteur on Trafficking in Human Beings and Sexual Violence against Children. "National Rapporteur presents First Report on Child Pornography to United Nations," National Rapporteur Press Release, May 6, 2012.

E.H. "Why does liberal Iceland want to ban online pornography?" *The Economist,* April 24, 2013.

Ecenbarger, William. *Kids for Cash: Two Judges, Thousands of Children, and a $2.8 Million Kickback Scheme.* New York: The New Press, 2014.

Egelberg, Scott. "Local Doctor Pleads Guilty to Child Pornography Charge." *South Orange Patch,* January 4, 2012.

Eisinger, Jesse. *The Chickenshit Club: Why the Justice Department Fails to Prosecute Executives.* New York: Simon & Schuster, 2017.

European Parliamentary Research Service. "Combating Sexual Abuse of Children," Directive 2011/93/EU, April 2017.

Europol. "New cybercrime report examines disturbing trends in commercial online child sex abuse." October 15, 2013.

Europol. "Serious and Organised Crime Threat Assessment (SOCTA)." 2017.

Evelly, Jeanmarie. "LIC Restaurateur and Child Sex Abuse Survivor Pushes for Changes to NY Law." *DNA Info,* May 12, 2017.

Fairfax County Police Department. *Daniel Rosen Search Warrant* Case No. 2015001232 Offense Tracking Number 059GM1500012254. Fairfax, Virginia, February 24, 2015.

Farmer, Paul. *Pathologies of Power: Health, Human Rights, and the New War on the Poor.* Berkeley: University of California Press, 2004.

Farrell, Paul, "Daniel Rosen: 5 Fast Facts You Need to Know." Heavy.com, April 17, 2015.

Fifield, Jen. "One Major Reason Why Child Abuse in Military Families Goes Unreported," *Task & Purpose,* June 12, 2017.

Federal Bureau of Investigations (FBI). "'Playpen' Creator Sentenced to 30 Years: Dark Web 'Hidden Service' Case Spawned Hundreds of Child Porn Investigations." May 5, 2017.

Federal Bureau of Investigations (FBI). "Carmel Man Petitions to Plead Guilty to Charges of Possession, Distribution of Child Pornography." Southern District of Indiana: United States Government, May 14, 2013.

Federal Bureau of Investigations (FBI). "Child Pornography Case Results in Lengthy Prison Sentences: Couple Abused Child in Their Care." November 13, 2014.

Federal Bureau of Investigations (FBI). "Former Bakersfield Police Detective Pleads Guilty to Possession of Child Pornography." Eastern District of California: United States Government, February 19, 2013.

Feehan, Jennifer. "TPS teacher gets 75 months for child porn: Bruce Omlor had pleaded guilty in May to receiving the material on his home computer." *Toledo Blade,* September 9, 2013.

Field, Susan. "Mark Ranzenberger waives preliminary hearing in CSC case." *Morning Sun News,* October 10, 2016.

Field, Susan. "Mt. Pleasant child rapist gets 14 to 45 years in prison." *The News Herald*, January 26, 2017.

Flatow, Nicole. "Rochester Teens Arrested for Obstructing the Sidewalk While Waiting For School Bus." *Think Progress*, December 2, 2013.

Fortier, Marc. "Ex-TSA Employee Indicted on Child Porn Charges." Patch.com, September 17, 2013.

Fortin, Francis and Patrice Corriveau, *Who Is Bob34? Investigating Child Cyberpornography*. British Columbia: University of British Columbia Press, 2015.

Foster, Peter and video by Dermot Tatlow. "John Grisham: men who watch child porn are not all paedophiles." *The Telegraph*, October 15, 2014.

FOX 19 News, Digital Media Staff. "Former Campbell County judge indicted on rape, human trafficking charges." May 4, 2017.

Fox News. "12 arrested in largest child pornography case in Puerto Rico." April 9, 2015.

Fox, Peter. "Don't Block Your Ears to Abuse Mr. Premier." *The Herald*, November 8, 2012.

Francis Allen, "Hebephilia is a Crime, Not a Mental Disorder." *Psychiatric Times*, December 15, 2011.

Franceschina, Peter, Linda Trischitta and Jon Burstein, "Leader of ICE in South Florida pleads not guilty to child porn charges," *South Florida Sun-Sentinel*, September 28, 2011.

Frontline: Public Broadcasting Service (PBS). "The Untouchables." January 22, 2013.

Gafni, Matthias. "Captured: Child porn producer arrested in Florida, toddler victim rescued." *Contra Costa Times*, December 21, 2012.

Gallagher, Paul. "Live streamed videos of abuse and pay-per-view child rape among 'disturbing' cybercrime trends, Europol report reveals." *The Independent*, October 16, 2013.

Gambacorta, David. "The Great Pennsylvania Government Porn Caper." *Esquire*, February 24, 2016.

Gansler, Douglas. *Report of the Special Deputy Attorney General Douglas F. Gansler on Misuse of Commonwealth of Pennsylvanian Government Email Communication Systems*. August 18, 2016.

Garske, Monica. "Local Marine Pilot Sentenced on Child Porn Charges." NBC San Diego, October 20, 2012.

Guardian, The. "NYPD officer accused of plot to kill and eat women has conviction overturned." July 1, 2014.

Gearty, Robert and Bill Hutchinson. "'Cannibal Cop' partner Michael Van Hise wanted to keep children as sex slaves: prosecutors." *New York Daily News*, January 7, 2013.

Gelber, Alexandra. *Response to A Reluctant Rebellion*. Washington DC: Department of Justice, July 1, 2009.

Ghose, Tia. "On Polygraph Tests, Would-Be Border Patrol Agents Confess to Crimes." *The Daily Beast*, March 4, 2013.

Gilbert, David. "Rising Trend of Live Streaming Child Abuse of 'Particular Concern." *IBTimes*, October 16, 2013.

Gillespie Alisdair. *Child Pornography: Law and Policy*, New York: Routledge, 2012.

Gilliam, Derek. "Child porn: Reaching epidemic status in Florida." *Jacksonville*, November 14, 2014.

Goff, Liz. "Cannibal Cop Seeking New Trial." *Queens Gazette*, June 26, 2013.

Goldberg, Jeff. "James Daniel Howard charged with child pornography offenses." WJLA News, May 2, 2013.

Goldthwait, Bob. *Call Me Lucky*, Type 55 Films, MPI Media Group.

Gordon, Olivia. "The Young Woman Behind the Software that Catches Child Predators." *VICE*, July 22, 2016.

Gould, Pamela. "Child porn convictions worry area parents." Fredericksburg.com, February 2, 2013.

Gould, Joe. "Soldier gets 28 years for sexually assaulting her son." *USA Today*, January 2, 2014.

Grant, Jason. "N.J. doctor admits to distributing sadistic, violent child pornography." *New Jersey On-Line*, January 5, 2012.

Greenberg, Andy. "How an Entire Nation Became Russia's Test Lab for Cyberwar." *Wired*, June 20, 2017.

Greenaway, Samantha. "4 Disturbing Ways Child Molesters Use Tech to Commit Crimes," *Business Insider*, March 15, 2014.

Gyan Jr., Joe. "Baton Rouge lawyer says 'crude joke' led to child porn charges." *The Advocate*, September 15, 2016.

Gyan Jr., Joe. "More to story than Christopher Young allegedly distributing child porn, ex-Jefferson Parish president's brother argues." *The Advocate*, December 26, 2016.

Handrahan, Lori. "Executive Branch Porn Problem." *Washington Times*, August 10, 2012.

Handrahan, Lori. "Mark Thompson: From Pedophile Cover-Up to the *New York Times*." *FrontPage Magazine*, November 20, 2012.

Handrahan, Lori. "To Catch Government Workers with Ties to Child Porn, call the IRS." *Forbes Magazine*, 19 September 19, 2012.

Hanning, James. "Tom Watson: Why Labour's deputy leader won't stop speaking up for the victims of child abuse." *The Independent*, October 17, 2015.

Hansen, Haley. "Former Chanhassen High principal charged with 10 more counts of child porn." *Star Tribune*, March 30, 2017.

Harlan Reynolds, Glenn. "Our criminal justice system has become a crime." *USA Today*, March 19, 2014.

Harris, Alex. "Ex-Miami Beach assistant principal gets nearly 5 years in prison for child porn." *Miami Herald*, July 17, 2017.

Harris, Chris. "Utah Teacher Allegedly Brought 'Meticulous' Child Porn Scrapbooks to His Middle School." *People Magazine*, May 2, 2017.

Harris, Shane. "3rd U.S. Official Hit with Child Sex and Porn Charges." *The Daily Beast*, February 25, 2015.

Hastings, Deborah. "Bailey Joe Mills, 33, was the alleged ringleader of the child pornography production operation he ran from his North Carolina home, which he billed as a daycare service." *New York Daily News*, June 25, 2014.

Hawaii News Now. "President Obama signs 'Talia's law,' aimed at protecting children on military bases." December 27, 2016.

Hazzard, Andrew. "Former principal charged with child porn had many roles close to children." *Grand Forks Herald*, April 13, 2017.

Hermann, Peter. "Crime Scenes: Neighbors angry at delay in child porn arrests." *Baltimore Sun*, April 9, 2011.

Hessler Jr., Carl. "Kane: 'I will not stop until the truth comes out.'" *Delaware County Daily Times*, October 2, 2015.

Hickman, Matthew J. "Citizen Complaints about Police Use of Force," NCJ 210296, Washington DC: United States Government, June 2006.

Hogan, John. "Former CMU faculty member arrested, charged with possession of child pornography." *Central Michigan Life*, May 20, 2016.

Huffington Post. "Moshe Gerstein, Attorney Charged in Sweep, Found Dead in Mexico." August 23, 2011.

Huffman, Charlotte. "Two child sex offenders explain how they picked their targets." ABC News WFAA 8, April 27, 2017.

Huron Daily Tribune. "Former prosecutor gets more prison time for child rape." March 22, 2016.

Hyland, Shelley, Lynn Langton, and Elizabeth Davis, "Police Use of Nonfatal Force, 2002–11 NCJ 249216." Washington DC: United States Government, November 2015.

Immigration and Customs Enforcement (ICE). "Child predator sentenced to life imprisonment in Louisiana." Louisiana, United States Government, July 18, 2012.

Independent.ie. "Exposed: Ireland's vile child-sex rings." July 11, 1998.

Indiana Police Department. *Officer Report Incident B15-12856*. Probable Cause Affidavit. Bloomington, May 18, 2015.

Internet Watch Foundation. *Annual Report 2016*. United Kingdom, 2016.

Interpol, "Interpol network identifies 10,000 child sexual abuse victims," Interpol Press Release, January 9, 2017,

Interpol. "Global operation targets child sexual abuse material exchanged via messaging apps." April 18, 2017.

Jauregui, Andres. "Gordon Oehmig, Former Wrestling 'Coach of The Year,' Arrested on Child Porn Charges." *Huffington Post*, October 23, 2012.

Jauregui, Andres. "Jonathan Adleta, Former Marine, Gets 2 Life Sentences for Sexually Abusing Children." *Huffington Post*, January 23, 2014.

Jefferson, Cord. "Born This Way: Sympathy and Science for Those Who Want to Have Sex with Children." *Gawker*, September 7, 2012.

Jeffrey, Terence. "21,995,000 to 12,329,000: Government Employees Outnumber Manufacturing Employees 1.8 to 1." *CNS News*, September 8, 2015.

Jenkins, Philip. *Beyond Tolerance: Child Pornography on the Internet*. New York: New York University, 2003.

Jennings, Julie. "Federal Workforce Statistics Sources: OPM and OMB." Congressional Research Service, December 7, 2016.

John Shiffman, "Airport passenger screener charged in distributing child pornography," *The Inquirer*, April 23, 2011.

Johnson, Alex. "Former Denver preschool teacher pleads guilty in horrifying child porn case." NBC News, May 30, 2013.

Johnson, Kevin. "Clandestine websites fuel 'alarming' increase in child porn." *USA Today*, May 15, 2014.

Jordon, Tracy. "Child pornography charges filed against former police chief." *The Morning Call*, December 12, 2013.

Journal, The. "New website will show clues from child sex abuse cases to help track down paedophiles." June 1, 2017.

Judd, Alan. "Doctor accused of violently molesting, raping 1,200 children recorded abuse." *Norwalk Reflector*, December 29, 2016.

Judicial Discipline & Disability Commission. *Joseph Boeckmann Statement of Allegations* JDDC Case No. 14-31-, 312, 313, 314. Arkansas: Judicial Discipline & Disability Commission, November 17, 2017.

Kaplan, Margo. "Pedophilia: A Disorder, Not a Crime" *New York Times,* October 5, 2014.

Keeler, Bob. "Bedminster resident Robert Geist sentenced for possessing child pornography." *Montgomery News,* September 29, 2014.

Keller, Jared. "A Disturbing Portion of Marine Corps' Courts-Martial In 2017 Are for Child Sexual Abuse." *Task & Purpose,* June 13, 2017.

Keloland Media Group. "Flynn Child Porn Trial Day 2." December 15, 2010.

Keloland Media Group. "Former SD Airman Sentenced for Child Pornography." May 7, 2013.

Kendall, Justin. "Samuel Logan, disbarred JoCo lawyer, pleads guilty to trying to have sex a teen girl over the Internet." *The Pitch*, May 26, 2011.

Kim, David. "UPDATED – UMR Professor Nabbed in Rochester Child Porn Bust; 7th Arrest." KROC AM 1340, February 6, 2015.

Kirby, Brendan. "No actual victim, judge rules in dismissing former Mobile prosecutor's enticement charges." AL.com, December 5, 2012.

Krause, Kevin. "The FBI ran a huge child porn site to catch predators. The accused are crying foul." *Miami Herald*, January 22, 2017.

Lardner, Richard and Eileen Sullivan. "Opaque military justice system shields child sex abuse cases." Associated Press (AP), November 24, 2015.

Lardner, Richard. Eileen Sullivan and Meghan Hoyer. "Military Children Sexual Assault Numbers Released." *US News & World Report,* January 4, 2016.

Lardner, Richard. Eileen Sullivan and Meghan Hoyer. "Pentagon: Hundreds of military kids sexually abused annually." Associated Press (AP), January 4, 2016.

Larimer, Sarah. "Disgraced ex-cop Daniel Holtzclaw sentenced to 263 years for on-duty rapes, sexual assaults." *Washington Post,* January 22, 2016.

Lehigh Valley Live. "Kane defiant after latest arrest, vows to expose officials." October 2, 2015.

Leijten, Jorg. "Politie: kinderporno bedreigt de Nederlandse samenleving Nationaal dreigingsbeeld De politie krijgt veel meer meldingen binnen van mogelijke kinderporno. Ze kan lang niet alle tips goed nagana." *NRC.nl*, May 31, 2017.

Leonnig, Carol. "Homeland Security inspector general who was under probe steps down." *Washington Post*, December 16, 2013.

Levesque, William R. "MacDill officer sought out 'pervs,' records in child porn case show." *Tampa Bay Times*, February 4, 2014.

Lin, Albert. "Arkansas Judge's Shocking Racist, Sexist, Homophobic Comments." *Diversity Inc.*, March 10, 2014.

Lincoln Journal Star. "Air Force sergeant sentenced to 10 years for child porn." May 4, 2006.

Lithwick, Dahlia. "Jack Weinstein." *The Atlantic*, November 2010.

Lo, Teresa. "9 Lawyers Associated with Child Pornography." *JD Journal*, January 1, 2016.

Lopeze, Rebecca and Jonathan Betz, "University Park Woman Faces Child Porn Charges." *Dallas News*, June 2, 2012.

Los Angeles Times. "Silver Star revoked for former Clinton defense official now in prison." July 28, 2011.

Maass, Dave. "States Introduce Dubious Anti-Pornography Legislation to Ransom the Internet." Electronic Freedom Foundation (EFF), April 12, 2017.

Marimow, Ann E. "Former FBI analyst sentenced to more than three years in prison in child pornography case." *Washington Post*, September 9, 2013.

Mary, Pulido. "Internet Child Pornography: Who is at the Keyboard?" *Huffington Post*, January 9, 2014.

Maryland Daily Record, Daily Record Staff. "Former Baltimore prosecutor gets jail for child porn." June 1, 2017.

Masulli Reyes, Jessica. "Former Delaware pediatrician Earl Bradley loses another appeal." DelmarvaNow.com, May 19, 2017.

May, Robert. *Kids for Cash.* SenArt Films, 2014.

Mayhew, Freddy. "Former Exaro chief launches podcast reporting on child sex abuse issues." *Press Gazette*, October 7, 2016.

McCabe, Scott. "FBI analyst busted in online child porn sting." *Washington Examiner*, December 4, 2012.

McConn. Terry. "Ex-Walla Walla judge, former minister sentenced in child porn case." *Tri-City Herald*, February 27, 2014.

McDonald, Henry. "Child abuse inquiry turns to Kincora home and claims of MI5 blackmail: Inquiry will hear from men abused as boys at Northern Ireland children's home and allegations that perpetrators were protected by working as spies." *The Guardian*, May 30, 2016.

McElhatton, Jim. "CIA able to keep its secrets on budgets, bad apples IG documents reveal porn, fraud, other misconduct." *Washington Times*, November 13, 2012.

McKelvey, Wallace. "Kathleen Kane's porn report: 5 things you need to know as AG's office releases email probe." PennLive.com, November 22, 2016.

Mears, Bill. "Former top FBI agent charged with child porn distribution." Cable News Network (CNN), May 15, 2012.

Mercer, Bob. "Accused of child sex and porn, Former state's attorney gives up his law license." *Black Hills Pioneer*, August 19, 2014.

Meredith Adams, Jane. "Schools failing to protect students from sexual abuse by school personnel, federal report says." *Ed Source*, February 5, 2014.

Military Times. "The Army's hidden child abuse epidemic." July 29, 2013.

Miller, Emily. "Local lawyer charged in child pornography case." Fox News 5, June 29, 2015.

Montanaro, Julie. "Former Department of Agriculture Worker Sentenced for Child Porn." WCTV.TV, February 10, 2015.

Moon Cronk, Terri. "Sexual Assaults in Military Drop, Reporting Goes Up, Annual Report Reveals." US Department of Defense, May 1, 2017.

Moor, Keith. "'Snuff films alarm: AFP warns of growing paedophile problem." *Herald Sun,* June 4, 2017.

Moyer, Justin Wm. "Army lieutenant colonel gets 20 years in child pornography case." *Washington Post,* November 8, 2016.

Moyer, Justin Wm. "Former HHS official sentenced to 25 years in prison for child pornography charges." *Washington Post,* January 6, 2015.

Naples Daily News. "Perverted justice? Child pornography sentences vary widely in federal, state courts." May 18, 2013.

National Conference of State Legislatures. "Children and the Internet Laws Relating to Filtering, Blocking and Usage Policies in Schools and Libraries." November 16, 2016.

National Rapporteur on Trafficking in Human Beings. "Child Pornography: First Report of the Dutch National Rapporteur. The Netherlands: Dutch Government, 2011.

Navy Times. "March courts-martial results announced." April 15, 2015.

NBC News Portland KGW Staff. "Former Ore. man gets 30 mos. for child porn on gov't computer." October 4, 2012.

NBC News WJHG 7. "Child Porn Defendant Dies in Federal Prison." March 1, 2014.

NBC News. "123 child victims of Internet sex abuse identified -- one just 19 days old, US officials say." January 3, 2013.

Neal, David. "Child-porn arrest of a Miami Beach educator started with a 'room' flagged in Arizona." *Miami Herald,* February 6, 2017.

Neil, Martha. "Former Attorney Takes Plea in Child Porn Case, Will Get 24 to 37 Months." *ABA Journal,* May 24, 2011.

NetClean. *NetClean Report 2016.* Sweden, 2016.

New York Daily News. "Accused NYPD 'cannibal cop' Gilberto Valle: Facebook postings, instant messages paint picture of twisted mind." October 25, 2012.

New York Times. "Disability Expansion Raises Ire in Greece." January 9, 2012.

New York Times-Editorial Board. "Rampant Prosecutorial Misconduct." January 4, 2014.

News24. "Huge Canada child sex ring bust." April 22, 2017.

Nixon, Ron. "Claims of Corrupt Immigration Contractors Go Unexamined, Investigators Say." *New York Times,* January 23, 2017.

Noah, Timothy. "The Justice Gap: 'The Divide,' by Matt Taibbi." *New York Times,* April 10, 2014.

Nsubuga, Jimmy. "Children's doctor used 'military-grade' software to hide child porn on his computer." *Metro UK,* March 20, 2017.

NTB/The Local NO. "Police break up massive Norwegian paedophilia ring." November 21, 2016.

O'Connor, Phillip. "Oklahoma airman found guilty of possessing child pornography." *News OK*, November 26, 2012.

Office of the Inspector General (OIG) Department of Justice. *The Handling of Sexual Harassment and Misconduct by the Department's Law Enforcement Components*. Washington DC: United States Government, 2015.

Office of the Inspector General Department of Homeland Security. "Statement of Charles K. Edwards Acting Inspector General US Department of Homeland Security Before the Subcommittee on Oversight, Investigations and Management, U.S. House of Representatives." Washington DC: United States Government, May 17, 2012.

Office of the Inspector General Department of Transportation. "Air Traffic Control Specialist Sentenced to 78 Months Imprisonment for Charges of Child Pornography." Washington DC: United States Government, November 14, 2008.

Ontario Court of Justice. "Ben Levin's Statement of Facts." Her Majesty the Queen, Canadian Government.

Pachico, Elyssa. "Putting Salacious DEA Sex Party Report in Perspective." *Insight Crime,* March 27, 2015.

Palmer, Brian. "How Many Kids Are Sexually Abused by Their Teachers?" *Slate*, February 8, 2012.

Paphitis, Nicholas. "Furor in Greece over pedophilia as a disability." Associated Press (AP), January 9, 2012.

Paterson, Kirsteen. "Australian TV show 60 Minutes alleges child abuse in Westminster." *The National*, July 20, 2015.

Patrick, Robert and Ashley Jost, "Washington University dean of students indicted on child pornography charge." *St. Louis Post-Dispatch*, January 30, 2017.

Patrick, Robert. "Former prosecutor gets two years in child porn case." *St. Louis Post-Dispatch*, May 12, 2010.

Pavuk, Amy. "Retired Navy officer gets one-year prison in child-porn case." *Orlando Sentinel,* January 27, 2014.

Pieters, Janene. "Explosive increase in child pornography forms national threat: Dutch police." NLTimes.nl, May 31, 2017.

Pohl, Ines. "Child pornography in doubt for the child." *Deutschlandfunk*, February 22, 2014.

Pompilio, Natalie. "Pornographic email scandal roils Pennsylvania politics." *Washington Post*, December 26, 2015.

Ponder, Doug. "Child porn trial set for principal accused of taking students' phone photos." *LaRue County Herald-News*, March 29, 2017.

Popham, Peter. "Ten charged in Portuguese paedophile ring scandal." *The Independent,* December 31, 2003.

Portland Press Herald. "LePage issues order prohibiting state workers from viewing porn." February 20, 2015.

Prine, Carl. "Navy SEAL accused of molesting girl on camera, raping a woman and hoarding a stash of child porn." *Los Angeles Times*, April 22, 2017.

Profita, Hillary. "Has Media Ignored Sex Abuse in School?" *CBS News*, August 24, 2006.

Pulkkinen, Levi. "Judge: FBI-tied child porn collector 'not a danger' to school." *SeattlePI*, April 8, 2016.

Q13 Fox News. "Middle school special ed teacher allegedly caught with child pornography." July 15, 2015.

Quayle, Ethel and Kurt Ribisl. *Understanding and Preventing Online Sexual Exploitation of Children*. New York, Routledge, 2012.

Quayle, Ethel and Max Taylor. *Child Pornography: An Internet Crime*. New York: Routledge, 2003.

Ramirez, Carlos. "Dunellen Board of Education President Arrested on Charges of Child Pornography." *New Brunswick Today*, August 25, 2016.

Raymond, Nate. "FBI seized child porn website with 215,000 users: court filing." Reuters, July 7, 2015.

Reaves, Brian. "Federal Law Enforcement Officers, 2008." *Bureau of Justice Statistics*, June 26, 2012.

Reavy, Pat. "West Valley teacher had 'meticulous' child porn scrapbook in class, police say." *Desert News*, May 1, 2017.

Reilly, Steve and John Kelly, "How USA TODAY audited the country's broken systems for tracking teacher discipline." *USA Today*, February 14, 2016.

Reilly, Steve. "Broken discipline tracking systems let teachers flee troubled pasts." *USA Today*, 2017.

Reilly, Steve. "Teachers who sexually abuse students still find classroom jobs: Despite decades of scandals, America's schools still hide actions of dangerous educators." *USA Today*, 2017.

Reuters. "Police arrest 348 in global child porn investigation, rescue 386 children." November 14, 2013.

Robinson, Lisa. "Victim in Netflix's 'The Keepers' speaks out: Woman details alleged abuse." NBC News WBLATV11, June 7, 2017.

Rocha, Veronica. "238 arrested in sweep of suspected child sex predators." *Los Angeles Times*, June 21, 2016.

Rockett, Ali. "Child testifies against former Richmond police officer accused of sex crimes." *Richmond Times-Dispatch*, July 11, 2017.

Rockett, Ali. "Former Richmond police officer to serve life in prison for sexual abuse of child." *Richmond Times-Dispatch*, July 13, 2017.

Rollins, Ernest. "Former IU ethics office employee sentenced to 2-1/2 years for possession of child pornography." *Herald Times On-Line*, February 28, 2017.

Rose, David. "The scandal of the sex crime 'cure' hubs: How minister buried report into £100 million prison programme to treat paedophiles and rapists that INCREASED re-offending rates." *The Mail on Sunday*, June 24, 2017.

Ryan, Jeremy. "Former cop, child caseworker accused of possessing child porn." CNY Central.com, December 21, 2010.

Ryan, Patty. "Former Tampa officer gets nearly 5 years for child porn." *Tampa Bay Times*, May 8, 2013.

Ryan, Patty. "Ex-Tampa police officer takes plea deal in child porn case." *Tampa Bay Times*, February 4, 2013.

Salem News.com. "West Point Army Officer Receives 37 Years in Prison." January 7, 2011.

Sapien, Joaquin and Sergio Hernandez, "Who Polices Prosecutors Who Abuse Their Authority? Usually Nobody." *ProPublica,* April 3, 2013.

Sarnoff, Conchita. *TraffKing.* Washington DC: Conchita Sarnoff, 2016.

Schuppe, John. "Pennsylvania Seeks to Close Books on "Kids for Cash" Scandal." NBC News, August 12, 2015.

Schwartz, John. "Congress Passes Bill Extending Definition of Child Pornography." *Washington Post,* October 4, 1996.

Seattle Times. "Ex-judge in Wash. charged with having child porn." December 27, 2013.

Serna, Joseph and Christine Mai-Duc, "Special education aide arrested in alleged Riverside child porn ring." *Los Angeles Times,* February 15, 2015.

Seto, Michael. "Is pedophilia a sexual orientation?" Archives of Sexual Behavior 41 (1), (2012):231-6.

Seto, Michael. *Internet Sex Offenders.* Washington DC: American Psychological Association, 2013.

Seto, Michael. *Pedophilia and Sexual Offending Against Children: Theory, Assessment, and Intervention.* Washington DC: American Psychological Association, 2008.

Sher, Julian. "Child porn bust: The U.S. postal investigator who helped Toronto police." *The Star,* November 14, 2013.

Sher, Julian. *Caught in the Web: Inside the Police Hunt to Rescue Children from Online Predators.* New York: Carroll & Graf Publisher, 2007.

Sheridan, Mary Beth and Jerry Markon, "Official at Children's Museum Is Charged in Child Pornography Case." *Washington Post,* November 7, 2007.

Sherman, Christopher. "Abel Limas, Ex-Judge Involved in Racketeering, Gets 6 Years." *Huffington Post,* August 21, 2013.

Silberg, Joyanna. "How Many Children Are Court -Ordered into Unsupervised Contact with an Abusive Parent After Divorce?" The Leadership Council, Press Release, September 22, 2008.

Silmalis, Linda. "Child sex abuse reports on rise and should not be taboo subject." *The Sunday Telegraph,* June 10, 2017.

Simmoneau, Ben. "I-Team: Priest Removed from Ministry Due to Sex Abuse Allegations Now Works At PHL." CBS Philly, May 24, 2012.

Simons, Abby. "Disgraced attorney owes $15 million to teenager he raped." *Star Tribune,* May 25, 2011.

Simons, Marlise. "Dutch Say a Sex Ring Used Infants on Internet." *New York Times,* July 19, 1998.

Sioux City Journal. "South Dakota lawyer acquitted of child porn charges." December 18, 2010.

Smith, Simon. "Europol shares 20 tiny details from vile images of child sex abuse in a bid to track down perpetrators and victims." *Manchester Evening News,* June 1, 2017.

Sommer, Will. "Where the Sidewalk Ends." *Washington City Paper,* May 22, 2015.

South Bend Tribune. "Granger Army cadet accused of emailing porn." December 19, 2013.

Space Coast Daily. "Former Brevard County Principal, Ricky Sheppard To Plead Guilty to Child Porn Charges." August 9, 2016.

Standen, Camille. "The Journalist Who Was Arrested for Investigating a Pedophile Orphanage." *VICE*, February 27, 2013.

Stars & Stripes. "Navy revokes imprisoned Vietnam veteran's Silver Star." July 27, 2011.

State of Maine. "An Order Clarifying State Management's Response to Certain Prohibited Misconduct." No. 2015-002, February 5, 2015.

Steel, Chad. *Digital Child Pornography: A Practical Guide for Investigators,* Lily Shiba Press, 2014.

Stennett, Desiree. "Patrick Air Force Base: Chief scientist held on $250K bond after child-porn arrest." *Orlando Sentinel,* May 10, 2013.

Stepzinski, Terry. "Ex-judge gets jail for child porn." *Florida Times-Union,* December 17, 2005.

Sterman, Joce. "Former TSA agent from Baltimore County indicted on federal porn charges." ABC News 2, March 18, 2012.

Sternstein, Aliya. "Child porn on government devices: A hidden security threat." *The Christian Science Monitor,* December 5, 2016.

Stetson University. "Statement from Stetson University Regarding Clyde E. Fant." March 9, 2017.

Stevenson Bryon. *Just Mercy: A Story of Justice and Redemption,* (New York: Random House, 2014.

Stinson Jill, and Judith V. Becker. *Treating Sex Offenders: An Evidence-Based Manual.* New York: Guilford Press, 2013.

Stockinger, Josh. "Should Navy vet get prison for 'staggering' child porn collection?" *Daily Herald,* January 17, 2012.

Stuart, Courtney. "Former UVA associate dean Michael Morris pleads guilty to child porn charges." *C-Ville,* April 22, 2014.

Suffolk County Court. *Andrew Cheever Criminal Complaint* Case: 1:11-cr-10398-NMG Document 1-1. Boston Massachusetts: Suffolk County Court, September 1, 2011.

Sulzberger, A.G. "Defiant Judge Takes on Child Pornography Law." *New York Times,* May 21, 2010.

Taibbi, Matt. *The Divide, American Injustice in the Age of the Wealth Gap.* New York: Spiegel & Grau, 2014.

Talamo, Lex. "Child porn offenders in technological arms race with cops." *USA Today,* 2017.

Tanner, Jeremey and Monica Morales, "Disturbing viral Facebook post shows man sexually abusing child," PIX11, March 22, 2013.

Taylor, Jerome. "Guilty after six-year trial, Portugal's high-society paedophile ring." *The Independent,* September 3, 2010.

Taylor, Marisa. "National Reconnaissance Office hasn't told police of crime confessions." McClatchy Newspapers, July 10, 2012.

Third Judicial District Court. *Christopher DeZutter Criminal Complaint* Court File No. 55-CR-15-828. Third Judicial District Court. State of Minnesota: County of Olmsted, February 6, 2015.

Thorne, Dan. "MP Tom Watson warns of 'powerful paedophile network linked to Parliament and Number 10.'" *TNT Magazine,* October 24, 2012.

Topping, Alexandra. "Online child abuse images 'becoming more extreme, sadistic and violent.'" *The Guardian,* June 13, 2012.

Torralva, Krista. "German man indicted after traveling to Orlando for sex with minor, feds say." *Orlando Sentinel,* July 12, 2017.

Turley, Jonathan. "Charges Dismissed Against Former Child Sex Crimes Prosecutor for Lack Of Actual Minor In FBI Sting." *Jonathan Turley Blog,* December 7, 2012.

Udesky, Laurie. "Custody in Crisis: How Family Courts Nationwide Put Children in Danger." *100 Reporters,* December 1, 2016.

UNICEF. "National Responses to Online Child Sexual Abuse and Exploitation in ASEAN Member States." 2016.

United Nations. "Convention against Torture and Other Cruel, Inhuman or Degrading Treatment or Punishment." General Assembly Resolution 39/46, December 10, 1984.

United Nations. "Child pornography flourishes in a world with no borders." Office of the High Commissioner for Human Rights (OHCHR), Geneva, February 11, 2014.

United Nations. "Report of the Special Rapporteur on the Sale of Children, Child Prostitution and Child Pornography." Document A/HRC/31/158, December 30, 2015.

United Nations. "UN Global Initiative to Fight Human Trafficking." February 9, 2014.

United States Congress. "Protection of Children Against Sexual Exploitation Act," S. 1585 (95th). Washington DC: United States Government, February 6, 1978.

United States Congress. "Testimony of Barry F. Crimmins, Hearing on Child Pornography on the Internet." Senate Judiciary Committee, 104th United States Congress, July 24, 1995.

United States Senate Senator Charles Grassley. "Justice Department Silent on Pornography Found on Assistant U.S. Attorney's Computer." October 14, 2011.

United States Senate Senator Charles Grassley. "Q&A: Holding the Pentagon Accountable." Washington DC: United States Government, November 24, 2010.

United States Sentencing Commission. *2012 Report to the Congress: Federal Child Pornography Offenses.* Washington DC: United States Government, 2012.

Unites States Congress. "Statement of Chairman Lamar Smith on the House Floor, H.R. 6063, the Child Protection Act." Washington DC: United States Government, July 31, 2012.

United States Congress. "H.R.244 - Consolidated Appropriations Act, 2017." Congress. gov.

United States Congress. "H.R.680 - Eliminating Pornography from Agencies Act 115th Congress (2017-2018)." Congress.gov.

United States Court of Appeals for the Ninth Circuit. *Lawson Hardrick Appellate Decision United States v. Lawson Hardrick, Jr.,* No. 13-50195. D.C. No. 3:12-cr-03061-H- (9th Cir. 2014). United States Government, September 4, 2014.

University of Technology Sydney (UTS). "Live-streamed child sex abuse part of a global crime pandemic." Press Release, May 30, 2017.

USA Today. "Penis pump judge gets 4-year jail term." August 18, 2006.

Wagner, Andy. "Lawmakers Want Digital Devices to Block "Obscene" Websites Including Some Social Media Platforms." *Multi-State*, April 4, 2017.

Waterman, Cole. "Victim calls CMU pedophile professor a psychopath, monster at sentencing." *MLive*, January 20, 2017.

Waters, Flint. *Congressional Testimony, Committee on the Judiciary House Hearing 110 Congress Sex Crimes and The Internet* Serial No. 110-87, Washington DC: US Government Printing Office, October 17, 2007,

Watt, Nicholas and Patrick Wintour, "Children's homes were 'supply line' for paedophiles, says ex-minister." *The Guardian*, 8 July 2014.

Weinreb, Arthur. "Ben Levin: Child pornography charges were the least of it." *Canadian Free Press*, June1, 2015.

Welborn, Larry. "Ex-judge Kline gets prison." *Orange County Register*, February 20, 2007.

West, Evan. "Explosive Charges: The Donald Sachtleben Case." *Indianapolis Monthly*, July 11, 2014.

WHIO News 7 Breaking News Staff. "James Uphoff sentenced in child porn case." September 10, 2014.

White, Ryan. "Making 'The Keepers' Taught Me the Power of Believing Survivors." *Huffington Post*, June 5, 2017.

White, Ryan. "The Keepers." Netflix, May 2017.

Wood, Paddy. "Online child porn inquiries rise five-fold." *The Australian*, July 21, 2014.

WRAL.com. "Deputies: Day care, mentoring program a front for Sanford child porn operation." November 21, 2014.

WRAL.com. "With third strike, Sanford sex offender faces life in prison." August 12, 2014.

Zarembo, Alan. "In Focus: The pedophile next door." *Portland Press Herald*, 20 January 2013.

Zauzmer, Julie. "Defendant allegedly asked about hit man to kill child witnesses." *Washington Post*, February 19, 2015.

Text Boxes, Tables, Pictures & Graphs

[Page 3] – Justin Wm. Moyer, "Former HHS official sentenced to 25 years in prison for child pornography charges," Washington Post, January 6, 2015, accessed July 13, 2017, https://www.washingtonpost.com/news/morning-mix/wp/2015/01/06/former-hhs-official-sentenced-to-25-years-in-prison-for-child-pornography-charges/?utm_term=.dfb6ca3e9552.

[Page 4] – "123 child victims of Internet sex abuse identified -- one just 19 days old, US officials say," NBC News, January 3, 2013, accessed July 13, 2017, https://usnews.newsvine.com/_news/2013/01/03/16327023-123-child-victims-of-internet-sex-abuse-identified-one-just-19-days-old-us-officials-say.

[Page 5] – Lori Handrahan Medium Profile, July 13, 2017, https://medium.com/@LoriHandrahan2.

[Page 9] – "Ben Levin's Statement of Facts," Ontario Court of Justice, Her Majesty the Queen, Canadian Government, accessed July 13, 2017, https://www.scribd.com/document/257879990/Agreed-Statement-of-Facts-Her-Majesty-the-Queen-v-Benjamin-Levin, 5.

[Page 9] – "Ben Levin's Statement of Facts," Ontario Court of Justice, 8.

[Page 10] – "Investigators: Berkeley County man asked for pics of infant rape," ABC News, December 20, 2012, accessed July 13, 2017, http://abcnews4.com/archive/court-docs-kiddie-porn.

[Page 11] – "Former USF dean sentenced for child porn," Bay City News, March 28, 2007, accessed 13 July 2017, http://www.sfgate.com/news/article/Former-USF-dean-sentenced-for-child-porn-3325965.php.

[Page 12] – "Former Police Chief In Berks County Pleads Guilty To Child Porn," CBS Philly, April 8, 2014, accessed July 13, 2017, http://philadelphia.cbslocal.com/2014/04/08/former-police-chief-in-berks-county-pleads-guilty-to-child-porn.

[Page 14] – "United States Sentencing Commission," United States Government, accessed July 13, 2017, http://www.ussc.gov/about/who-we-are/organization/contact-us.

[Page 15] – Joe Gould, "Soldier gets 28 years for sexually assaulting her son," USA Today, January 2, 2014, accessed July 13, 2017, https://www.usatoday.com/story/news/nation/2014/01/02/sergeant-child-pornography-son/4288709.

[Page 17] – Internet Watch Foundation, IWF Annual Report 2016 (United Kingdom: IWF, 3 April 2017) accessed July 13, 2017, https://www.iwf.org.uk/report/2016-annual-report, 12.

[Page 19] – Europol, "Strategic Assessment," 15.

[Page 20] – Bureau of Justice Statistics, e-mail message to author May 15, 2017.

[Page 21] – Department of Justice, email message to author in response to FOIA No. 15-00305 request February 3, 2017.

[Page 23] – Anti-Slavery Australia. Interpol Chart International Child Sexual Exploitation (ICSE) image database as displayed in Anti-Slavery Australia, Behind the Screen: On-Line Child Exploitation in Australia, (Broadway: Anti-Slavery Australia, 2017) accessed July 13, 2017, http://www.antislavery.org.au/newsflash/286-new-report-behind-the-screen-online-child-exploitation-in-australia.html, 10.

[Page 31] – Charlotte Huffman, "Two child sex offenders explain how they picked their targets," ABC News WFAA 8, April 27, 2017, accessed July 13, 2017, http://www.wfaa.com/news/two-child-sex-offenders-explain-how-they-picked-their-targets-1/434667495.

[Page 32] – Lex Talamo, "Child porn offenders in technological arms race with cops," USA Today, 2017, accessed July 13, 2017, https://www.usatoday.com/story/news/investigations/2017/05/22/child-porn-offenders-technological-arms-race-cops/101527462.

[Page 33] – Department of Justice, United States Government, "Air Force NCO Indicted For Sexually Exploiting Toddlers And Children To Produce Child Pornography," September 12, 2013, accessed July 13, 2017, https://www.justice.gov/usao-md/pr/air-force-nco-indicted-sexually-exploiting-toddlers-and-children-produce-child.

[Page 41] – Alexandra Gelber. Response to A Reluctant Rebellion (Washington DC: Department of Justice, 1 July 2009), accessed July 13, 2017, https://www.justice.gov/sites/default/files/criminal-ceos/legacy/2012/03/19/ReluctantRebellionResponse.pdf

[Page 41] – Andres Jauregui, "Gordon Oehmig, Former Wrestling 'Coach Of The Year,' Arrested On Child Porn Charges," Huffington Post, October 23, 2012, accessed July 13, 2017, http://www.huffingtonpost.com/2012/10/23/gordon-oehmig-former-texas-wrestling-coach-child-pornography_n_2005175.html?ncid=edlinkusaolp00000003.

[Page 42] – "Moshe Gerstein, Attorney Charged in Sweep, Found Dead In Mexico," Huffington Post, August 23, 2011, accessed July 13, 2017, http://www.huffingtonpost.com/2011/06/23/moshe-gersteinm-child-porn_n_883250.html.

[Page 43] – Emily Miller, "Local lawyer charged in child pornography case," Fox News 5, June 29 2015, accessed July 13, 2017, http://www.fox5dc.com/news/2280203-story.

[Page 44] – "International child-porn network busted, aided by clue of toy bunny, say feds," CBS News Crimesider Staff, August 6, 2012, accessed July 13, 2017, http://www.cbsnews.com/news/international-child-porn-network-busted-aided-by-clue-of-toy-bunny-say-feds.

[Page 46] – Officer Report Incident B15-12856. Probable Cause Affidavit (Bloomington: Bloomington, Indiana Police Department, May 18, 2015), 1.

[Page 46] – Amy Pavuk, "Retired Navy officer gets one year prison in child-porn case," Orlando Sentinel, January 27, 2014, accessed July 13, 2017, http://articles.orlandosentinel.com/2014-01-27/news/os-child-porn-navy-officer-babchyck-20140127_1_navy-officer-federal-prison-exploited-children.

[Page 51] – US Sentencing Commission, "Report to the Congress: Federal Child Pornography Offenses," (Washington, DC: United States Government, 2012), accessed July 13, 2017, http://www.ussc.gov/research/congressional-reports/2012-report-congress-federal-child-pornography-offenses, 142.

[Page 53] – Flint Waters, Wyoming Internet Crimes Against Children (ICAC) Taskforce, Congressional Testimony, Committee on the Judiciary House Hearing 110 Congress Sex Crimes and The Internet Serial No. 110-87 (Washington DC: US Government Printing Office), October 17, 2007, accessed July 13, 2017, https://www.gpo.gov/fdsys/pkg/CHRG-110hhrg38335/html/CHRG-110hhrg38335.htm, 44.

[Page 53] – Susan Field, "Mark Ranzenberger waives preliminary hearing in CSC case," Morning Sun News, October 10, 2016, accessed July 13 2017, http://www.themorningsun.com/article/MS/20161028/NEWS/161029702 and John Hogan, "Ranzenberger admits sexual abuse of minor, pleads guilty to child porn possession," Central Michigan Life, September 27, 2017, accessed July 13, 2017, http://www.cm-life.com/article/2016/09/ranzenberger-pleads-guilty-admits-to-sexual-abuse-of-minor.

[Page 57] – United Nations, "Report of the Special Rapporteur on the Sale of Children, Child Prostitution and Child Pornography," Document A/HRC/31/158, December 30, 2015, accessed July 13, 2017, http://ap.ohchr.org/documents/dpage_e.aspx?si=A/HRC/31/58, 11. See also Special Rapporteur on the sale and sexual exploitation of children http://www.ohchr.org/EN/Issues/Children/Pages/ChildrenIndex.aspx.

[Page 58] – Jeff Goldberg, "James Daniel Howard charged with child pornography offenses,: WJLA News, May 2, 2013, accessed July 13, 2017, http://wjla.com/news/local/james-daniel-howard-charged-with-child-pornography-offenses-88304.

[Page 59] – Department of Justice, David O'Brien Plea Agreement. Case 6:13-cr-00194-RBD-GJK Document 59, May 30, 2014, (United States District Court Middle District of Florida Orlando Division: United States Government), 18

[Page 59] – "Former SD Airman Sentenced for Child Pornography, Keloland Media Group, May 7, 2013, accessed July 13, 2017, http://www.keloland.com/news/article/news/former-sd-airman-sentenced-for-child-pornography.

[Page 60] – Monica Garske, "Local Marine Pilot Sentenced on Child Porn Charges," NBC San Diego, October 20, 2012, accessed July 13, 2017, http://www.nbcsandiego.com/news/local/Local-Marine-Pilot-Sentenced-on-Child-Porn-Charges-175084751.html.

[Page 61] – Carl Prine, "Navy SEAL accused of molesting girl on camera, raping a woman and hoarding a stash of child porn," Los Angeles Times, April 22, 2017, accessed July 13, 2017, http://www.latimes.com/local/lanow/la-me-navy-seal-20170422-story.html.

[Page 62] – Department of Justice. Steven Jon Frederikson Criminal Complaint. Case 1:16-cr-00096-GBL Document 2, March 28, 2016, (US District Court for the Eastern District of Virginia, Alexandria Division: United States Government), 4.

[Page 63] – "Child Porn Defendant Dies in Federal Prison," NBC News WJHG 7, March 1, 2014, accessed July 13, 2017, http://www.wjhg.com/home/headlines/Child-Porn-Defendent-Is-Death-In-Federal-Prison-247970721.html.

[Page 64] – Department of Justice, David O'Brien Plea Agreement,18.

[Page 65] – "United States Air Force," United States Government, accessed July 13, 2017, http://www.publicaffairs.af.mil/Contact.

[Page 65] – "Senator Gillibrand," United States Government, accessed July 13, 2017, https://www.gillibrand.senate.gov.

[Page 66] – Department of Justice, Brian Fanelli Criminal Complaint 14MJ145, January 23, 2014, (US District Court. Southern District of New York: United States Government), 7.

[Page 69] – "Bureau of Justice Statistics," United States Government, accessed July 13, 2017, https://www.bjs.gov/index.cfm?ty=contactus.

[Page 73] – Department of Justice, Christopher McKee Criminal Complaint Case 3:13-cr-00039-REP Document 16, March 30, 2013, (US District Court. Eastern District of Virginia. Richmond Division: United States Government), 1.

[Page 75] – "US Senate Committee on Homeland Security and Government Affairs," United States Government, accessed July 13, 2017, https://www.hsgac.senate.gov.

[Page 75] – Department of Justice, Nicholas Bolden Criminal Complaint Case 1:13-cr-00033-WJG-RHW Document 1, March 26, 2103, (US District Court Southern District of Mississippi Southern Division: United States Government), 1.

[Page 76] – US Court of Appeals for the Ninth Circuit, Lawson Hardrick Appellate Decision United States v. Lawson Hardrick, Jr., No. 13-50195. D.C. No. 3:12-cr-03061-H- (9th Cir. 2014),

September 4, 2014, accessed July 13, 2017, https://www.courtlistener.com/opinion/2723744/united-states-v-lawson-hardrick-jr/, 5.

[Page 77] – Department of Justice, Christopher Craft Criminal Complaint Case1:16-cr-00047-TSE No. 1:16-CR-47 Document 9, April 21, 2016, (US District Court Eastern District of Virginia. Alexandria Division: United States Government), 3.

[Page 79] – Julie Carey, "Search Warrants in Case of State Dept. Official Charged with Soliciting Minor," NBC News 4 Washington, March 2, 2015, accessed July 13, 2017, http://www.nbcwashington.com/news/local/Daniel-Rosen-Search-Warrants-in-Case-of-State-Dept-Official-Charged-with-Soliciting-Minor-294735001.html and Fairfax County Police Department, Daniel Rosen Search Warrant Case No. 2015001232 Offense Tracking Number 059GM1500012254, February 24, 2015, accessed July 13, 2017, http://media.nbcwashington.com/documents/Rosen_court_docs.pdf, 2.

[Page 80] – "Congressman Gowdy," United States Government, accessed July 13, 2017, https://gowdy.house.gov.

[Page 82] – Department of Justice, Stephen Mantha Criminal Complaint Case 4:16-cr-40033-TSH Document 1-3, 22 September 2016, (Washington DC: United States Government), 7-8.

[Page 84] – Andres Jauregui, "Jonathan Adleta, Former Marine, Gets 2 Life Sentences For Sexually Abusing Children," Huffington Post, January 23, 2014, accessed July 13, 2017, http://www.huffingtonpost.com/2014/01/07/jonathan-adleta-2-life-sentences-sex-abuse_n_4553900.html.

[Page 96] – Judicial Discipline & Disability Commission, Joseph Boeckmann Statement of Allegations JDDC Case No. 14-31-, 312, 313, 314, November 17, 2017, (Arkansas: Judicial Discipline & Disability Commission), 8.

[Page 97] – Douglas Gansler, Report of the Special Deputy Attorney General Douglas F. Gansler on Misuse of Commonwealth of Pennsylvanian Government Email Communication Systems, August 18, 2016, accessed July 13, 2017, https://www.scribd.com/document/331955033/Report-of-Douglas-F-Gansler-on-Misuse-of-Commonwealth-E-mail-Systems#from_embed, 9.

[Page 98] – Gansler, Gansler Report, 2016, 26.

[Page 104] – Department of Justice, Christopher Jansen Criminal Complaint Case 3:14-cr-30089-RAL Document 59, November 4, 2015, (US District Court of South Dakota Central Division: United States Government), 2

[Page 113] – Department of Justice, Clyde Fant Plea Agreement Case 6:13-cr-00055-RBD-KRS Document 4, April 19, 2013, (US District Court Middle District of Florida Orlando Division: United States Government), 18.

[Page 113] – Lori Handrahan Medium Profile, July 13, 2017, https://medium.com/@LoriHandrahan2.

[Page 114] – "Department of Education," United States Government, accessed July 13, 2017, https://www2.ed.gov/about/contacts/gen/index.html.

[Page 115] – Third Judicial District Court, Christopher DeZutter Criminal Complaint Court File No. 55-CR-15-828, February 6, 2015, (Third Judicial District Court. State of Minnesota. County of Olmsted), 6.

[Page 116] – Department of Justice, Justin Carroll Indictment Case: 4:17-cr-00036-RWS-DDN Documenber 2, January 25, 2017, (US District Court Eastern District of Missouri Eastern Division: United States Government), 3-4.

[Page 116, 117] – Department of Justice, Michael Morris Sentencing Memo Case 3:13-cr-00021-NKM Document 48, July 10, 2014, (US District Court for the Western District of Virgina Charlottesville Division: United States Government), 4.

[Page 118] – Steve Reilly, "Teachers who sexually abuse students still find classroom jobs," USA Today, 2017, accessed July 13, 2017, https://www.usatoday.com/story/news/2016/12/22/teachers-who-sexually-abuse-students-still-find-classroom-jobs/95346790.

[Page 121] – Department of Justice, Jay Michaud Criminal Complaint Case 3:15-cr-05351-RJB Document No. MJ15-5113, July 10, 2105, (US District Court for the Western District of Washington at Tacoma: United States Government), 8.

[Page 122] – Department of Justice, United States Government, "Former High School Teacher Pleads Guilty To Possessing Child Pornography," June 29, 2015, accessed July 13, 2017, https://www.justice.gov/usao-md/pr/former-high-school-teacher-pleads-guilty-possessing-child-pornography.

[Page 123] – Department of Justice, James McGlothlin Criminal Complaint Case 3:16-cr-00115-MO Document 1, February 19, 2016, (US District Court for the District of Oregon: United States Government), 7.

[Page 124] – Department of Justice, Jay Michaud Criminal Complaint, 5.

[Page 125] – Federal Bureau of Investigations (FBI), "'Playpen' Creator Sentenced to 30 Years: Dark Web 'Hidden Service' Case Spawned Hundreds of Child Porn Investigations," May 5, 2017, accessed July 13, 2017, https://www.fbi.gov/news/stories/playpen-creator-sentenced-to-30-years.

[Page 126] – Department of Justice, Carl McBride Criminal Complaint Case No. 13-195M, November 5, 2013. (US District Court for the District of Delaware: United States Government), 6.

[Page 126] – Department of Justice, David Moe Plea Agreement Criminal Action No. 12-cr-00363-WJM, May 23, 2013, (US District Court for the District of Colorado: United States Government), 17.

[Page 127] – Department of Justice, Carl McBride Criminal Complaint, 7.

[Page 128] – Department of Justice, James Douglas Manring Statement of Facts Case 1:13-cr-00013-CMH Document 22, January 28, 2013, (US District Court for the Eastern District of Virginia Alexandria Division: United States Government), 4.

[Page 133] – Department of Justice, "The National Strategy for Child Exploitation Prevention and Interdiction 2016," (Washington DC: United States Government), April 8, 2016, accessed July 16, 2017, https://www.justice.gov/psc/file/842411/download.

[Page 134] – 73. Louis Casiano, "Former Marine sergeant from Spring sentenced for child porn," Houston Chronicle, March 19, 2012, accessed July 13, 2017, http://www.chron.com/news/houston-texas/article/Former-Marine-sergeant-from-Spring-sentenced-for-3418795.php?utm_source=twitterfeed&utm_medium=twitter.

[Page 135] – Scott Egelberg, "Local Doctor Pleads Guilty to Child Pornography Charge," South Orange Patch, January 4, 2012, accessed July 13, 2017, https://patch.com/new-jersey/southorange/local-doctor-pleads-guilty-to-child-pornography-charge and Jason Grant, "N.J. doctor admits to distributing sadistic, violent child pornography," New Jersey On-Line, January 05, 2012, accessed July 13, 2017, http://www.nj.com/news/index.ssf/2012/01/nj_doctor_admits_to_possessing.html.

[Page 136] – Ali Rockett, "Former Richmond police officer to serve life in prison for sexual abuse of child," Richmond Times-Dispatch, July 13, 2017, accessed July 18, 2017, http://www.richmond.com/news/local/crime/former-richmond-police-officer-to-serve-life-in-prison-for/article_3b148708-a2f5-54b4-9c86-42349b4e0da6.html and Ali Rockett, "Child testifies against former Richmond police officer accused of sex crimes," Richmond Times-Dispatch, July 11, 2017, accessed July 18, 2017,http://www.richmond.com/news/local/crime/child-testifies-against-for-mer-richmond-police-officer-accused-of-sex/article_ce07e192-4b9f-59ec-8d82-02888198b851. html?utm_medium=social&utm_source=twitter&utm_campaign=user-share

[Page 138] – Suffolk County Court, Andrew Cheever Criminal Complaint Case: 1:11-cr-10398-NMG Document 1-1, September 1, 2011, (Boston Massachusetts: Suffolk County Court), 16.,jusd

[Page 140] – Alan Judd, "Doctor accused of violently molesting, raping 1,200 children re-corded abuse," Norwalk Reflector, December 29, 2016, accessed July 17, 2017, http://www. norwalkreflector.com/Health-Care/2016/12/29/Doctor-accused-of-violently-molesting-rap-ing-1-200-children-recorded-abuse and Jessica Masulli Reyes, "Former Delaware pediatrician Earl Bradley loses another appeal," DelmarvaNow.com, May 19, 2017, accessed July 17, 2017, https:// www.delmarvanow.com/story/news/crime/2017/05/19/former-pediatrician-earl-bradley-los-es-another-state-appeal/333067001

[Page 141] – Joe Dolinsky, "Former Dupont cop David Turkos pleads guilty in child sex as-sault case," Times Leader, June 12, 2017, accessed July 17, 2017, http://timesleader.com/ news/663009/former-dupont-cop-pleads-guilty-in-child-sex-assault-case

[Page 142] – Krista Torralva, "German man indicted after traveling to Orlando for sex with minor, feds say," Orlando Sentinel, July 12, 2017, accessed July 18, 2017, http://www.orlandosentinel. com/news/breaking-news/os-german-man-indicted-20170712-story.html